Manager As Leaders

MANAGERS AS LEADERS

A Harvard Business Review Paperback

ISBN 0-87584-260-7

The *Harvard Business Review* articles in this collection are available individually. Discounts apply to quantity purchases. For information and ordering, contact Operations Department, Harvard Business School Publishing Division, Boston, MA 02163. Telephone: (617) 495-6192. Fax: (617) 495-6985.

Editor's Note: Some articles included in this book may have been written before authors and editors began to take into consideration the role of women in management. We hope the archaic usage representing all managers as male does not detract from the usefulness of the collection.

Printed in the United States of America.
93 92 91 5 4 3 2

Contents

How Leaders Think and Act

Leaders Reflect on Leadership

How Leaders Think and Act

Good management controls complexity; effective leadership produces useful change.

What Leaders Really Do

by John P. Kotter

Leadership is different from management, but not for the reasons most people think. Leadership isn't mystical and mysterious. It has nothing to do with having "charisma" or other exotic personality traits. It is not the province of a chosen few. Nor is leadership necessarily better than management or a replacement for it.

Rather, leadership and management are two distinctive and complementary systems of action. Each has its own function and characteristic activities. Both are necessary for success in an increasingly complex and volatile business environment.

Most U.S. corporations today are overmanaged and underled. They need to develop their capacity to exercise leadership. Successful corporations don't wait for leaders to come along. They actively seek out people with leadership potential and expose them to career experiences designed to develop that potential. Indeed, with careful selection, nurturing, and encouragement, dozens of people can play important leadership roles in a business organization.

Leadership complements management; it doesn't replace it.

But while improving their ability to lead, companies should remember that strong leadership with weak management is no better, and is sometimes actually worse, than the reverse. The real challenge is to combine strong leadership and strong management and use each to balance the other.

Of course, not everyone can be good at both leading and managing. Some people have the capacity to become excellent managers but not strong leaders. Others have great leadership potential but, for a variety of

John P. Kotter is professor of organizational behavior at the Harvard Business School and the author of The General Managers *(Free Press, 1982),* Power and Influence *(Free Press, 1985), and* The Leadership Factor *(Free Press, 1988). His most recent book is* A Force for Change: How Leadership Differs from Management *(Free Press, 1990).*

DRAWING BY MICHAEL WITTE

reasons, have great difficulty becoming strong managers. Smart companies value both kinds of people and work hard to make them a part of the team.

But when it comes to preparing people for executive jobs, such companies rightly ignore the recent literature that says people cannot manage *and* lead. They try to develop leader-managers. Once companies understand the fundamental difference between leadership and management, they can begin to groom their top people to provide both.

The Difference Between Management and Leadership

Management is about coping with complexity. Its practices and procedures are largely a response to one of the most significant developments of the twentieth century: the emergence of large organizations. Without good management, complex enterprises tend to become chaotic in ways that threaten their very existence. Good management brings a degree of order and consistency to key dimensions like the quality and profitability of products.

Leadership, by contrast, is about coping with change. Part of the reason it has become so important in recent years is that the business world has become more competitive and more volatile. Faster technological change, greater international competition, the deregulation of markets, overcapacity in capital-intensive industries, an unstable oil cartel, raiders with junk bonds, and the changing demographics of the work force are among the many factors that have contributed to this shift. The net result is that doing what was done yesterday, or doing it 5% better, is no longer a formula for success. Major changes are more and more necessary to survive and compete effectively in this new environment. More change always demands more leadership.

Consider a simple military analogy: a peacetime army can usually survive with good administration and management up and down the hierarchy, coupled with good leadership concentrated at the very top. A wartime army, however, needs competent leadership at all levels. No one yet has figured out how to manage people effectively into battle; they must be *led*.

These different functions–coping with complexity and coping with change–shape the characteristic activities of management and leadership. Each system of action involves deciding what needs to be done, creating networks of people and relationships that can accomplish an agenda, and then trying to ensure that those people actually do the job. But each accomplishes these three tasks in different ways.

Companies manage complexity first by *planning and budgeting*–setting targets or goals for the future (typically for the next month or year), establishing detailed steps for achieving those targets, and then allocating resources to accomplish those plans. By contrast, leading an organization to constructive change begins by *setting a direction*–developing a vision of the future (often the distant future) along with strategies for producing the changes needed to achieve that vision.

Management develops the capacity to achieve its plan by *organizing and staffing*–creating an organizational structure and set of jobs for accomplishing plan requirements, staffing the jobs with qualified individuals, communicating the plan to those people, delegating responsibility for carrying out the plan, and devising systems to monitor implementation. The equivalent leadership activity, however, is *aligning people.* This means communicating the new direction to those who can create coalitions that understand the vision and are committed to its achievement.

Finally, management ensures plan accomplishment by *controlling and problem solving*–monitoring results versus the plan in some detail, both formally and informally, by means of reports, meetings, and other tools; identifying deviations; and then planning and organizing to solve the problems. But for leadership, achieving a vision requires *motivating and inspiring*–keeping people moving in the right direction, despite major obstacles to change, by appealing to basic but often untapped human needs, values, and emotions.

A closer examination of each of these activities will help clarify the skills leaders need.

Setting a Direction vs. Planning and Budgeting

Since the function of leadership is to produce change, setting the direction of that change is fundamental to leadership.

Setting direction is never the same as planning or even long-term planning, although people often confuse the two. Planning is a management process, deductive in nature and designed to produce orderly results, not change. Setting a direction is more inductive. Leaders gather a broad range of data and look for patterns, relationships, and linkages that help explain things. What's more, the direction-setting aspect of leadership does not produce plans; it creates vision and strategies. These describe a business, technology, or corporate culture in terms of what it should become over the long term and articulate a feasible way of achieving this goal.

Most discussions of vision have a tendency to degenerate into the mystical. The implication is that a vision is something mysterious that mere mortals, even talented ones, could never hope to have. But developing good business direction isn't magic. It is a tough, sometimes exhausting process of gathering and analyzing information. People who articulate such visions aren't magicians but broad-based strategic thinkers who are willing to take risks.

Nor do visions and strategies have to be brilliantly innovative; in fact, some of the best are not. Effective business visions regularly have an almost mundane quality, usually consisting of ideas that are already well known. The particular combination or patterning of the ideas may be new, but sometimes even that is not the case.

For example, when CEO Jan Carlzon articulated his vision to make Scandinavian Airline Systems (SAS) the best airline in the world for the frequent business traveler, he was not saying anything that everyone in the airline industry didn't already know. Business travelers fly more consistently than other market segments and are generally willing to pay higher fares. Thus focusing on business customers offers an airline the possibility of high margins, steady business, and considerable growth. But in an industry known more for bureaucracy than vision, no company had ever put these simple ideas together and dedicated itself to implementing them. SAS did, and it worked.

What's crucial about a vision is not its originality but how well it serves the interests of important constituencies – customers, stockholders, employees – and how easily it can be translated into a realistic competitive strategy. Bad visions tend to ignore the legitimate needs and rights of important constituencies – favoring, say, employees over customers or stockholders. Or they are strategically unsound. When a company that has never been better than a weak competitor in an industry suddenly starts talking about becoming number one, that is a pipe dream, not a vision.

One of the most frequent mistakes that overmanaged and underled corporations make is to embrace "long-term planning" as a panacea for their lack of direction and inability to adapt to an increasingly competitive and dynamic business environment. But such an approach misinterprets the nature of direction setting and can never work.

Long-term planning is always time consuming. Whenever something unexpected happens, plans have to be redone. In a dynamic business environment, the unexpected often becomes the norm, and long-term planning can become an extraordinarily burdensome activity. This is why most successful corporations limit the time frame of their planning activities. Indeed, some even consider "long-term planning" a contradiction in terms.

In a company without direction, even short-term planning can become a black hole capable of absorbing an infinite amount of time and energy. With no vision and strategy to provide constraints around the planning process or to guide it, every eventuality deserves a plan. Under these circumstances, contingency planning can go on forever, draining time and attention from far more essential activities, yet without ever providing the clear sense of direction that a company desperately needs. After awhile, managers inevitably become cynical about all this, and the planning process can degenerate into a highly politicized game.

Planning works best not as a substitute for direction setting but as a complement to it. A competent planning process serves as a useful reality check on direction-setting activities. Likewise, a competent direction-setting process provides a focus in which planning can then be realistically carried out. It helps clarify what kind of planning is essential and what kind is irrelevant.

Aligning People vs. Organizing and Staffing

A central feature of modern organizations is interdependence, where no one has complete autonomy, where most employees are tied to many others by their work, technology, management systems, and hierarchy. These linkages present a special challenge when organizations attempt to change. Unless many individuals line up and move together in the same direction, people will tend to fall all over one another. To executives who are overeducated in management and undereducated in leadership, the idea of getting people moving in the same direction appears to be an organizational problem. What executives need to do, however, is not organize people but align them.

Managers "organize" to create human systems that can implement plans as precisely and efficiently as possible. Typically, this requires a number of potentially complex decisions. A company must choose a structure of jobs and reporting relationships, staff it with individuals suited to the jobs, provide training for those who need it, communicate plans to the work force, and decide how much authority to delegate and to whom. Economic incentives also need to be constructed to accomplish the

Setting Direction: Lou Gerstner at American Express

When Lou Gerstner became president of the Travel Related Services (TRS) arm at American Express in 1979, the unit was facing one of its biggest challenges in AmEx's 130-year history. Hundreds of banks were offering or planning to introduce credit cards through Visa and MasterCard that would compete with the American Express card. And more than two dozen financial service firms were coming into the traveler's checks business. In a mature marketplace, this increase in competition usually reduces margins and prohibits growth.

But that was not how Gerstner saw the business. Before joining American Express, he had spent five years as a consultant to TRS, analyzing the money-losing travel division and the increasingly competitive card operation. Gerstner and his team asked fundamental questions about the economics, market, and competition and developed a deep understanding of the business. In the process, he began to craft a vision of TRS that looked nothing like a 130-year-old company in a mature industry.

Gerstner thought TRS had the potential to become a dynamic and growing enterprise, despite the onslaught of Visa and MasterCard competition from thousands of banks. The key was to focus on the global marketplace and, specifically, on the relatively affluent customer American Express had been traditionally serving with top-of-the-line products. By further segmenting this market, aggressively developing a broad range of new products and services, and investing to increase productivity and to lower costs, TRS could provide the best service possible to customers who had enough discretionary income to buy many more services from TRS than they had in the past.

Within a week of his appointment, Gerstner brought together the people running the card organization and questioned all the principles by which they conducted their business. In particular, he challenged two widely shared beliefs – that the division should have only one product, the green card, and that this product was limited in potential for growth and innovation.

Gerstner also moved quickly to develop a more entrepreneurial culture, to hire and train people who would thrive in it, and to clearly communicate to them the overall direction. He and other top managers rewarded intelligent risk taking. To make entrepreneurship easier, they discouraged unnecessary bureaucracy. They also upgraded hiring standards and created the TRS Graduate Management Program, which offered high-potential young people special training, an enriched set of experiences, and an unusual degree of exposure to people in top management. To encourage risk taking among all TRS employees, Gerstner also established something called the Great Performers program to recognize and reward truly exceptional customer service, a central tenet in the organization's vision.

These initiatives led quickly to new markets, products, and services. TRS expanded its overseas presence dramatically. By 1988, AmEx cards were issued in 29 currencies (as opposed to only 11 a decade earlier). The unit also focused aggressively on two market segments that had historically received little attention: college students and women. In 1981, TRS combined its card and travel-service capabilities to offer corporate clients a unified system to monitor and control travel expenses. And by 1988, AmEx had grown to become the fifth largest direct-mail merchant in the United States.

Other new products and services included 90-day insurance on all purchases made with the AmEx card, a Platinum American Express card, and a revolving credit card known as Optima. In 1988, the company also switched to image-processing technology for billing, producing a more convenient monthly statement for customers and reducing billing costs by 25%.

As a result of these innovations, TRS's net income increased a phenomenal 500% between 1978 and 1987 – a compounded annual rate of about 18%. The business outperformed many so-called high-tech/high-growth companies. With a 1988 return on equity of 28%, it also outperformed most low-growth but high-profit businesses.

plan, as well as systems to monitor its implementation. These organizational judgments are much like architectural decisions. It's a question of fit within a particular context.

Aligning is different. It is more of a communications challenge than a design problem. First, aligning invariably involves talking to many more individuals than organizing does. The target population can involve not only a manager's subordinates but also bosses, peers, staff in other parts of the organization, as well as suppliers, governmental officials, or even customers. Anyone who can help implement the vision and strategies or who can block implementation is relevant.

Trying to get people to comprehend a vision of an alternative future is also a communications challenge of a completely different magnitude from organizing them to fulfill a short-term plan. It's much like the difference between a football quarterback attempting to describe to his team the next two or three plays versus his trying to explain to them a totally new approach to the game to be used in the second half of the season.

Whether delivered with many words or a few carefully chosen symbols, such messages are not necessarily accepted just because they are understood. Another big challenge in leadership efforts is credibility–getting people to believe the message. Many things contribute to credibility: the track record of the person delivering the message, the content of the message itself, the communicator's reputation for integrity and trustworthiness, and the consistency between words and deeds.

Finally, aligning leads to empowerment in a way that organizing rarely does. One of the reasons some organizations have difficulty adjusting to rapid changes in markets or technology is that so many people in those companies feel relatively powerless. They have learned from experience that even if they correctly perceive important external changes and then initiate appropriate actions, they are vulnerable to someone higher up who does not like what they have done. Reprimands can take many different forms: "That's against policy" or "We can't afford it" or "Shut up and do as you're told."

> Management controls people by pushing them in the right direction; leadership motivates them by satisfying basic human needs.

Alignment helps overcome this problem by empowering people in at least two ways. First, when a clear sense of direction has been communicated throughout an organization, lower level employees can initiate actions without the same degree of vulnerability. As long as their behavior is consistent with the vision, superiors will have more difficulty reprimanding them. Second, because everyone is aiming at the same target, the probability is less that one person's initiative will be stalled when it comes into conflict with someone else's.

Motivating People vs. Controlling and Problem Solving

Since change is the function of leadership, being able to generate highly energized behavior is important for coping with the inevitable barriers to change. Just as direction setting identifies an appropriate path for movement and just as effective alignment gets people moving down that path, successful motivation ensures that they will have the energy to overcome obstacles.

According to the logic of management, control mechanisms compare system behavior with the plan and take action when a deviation is detected. In a well-managed factory, for example, this means the planning process establishes sensible quality targets, the organizing process builds an organization that can achieve those targets, and a control process makes sure that quality lapses are spotted immediately, not in 30 or 60 days, and corrected.

For some of the same reasons that control is so central to management, highly motivated or inspired behavior is almost irrelevant. Managerial processes must be as close as possible to fail-safe and risk-free. That means they cannot be dependent on the unusual or hard to obtain. The whole purpose of systems and structures is to help normal people who behave in normal ways to complete routine jobs successfully, day after day. It's not exciting or glamorous. But that's management.

Leadership is different. Achieving grand visions always requires an occasional burst of energy. Motivation and inspiration energize people, not by pushing them in the right direction as control mechanisms do but by satisfying basic human needs for achievement, a sense of belonging, recognition, self-esteem, a feeling of control over one's life, and the ability to live up to one's ideals. Such feelings touch us deeply and elicit a powerful response.

Good leaders motivate people in a variety of ways. First, they always articulate the organization's vision

Aligning People: Chuck Trowbridge and Bob Crandall at Eastman Kodak

Eastman Kodak entered the copy business in the early 1970s, concentrating on technically sophisticated machines that sold, on average, for about $60,000 each. Over the next decade, this business grew to nearly $1 billion in revenues. But costs were high, profits were hard to find, and problems were nearly everywhere. In 1984, Kodak had to write off $40 million in inventory.

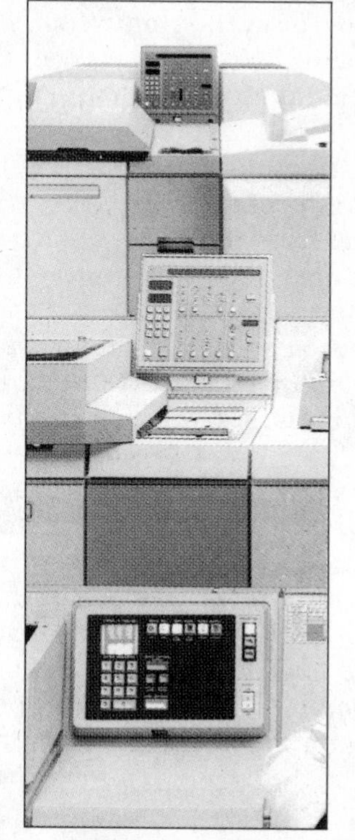

Most people at the company knew there were problems, but they couldn't agree on how to solve them. So, in his first two months as general manager of the new copy products group, established in 1984, Chuck Trowbridge met with nearly every key person inside his group, as well as with people elsewhere at Kodak who could be important to the copier business. An especially crucial area was the engineering and manufacturing organization, headed by Bob Crandall.

Trowbridge and Crandall's vision for engineering and manufacturing was simple: to become a world-class manufacturing operation and to create a less bureaucratic and more decentralized organization. Still, this message was difficult to convey because it was such a radical departure from previous communications, not only in the copy products group but throughout most of Kodak. So Crandall set up dozens of vehicles to emphasize the new direction and align people to it: weekly meetings with his own 12 direct reports; monthly "copy product forums" in which a different employee from each of his departments would meet with him as a group; quarterly meetings with all 100 of his supervisors to discuss recent improvements and new projects to achieve still better results; and quarterly "State of the Department" meetings, where his managers met with everybody in their own departments.

Once a month, Crandall and all those who reported to him would also meet with 80 to 100 people from some area of his organization to discuss anything they wanted. To align his biggest supplier – the Kodak Apparatus Division, which supplied one-third of the parts used in design and manufacturing – he and his managers met with the top management of that group over lunch every Thursday. More recently, he has created a format called "business meetings," where his managers meet with 12 to 20 people on a specific topic, such as inventory or master scheduling. The goal is to get all of his 1,500 employees in at least one of these focused business meetings each year.

Trowbridge and Crandall also enlisted written communication in their cause. A four- to eight-page "Copy Products Journal" was sent to employees once a month. A program called "Dialog Letters" gave employees the opportunity to anonymously ask questions of Crandall and his top managers and be guaranteed a reply. But the most visible, and powerful, form of written communication were the charts. In a main hallway near the cafeteria, these huge charts vividly reported the quality, cost, and delivery results for each product, measured against difficult targets. A hundred smaller versions of these charts were scattered throughout the manufacturing area, reporting quality levels and costs for specific work groups.

Results of this intensive alignment process began to appear within six months and still more after a year. These successes made the message more credible and helped get more people on board. Between 1984 and 1988, quality on one of the main product lines increased nearly one-hundredfold. Defects per unit went from 30 to 0.3. Over a three-year period, costs on another product line went down nearly 24%. Deliveries on schedule increased from 82% in 1985 to 95% in 1987. Inventory levels dropped by over 50% between 1984 and 1988, even though the volume of products was increasing. And productivity, measured in units per manufacturing employee, more than doubled between 1985 and 1988.

in a manner that stresses the values of the audience they are addressing. This makes the work important to those individuals. Leaders also regularly involve people in deciding how to achieve the organization's vision (or the part most relevant to a particular individual). This gives people a sense of control. Another important motivational technique is to support employee efforts to realize the vision by providing coaching, feedback, and role modeling, thereby helping people grow professionally and enhancing their self-esteem. Finally, good leaders recognize and reward success, which not only gives people a sense of accomplishment but also makes them feel like they belong to an organization that cares about them. When all this is done, the work itself becomes intrinsically motivating.

The more that change characterizes the business environment, the more that leaders must motivate people to provide leadership as well. When this works, it tends to reproduce leadership across the entire organization, with people occupying multiple leadership roles throughout the hierarchy. This is highly valuable, because coping with change in any complex business demands initiatives from a multitude of people. Nothing less will work.

Of course, leadership from many sources does not necessarily converge. To the contrary, it can easily conflict. For multiple leadership roles to work together, people's actions must be carefully coordinated by mechanisms that differ from those coordinating traditional management roles.

Strong networks of informal relationships – the kind found in companies with healthy cultures – help coordinate leadership activities in much the same way that formal structure coordinates managerial activities. The key difference is that informal networks can deal with the greater demands for coordination associated with nonroutine activities and change. The multitude of communication channels and the trust among the individuals connected by those channels allow for an ongoing process of accommodation and adaptation. When conflicts arise among roles, those same relationships help resolve the conflicts. Perhaps most important, this process of dialogue and accommodation can produce visions that are linked and compatible instead of remote and competitive. All this requires a great deal more communication than is needed to coordinate managerial roles, but unlike formal structure, strong informal networks can handle it.

> Despite leadership's growing importance, the on-the-job experiences of most people undermine their ability to lead.

Of course, informal relations of some sort exist in all corporations. But too often these networks are either very weak – some people are well connected but most are not – or they are highly fragmented – a strong network exists inside the marketing group and inside R&D but not across the two departments. Such networks do not support multiple leadership initiatives well. In fact, extensive informal networks are so important that if they do not exist, creating them has to be the focus of activity early in a major leadership initiative.

Creating a Culture of Leadership

Despite the increasing importance of leadership to business success, the on-the-job experiences of most people actually seem to undermine the development of attributes needed for leadership. Nevertheless, some companies have consistently demonstrated an ability to develop people into outstanding leader-managers. Recruiting people with leadership potential is only the first step. Equally important is managing their career patterns. Individuals who are effective in large leadership roles often share a number of career experiences.

Perhaps the most typical and most important is significant challenge early in a career. Leaders almost always have had opportunities during their twenties and thirties to actually try to lead, to take a risk, and to learn from both triumphs and failures. Such learning seems essential in developing a wide range of leadership skills and perspectives. It also teaches people something about both the difficulty of leadership and its potential for producing change.

Later in their careers, something equally important happens that has to do with broadening. People who provide effective leadership in important jobs always have a chance, before they get into those jobs, to grow beyond the narrow base that characterizes most managerial careers. This is usually the result of lateral career moves or of early promotions to unusually broad job assignments. Sometimes other vehicles help, like special task-force assignments or a lengthy general management course. Whatever the case, the breadth of knowledge developed in this way seems to be helpful in all aspects of leadership. So does the network of relationships that is often acquired both inside and outside the company. When

Motivating People: Richard Nicolosi at Procter & Gamble

For about 20 years since its founding in 1956, Procter & Gamble's paper products division had experienced little competition for its high-quality, reasonably priced, and well-marketed consumer goods. By the late 1970s, however, the market position of the division had changed. New competitive thrusts hurt P&G badly. For example, industry analysts estimate that the company's market share for disposable diapers fell from 75% in the mid-1970s to 52% in 1984.

That year, Richard Nicolosi came to paper products as the associate general manager, after three years in P&G's smaller and faster moving soft-drink business. He found a heavily bureaucratic and centralized organization that was overly preoccupied with internal functional goals and projects. Almost all information about customers came through highly quantitative market research. The technical people were rewarded for cost savings, the commercial people focused on volume and share, and the two groups were nearly at war with each other.

During the late summer of 1984, top management announced that Nicolosi would become the head of paper products in October, and by August he was unofficially running the division. Immediately he began to stress the need for the division to become more creative and market driven, instead of just trying to be a low-cost producer. "I had to make it very clear," Nicolosi later reported, "that the rules of the game had changed."

The new direction included a much greater stress on teamwork and multiple leadership roles. Nicolosi pushed a strategy of using groups to manage the division and its specific products. In October, he and his team designated themselves as the paper division "board" and began meeting first monthly and then weekly. In November, they established "category teams" to manage their major brand groups (like diapers, tissues, towels) and started pushing responsibility down to these teams. "Shun the incremental," Nicolosi stressed, "and go for the leap."

In December, Nicolosi selectively involved himself in more detail in certain activities. He met with the advertising agency and got to know key creative people. He asked the marketing manager of diapers to report directly to him, eliminating a layer in the hierarchy. He talked more to the people who were working on new product-development projects.

In January 1985, the board announced a new organizational structure that included not only category teams but also new-brand business teams. By the spring, the board was ready to plan an important motivational event to communicate the new paper products vision to as many people as possible. On June 4, 1985, all the Cincinnati-based personnel in paper plus sales district managers and paper plant managers—several thousand people in all—met in the local Masonic Temple. Nicolosi and other board members described their vision of an organization where "each of us is a leader." The event was videotaped, and an edited version was sent to all sales offices and plants for everyone to see.

All these activities helped create an entrepreneurial environment where large numbers of people were motivated to realize the new vision. Most innovations came from people dealing with new products. Ultra Pampers, first introduced in February 1985, took the market share of the entire Pampers product line from 40% to 58% and profitability from break-even to positive. And within only a few months of the introduction of Luvs Delux in May 1987, market share for the overall brand grew by 150%.

Other employee initiatives were oriented more toward a functional area, and some came from the bottom of the hierarchy. In the spring of 1986, a few of the division's secretaries, feeling empowered by the new culture, developed a Secretaries Network. This association established subcommittees on training, on rewards and recognition, and on the "secretary of the future." Echoing the sentiments of many of her peers, one paper products secretary said: "I don't see why we too can't contribute to the division's new direction."

By the end of 1988, revenues at the paper products division were up 40% over a four-year period. Profits were up 66%. And this happened despite the fact that the competition continued to get tougher.

enough people get opportunities like this, the relationships that are built also help create the strong informal networks needed to support multiple leadership initiatives.

One way to develop leadership is to create challenging opportunities for young employees.

Corporations that do a better-than-average job of developing leaders put an emphasis on creating challenging opportunities for relatively young employees. In many businesses, decentralization is the key. By definition, it pushes responsibility lower in an organization and in the process creates more challenging jobs at lower levels. Johnson & Johnson, 3M, Hewlett-Packard, General Electric, and many other well-known companies have used that approach quite successfully. Some of those same companies also create as many small units as possible so there are a lot of challenging lower level general management jobs available.

Sometimes these businesses develop additional challenging opportunities by stressing growth through new products or services. Over the years, 3M has had a policy that at least 25% of its revenue should come from products introduced within the last five years. That encourages small new ventures, which in turn offer hundreds of opportunities to test and stretch young people with leadership potential.

Such practices can, almost by themselves, prepare people for small- and medium-sized leadership jobs. But developing people for important leadership positions requires more work on the part of senior executives, often over a long period of time. That work begins with efforts to spot people with great leadership potential early in their careers and to identify what will be needed to stretch and develop them.

Again, there is nothing magic about this process. The methods successful companies use are surprisingly straightforward. They go out of their way to make young employees and people at lower levels in their organizations visible to senior management. Senior managers then judge for themselves who has potential and what the development needs of those people are. Executives also discuss their tentative conclusions among themselves to draw more accurate judgments.

Armed with a clear sense of who has considerable leadership potential and what skills they need to develop, executives in these companies then spend time planning for that development. Sometimes that is done as part of a formal succession planning or high-potential development process; often it is more informal. In either case, the key ingredient appears to be an intelligent assessment of what feasible development opportunities fit each candidate's needs.

Institutionalizing a leadership-centered culture is the ultimate act of leadership.

To encourage managers to participate in these activities, well-led businesses tend to recognize and reward people who successfully develop leaders. This is rarely done as part of a formal compensation or bonus formula, simply because it is so difficult to measure such achievements with precision. But it does become a factor in decisions about promotion, especially to the most senior levels, and that seems to make a big difference. When told that future promotions will depend to some degree on their ability to nurture leaders, even people who say that leadership cannot be developed somehow find ways to do it.

Such strategies help create a corporate culture where people value strong leadership and strive to create it. Just as we need more people to provide leadership in the complex organizations that dominate our world today, we also need more people to develop the cultures that will create that leadership. Institutionalizing a leadership-centered culture is the ultimate act of leadership.

Reprint 90309

Managers and leaders: Are they different?

Abraham Zaleznik

A bureaucratic society which breeds managers may stifle young leaders who need mentors and emotional interchange to develop

Most societies, and that includes business organizations, are caught between two conflicting needs: one, for managers to maintain the balance of operations, and one for leaders to create new approaches and imagine new areas to explore. One might well ask why there is a conflict. Cannot both managers and leaders exist in the same society, or even better, cannot one person be both a manager and a leader? The author of this article does not say that is impossible but suggests that because leaders and managers are basically different types of people, the conditions favorable to the growth of one may be inimical to the other. Exploring the world views of managers and leaders, the author illustrates, using Alfred P. Sloan and Edwin Land among others as examples, that managers and leaders have different attitudes toward their goals, careers, relations with others, and themselves. And tracing their different lines of development, the author shows how leaders are of a psychologically different type than managers; their development depends on their forming a one-to-one relationship with a mentor.

Abraham Zaleznik is the Cahners-Rabb Professor of Social Psychology of Management at the Harvard Business School. He is also a psychoanalyst and an active member, American Psychoanalytic Association. This is Dr. Zaleznik's fifth article for HBR, the last one being "Power and Politics in Organizational Life," which appeared in the May-June 1970 issue. The present article is based on a working paper prepared for Time Inc.'s conference on leadership, held in Washington in September, 1976.

Illustration by Hans-Georg Rauch

What is the ideal way to develop leadership? Every society provides its own answer to this question, and each, in groping for answers, defines its deepest concerns about the purposes, distributions, and uses of power. Business has contributed its answer to the leadership question by evolving a new breed called the manager. Simultaneously, business has established a new power ethic that favors collective over individual leadership, the cult of the group over that of personality. While ensuring the competence, control, and the balance of power relations among groups with the potential for rivalry, managerial leadership unfortunately does not necessarily ensure imagination, creativity, or ethical behavior in guiding the destinies of corporate enterprises.

Leadership inevitably requires using power to influence the thoughts and actions of other people. Power in the hands of an individual entails human risks: first, the risk of equating power with the ability to get immediate results; second, the risk of ignoring the many different ways people can legitimately accumulate power; and third, the risk of losing self-control in the desire for power. The need to hedge these risks accounts in part for the development of collective leadership and the managerial ethic. Consequently, an inherent conservatism dominates the culture of large organizations. In *The Second American Revolution*, John D. Rockefeller, 3rd. describes the conservatism of organizations:

"An organization is a system, with a logic of its own, and all the weight of tradition and inertia. The deck is stacked in favor of the tried and proven way of doing things and against the taking of risks and striking out in new directions."[1]

Out of this conservatism and inertia organizations provide succession to power through the development of managers rather than individual leaders. And the irony of the managerial ethic is that it fosters a bureaucratic culture in business, supposedly the last bastion protecting us from the encroachments and controls of bureaucracy in government and education. Perhaps the risks associated with power in the hands of an individual may be necessary ones for business to take if organizations are to break free of their inertia and bureaucratic conservatism.

Manager vs. leader personality

Theodore Levitt has described the essential features of a managerial culture with its emphasis on rationality and control:

"Management consists of the rational assessment of a situation and the systematic selection of goals and purposes (what is to be done?); the systematic development of strategies to achieve these goals; the marshalling of the required resources; the rational design, organization, direction, and control of the activities required to attain the selected purposes; and, finally, the motivating and rewarding of people to do the work."[2]

In other words, whether his or her energies are directed toward goals, resources, organization structures, or people, a manager is a problem solver. The manager asks himself, "What problems have to be solved, and what are the best ways to achieve results so that people will continue to contribute to this organization?" In this conception, leadership is a practical effort to direct affairs; and to fulfill his task, a manager requires that many people operate at different levels of status and responsibility. Our democratic society is, in fact, unique in having solved the problem of providing well-trained managers for business. The same solution stands ready to be applied to government, education, health care, and other institutions. It takes neither genius nor heroism to be a manager, but rather persistence, tough-mindedness, hard work, intelligence, analytical ability and, perhaps most important, tolerance and good will.

Another conception, however, attaches almost mystical beliefs to what leadership is and assumes that only great people are worthy of the drama of power and politics. Here, leadership is a psychodrama in which, as a precondition for control of a political structure, a lonely person must gain control of him or herself. Such an expectation of leadership contrasts sharply with the mundane, practical, and yet important conception that leadership is really managing work that other people do.

Two questions come to mind. Is this mystique of leadership merely a holdover from our collective childhood of dependency and our longing for good and heroic parents? Or, is there a basic truth lurking behind the need for leaders that no matter how competent managers are, their leadership stagnates because of their limitations in visualizing purposes and generating value in work? Without this imaginative capacity and the ability to communicate, managers, driven by their narrow purposes, perpetuate group conflicts instead of reforming them into broader desires and goals.

If indeed problems demand greatness, then, judging by past performance, the selection and development of leaders leave a great deal to chance. There are no known ways to train "great" leaders. Furthermore, beyond what we leave to chance, there is a deeper issue in the relationship between the need for competent managers and the longing for great leaders.

What it takes to ensure the supply of people who will assume practical responsibility may inhibit the development of great leaders. Conversely, the presence of great leaders may undermine the development of managers who become very anxious in the relative disorder that leaders seem to generate. The antagonism in aim (to have many competent managers as well as great leaders) often remains obscure in stable and well-developed societies. But the antagonism surfaces during periods of stress and change, as it did in the Western countries during both the Great Depression and World War II. The tension also appears in the struggle for power between the-

1. John D. Rockefeller, 3rd., *The Second American Revolution* (New York: Harper-Row, 1973), p. 72.

2. Theodore Levitt, "Management and the Post Industrial Society," *The Public Interest*, Summer 1976, p. 73.

orists and professional managers in revolutionary societies.

It is easy enough to dismiss the dilemma I pose (of training managers while we may need new leaders, or leaders at the expense of managers) by saying that the need is for people who can be *both* managers and leaders. The truth of the matter as I see it, however, is that just as a managerial culture is different from the entrepreneurial culture that develops when leaders appear in organizations, managers and leaders are very different kinds of people. They differ in motivation, personal history, and in how they think and act.

A technologically oriented and economically successful society tends to depreciate the need for great leaders. Such societies hold a deep and abiding faith in rational methods of solving problems, including problems of value, economics, and justice. Once rational methods of solving problems are broken down into elements, organized, and taught as skills, then society's faith in technique over personal qualities in leadership remains the guiding conception for a democratic society contemplating its leadership requirements. But there are times when tinkering and trial and error prove inadequate to the emerging problems of selecting goals, allocating resources, and distributing wealth and opportunity. During such times, the democratic society needs to find leaders who use themselves as the instruments of learning and acting, instead of managers who use their accumulation of collective experience to get where they are going.

The most impressive spokesman, as well as exemplar of the managerial viewpoint, was Alfred P. Sloan, Jr. who, along with Pierre du Pont, designed the modern corporate structure. Reflecting on what makes one management successful while another fails, Sloan suggested that "good management rests on a reconciliation of centralization and decentralization, or 'decentralization with coordinated control' ".[3]

Sloan's conception of management, as well as his practice, developed by trial and error, and by the accumulation of experience. Sloan wrote:

"There is no hard and fast rule for sorting out the various responsibilities and the best way to assign them. The balance which is struck . . . varies according to what is being decided, the circumstances of the time, past experience, and the temperaments and skills of the executive involved." [4]

In other words, in much the same way that the inventors of the late nineteenth century tried, failed, and fitted until they hit on a product or method, managers who innovate in developing organizations are "tinkerers." They do not have a grand design or experience the intuitive flash of insight that, borrowing from modern science, we have come to call the "breakthrough."

Managers and leaders differ fundamentally in their world views. The dimensions for assessing these differences include managers' and leaders' orientations toward their goals, their work, their human relations, and their selves.

Attitudes toward goals

Managers tend to adopt impersonal, if not passive, attitudes toward goals. Managerial goals arise out of necessities rather than desires, and, therefore, are deeply embedded in the history and culture of the organization.

Frederic G. Donner, chairman and chief executive officer of General Motors from 1958 to 1967, expressed this impersonal and passive attitude toward goals in defining GM's position on product development:

". . . To meet the challenge of the marketplace, we must recognize changes in customer needs and desires far enough ahead to have the right products in the right places at the right time and in the right quantity.

"We must balance trends in preference against the many compromises that are necessary to make a final product that is both reliable and good looking, that performs well and that sells at a competitive price in the necessary volume. We must design, not just the cars we would like to build, but more importantly, the cars that our customers want to buy." [5]

Nowhere in this formulation of how a product comes into being is there a notion that consumer tastes and preferences arise in part as a result of what manufacturers do. In reality, through product design, advertising, and promotion, consumers learn to like what they then say they need. Few would argue that people who enjoy taking snapshots *need* a camera that also develops pictures. But in response to novelty, convenience, a shorter interval between acting (taking the snap) and gaining pleasure (seeing the shot), the Polaroid camera succeeded in the marketplace. But it is inconceivable that Edwin Land responded to impressions of consumer need. Instead, he translated a technology (polarization of light) into a product, which proliferated and stimulated consumers' desires.

The example of Polaroid and Land suggests how leaders think about goals. They are active instead of reactive, shaping ideas instead of responding to them. Leaders adopt a personal and active attitude toward goals. The influence a leader exerts in altering moods, evoking images and expectations, and in establishing specific desires and objectives determines the direction a business takes. The net result of this influence is to change the way people think about what is desirable, possible, and necessary.

Conceptions of work

What do managers and leaders do? What is the nature of their respective work?

Leaders and managers differ in their conceptions. Managers tend to view work as an enabling process involving some combination of people and ideas interacting to establish strategies and make decisions. Managers help the process along by a range of skills, including calculating the interests in opposition, staging and timing the surfacing of controversial issues, and reducing tensions. In this enabling process, managers appear flexible in the use of tactics: they negotiate and bargain, on the one hand, and use rewards and punishments, and other forms of coercion, on the other. Machiavelli wrote for managers and not necessarily for leaders.

Alfred Sloan illustrated how this enabling process works in situations of conflict. The time was the early 1920s when the Ford Motor Co. still dominated the automobile industry using, as did General Motors, the conventional water-cooled engine. With the full backing of Pierre du Pont, Charles Kettering dedicated himself to the design of an air-cooled engine, which, if successful, would have been a great technical and market coup for GM. Kettering believed in his product, but the manufacturing division heads at GM remained skeptical and later opposed the new design on two grounds: first, that it was technically unreliable, and second, that the corporation was putting all its eggs in one basket by investing in a new product instead of attending to the current marketing situation.

In the summer of 1923 after a series of false starts and after its decision to recall the copper-cooled Chevrolets from dealers and customers, GM management reorganized and finally scrapped the project. When it dawned on Kettering that the company had rejected the engine, he was deeply discouraged and wrote to Sloan that without the "organized resistance" against the project it would succeed and that unless the project were saved, he would leave the company.

Alfred Sloan was all too aware of the fact that Kettering was unhappy and indeed intended to leave General Motors. Sloan was also aware of the fact that, while the manufacturing divisions strongly opposed the new engine, Pierre du Pont supported Kettering. Furthermore, Sloan had himself gone on record in a letter to Kettering less than two years earlier expressing full confidence in him. The problem Sloan now had was to make his decision stick, keep Kettering in the organization (he was much too valuable to lose), avoid alienating du Pont, and encourage the division heads to move speedily in developing product lines using conventional water-cooled engines.

The actions that Sloan took in the face of this conflict reveal much about how managers work. First, he tried to reassure Kettering by presenting the problem in a very ambiguous fashion, suggesting that he and the Executive Committee sided with Kettering, but that it would not be practical to force the divisions to do what they were opposed to. He presented the problem as being a question of the people, not the product. Second, he proposed to reorganize around the problem by consolidating all functions in a new division that would be responsible for the design, production, and marketing of the new car. This solution, however, appeared as ambiguous as his efforts to placate and keep Kettering in General Motors. Sloan wrote: "My plan was to create an independent pilot operation under the sole jurisdiction of Mr. Kettering, a kind of copper-cooled-car division. Mr. Kettering would designate his own chief engineer and his production staff to solve the technical problems of manufacture." [6]

While Sloan did not discuss the practical value of this solution, which included saddling an inventor

3. Alfred P. Sloan, Jr., *My Years with General Motors* (New York: Doubleday & Co. 1964), p. 429.

4. Ibid., p. 429.

5 Ibid. p. 440.

6. Ibid. p. 91.

with management responsibility, he in effect used this plan to limit his conflict with Pierre du Pont.

In effect, the managerial solution that Sloan arranged and pressed for adoption limited the options available to others. The structural solution narrowed choices, even limiting emotional reactions to the point where the key people could do nothing but go along, and even allowed Sloan to say in his memorandum to du Pont, "We have discussed the matter with Mr. Kettering at some length this morning and he agrees with us absolutely on every point we made. He appears to receive the suggestion enthusiastically and has every confidence that it can be put across along these lines." [7]

Having placated people who opposed his views by developing a structural solution that appeared to give something but in reality only limited options, Sloan could then authorize the car division's general manager, with whom he basically agreed, to move quickly in designing water-cooled cars for the immediate market demand.

Years later Sloan wrote, evidently with tongue in cheek, "The cooper-cooled car never came up again in a big way. It just died out, I don't know why." [8]

In order to get people to accept solutions to problems, managers need to coordinate and balance continually. Interestingly enough, this managerial work has much in common with what diplomats and mediators do, with Henry Kissinger apparently an outstanding practitioner. The manager aims at shifting balances of power toward solutions acceptable as a compromise among conflicting values.

What about leaders, what do they do? Where managers act to limit choices, leaders work in the opposite direction, to develop fresh approaches to longstanding problems and to open issues for new options. Stanley and Inge Hoffmann, the political scientists, liken the leader's work to that of the artist. But unlike most artists, the leader himself is an integral part of the aesthetic product. One cannot look at a leader's art without looking at the artist. On Charles de Gaulle as a political artist, they wrote: "And each of his major political acts, however tortuous the means or the details, has been whole, indivisible and unmistakably his own, like an artistic act." [9]

The closest one can get to a product apart from the artist is the ideas that occupy, indeed at times obsess, the leader's mental life. To be effective, however, the leader needs to project his ideas into images that excite people, and only then develop choices that give the projected images substance. Consequently, leaders create excitement in work.

John F. Kennedy's brief presidency shows both the strengths and weaknesses connected with the excitement leaders generate in their work. In his inaugural address he said, "Let every nation know, whether it wishes us well or ill, that we shall pay any price, bear any burden, meet any hardship, support any friend, oppose any foe, in order to assure the survival and the success of liberty."

This much-quoted statement forced people to react beyond immediate concerns and to identify with Kennedy and with important shared ideals. But upon closer scrutiny the statement must be seen as absurd because it promises a position which if in fact adopted, as in the Viet Nam War, could produce disastrous results. Yet unless expectations are aroused and mobilized, with all the dangers of frustration inherent in heightened desire, new thinking and new choice can never come to light.

Leaders work from high-risk positions, indeed often are temperamentally disposed to seek out risk and danger, especially where opportunity and reward appear high. From my observations, why one individual seeks risks while another approaches problems conservatively depends more on his or her personality and less on conscious choice. For some, especially those who become managers, the instinct for survival dominates their need for risk, and their ability to tolerate mundane, practical work assists their survival. The same cannot be said for leaders who sometimes react to mundane work as to an affliction.

Relations with others

Managers prefer to work with people; they avoid solitary activity because it makes them anxious. Several years ago, I directed studies on the psychological aspects of career. The need to seek out others with whom to work and collaborate seemed to stand out as important characterstics of managers. When asked, for example, to write imaginative stories in response to a picture showing a single figure (a boy contemplating a violin, or a man silhouetted in a state of reflection), managers populated their stories with people. The following is an example of a manager's imaginative story about the young boy contemplating a violin:

"Mom and Dad insisted that junior take music lessons so that someday he can become a concert musician. His instrument was ordered and had just arrived. Junior is weighing the alternatives of playing football with the other kids or playing with the squeak box. He can't understand how his parents could think a violin is better than a touchdown.

"After four months of practicing the violin, junior has had more than enough, Daddy is going out of his mind, and Mommy is willing to give in reluctantly to the men's wishes. Football season is now over, but a good third baseman will take the field next spring." [10]

This story illustrates two themes that clarify managerial attitudes toward human relations. The first, as I have suggested, is to seek out activity with other people (i.e. the football team), and the second is to maintain a low level of emotional involvement in these relationships. The low emotional involvement appears in the writer's use of conventional metaphors, even clichés, and in the depiction of the ready transformation of potential conflict into harmonious decisions. In this case, Junior, Mommy, and Daddy agree to give up the violin for manly sports.

These two themes may seem paradoxical, but their coexistence supports what a manager does, including reconciling differences, seeking compromises, and establishing a balance of power. A further idea demonstrated by how the manager wrote the story is that managers may lack empathy, or the capacity to sense intuitively the thoughts and feelings of others. To illustrate attempts to be empathic, here is another story written to the same stimulus picture by someone considered by his peers to be a leader:

"This little boy has the appearance of being a sincere artist, one who is deeply affected by the violin, and has an intense desire to master the instrument.

"He seems to have just completed his normal practice session and appears to be somewhat crestfallen at his inability to produce the sounds which he is sure lie within the violin.

"He appears to be in the process of making a vow to himself to expend the necessary time and effort to play this instrument until he satisfies himself that he is able to bring forth the qualities of music which he feels within himself.

"With this type of determination and carry through, this boy became one of the great violinists of his day." [11]

Empathy is not simply a matter of paying attention to other people. It is also the capacity to take in emotional signals and to make them mean something in a relationship with an individual. People who describe another person as "deeply affected" with "intense desire," as capable of feeling "crestfallen" and as one who can "vow to himself," would seem to have an inner perceptiveness that they can use in their relationships with others.

Managers relate to people according to the role they play in a sequence of events or in a decision-making *process*, while leaders, who are concerned with ideas, relate in more intuitive and empathetic ways. The manager's orientation to people, as actors in a sequence of events, deflects his or her attention away from the substance of people's concerns and toward their roles in a process. The distinction is simply between a manager's attention to *how* things get done and a leader's to *what* the events and decisions mean to participants.

In recent years, managers have taken over from game theory the notion that decision-making events can be one of two types: the win-lose situation (or zero-sum game) or the win-win situation in which everybody in the action comes out ahead. As part of the process of reconciling differences among people and maintaining balances of power, managers strive to convert win-lose into win-win situations.

As an illustration, take the decision of how to allocate capital resources among operating divisions in a large, decentralized organization. On the face of it, the dollars available for distribution are limited at any given time. Presumably, therefore, the more one division gets, the less is available for other divisions.

Managers tend to view this situation (as it affects human relations) as a conversion issue: how to make what seems like a win-lose problem into a win-win problem. Several solutions to this situation come to mind. First, the manager focuses others' attention

7. Ibid. p. 91.

8. Ibid. p. 93.

9. Stanley and Inge Hoffmann, "The Will for Grandeur: de Gaulle as Political Artist," *Daedalus*, Summer 1968, p. 849.

10. Abraham Zaleznik, Gene W. Dalton, and Louis B. Barnes, *Orientation and Conflict in Career*, (Boston: Division of Research, Harvard Business School, 1970), p. 316.

11. Ibid. p. 294.

on procedure and not on substance. Here the actors become engrossed in the bigger problem of *how* to make decisions, not *what* decisions to make. Once committed to the bigger problem, the actors have to support the outcome since they were involved in formulating decision rules. Because the actors believe in the rules they formulated, they will accept present losses in the expectation that next time they will win.

Second, the manager communicates to his subordinates indirectly, using "signals" instead of "messages." A signal has a number of possible implicit positions in it while a message clearly states a position. Signals are inconclusive and subject to reinterpretation should people become upset and angry, while messages involve the direct consequence that some people will indeed not like what they hear. The nature of messages heightens emotional response, and, as I have indicated, emotionally makes managers anxious. With signals, the question of who wins and who loses often becomes obscured.

Third, the manager plays for time. Managers seem to recognize that with the passage of time and the delay of major decisions, compromises emerge that take the sting out of win-lose situations; and the original "game" will be superseded by additional ones. Therefore, compromises may mean that one wins and loses simultaneously, depending on which of the games one evaluates.

There are undoubtedly many other tactical moves managers use to change human situations from win-lose to win-win. But the point to be made is that such tactics focus on the decision-making process itself and interest managers rather than leaders. The interest in tactics involves costs as well as benefits, including making organizations fatter in bureaucratic and political intrigue and leaner in direct, hard activity and warm human relationships. Consequently, one often hears subordinates characterize managers as inscrutable, detached, and manipulative. These adjectives arise from the subordinates' perception that they are linked together in a process whose purpose, beyond simply making decisions, is to maintain a controlled as well as rational and equitable structure. These adjectives suggest that managers need order in the face of the potential chaos that many fear in human relationships.

In contrast, one often hears leaders referred to in adjectives rich in emotional content. Leaders attract strong feelings of identity and difference, or of love and hate. Human relations in leader-dominated structures often appear turbulent, intense, and at times even disorganzied. Such an atmosphere intensifies individual motivation and often produces unanticipated outcomes. Does this intense motivation lead to innovation and high performance, or does it represent wasted energy?

Senses of self

In *The Varieties of Religious Experience*, William James describes two basic personality types, "once-born" and "twice-born."[12] People of the former personality type are those for whom adjustments to life have been straightforward and whose lives have been more or less a peaceful flow from the moment of their births. The twice-borns, on the other hand, have not had an easy time of it. Their lives are marked by a continual struggle to attain some sense of order. Unlike the once-borns they cannot take things for granted. According to James, these personalities have equally different world views. For a once-born personality, the sense of self, as a guide to conduct and attitude, derives from a feeling of being at home and in harmony with one's environment. For a twice-born, the sense of self derives from a feeling of profound separateness.

A sense of belonging or of being separate has a practical significance for the kinds of investments managers and leaders make in their careers. Managers see themselves as conservators and regulators of an existing order of affairs with which they personally identify and from which they gain rewards. Perpetuating and strengthening existing institutions enhances a manager's sense of self-worth: he or she is performing in a role that harmonizes with the ideals of duty and responsibility. William James had this harmony in mind—this sense of self as flowing easily to and from the outer world—in defining a once-born personality. If one feels oneself as a member of institutions, contributing to their well-being, then one fulfills a mission in life and feels rewarded for having measured up to ideals. This reward transcends material gains and answers the more fundamental desire for personal integrity which is achieved by identifying with existing institutions.

Leaders tend to be twice-born personalities, people who feel separate from their environment, including other people. They may work in organizations, but they never belong to them. Their sense of who they are does not depend upon memberships, work

12. William James, *Varieties of Religious Experience* (New York: Mentor Books, 1958).

roles, or other social indicators of identity. What seems to follow from this idea about separateness is some theoretical basis for explaining why certain individuals search out opportunities for change. The methods to bring about change may be technological, political, or ideological, but the object is the same: to profoundly alter human, economic, and political relationships.

Sociologists refer to the preparation individuals undergo to perform in roles as the socialization process. Where individuals experience themselves as an integral part of the social structure (their self-esteem gains strength through participation and conformity), social standards exert powerful effects in maintaining the individual's personal sense of continuity, even beyond the early years in the family. The line of development from the family to schools, then to career is cumulative and reinforcing. When the line of development is not reinforcing because of significant disruptions in relationships or other problems experienced in the family or other social institutions, the individual turns inward and struggles to establish self-esteem, identity, and order. Here the psychological dynamics center on the experience with loss and the efforts at recovery.

In considering the development of leadership, we have to examine two different courses of life history: (1) development through socialization, which prepares the individual to guide institutions and to maintain the existing balance of social relations; and (2) development through personal mastery, which impels an individual to struggle for psychological and social change. Society produces its managerial talent through the first line of development, while through the second leaders emerge.

Development of leadership

The development of every person begins in the family. Each person experiences the traumas associated with separating from his or her parents, as well as the pain that follows such frustration. In the same vein, all individuals face the difficulties of achieving self-regulation and self-control. But for some, perhaps a majority, the fortunes of childhood provide adequate gratifications and sufficient opportunities to find substitutes for rewards no longer available. Such individuals, the "once-borns," make moderate identifications with parents and find a harmony between what they expect and what they are able to realize from life.

But suppose the pains of separation are amplified by a combination of parental demands and the individual's needs to the degree that a sense of isolation, of being special, and of wariness disrupts the bonds that attach children to parents and other authority figures? Under such conditions, and given a special aptitude, the origins of which remain mysterious, the person becomes deeply involved in his or her inner world at the expense of interest in the outer world. For such a person, self-esteem no longer depends solely upon positive attachments and real rewards. A form a self-reliance takes hold along with expectations of performance and achievement, and perhaps even the desire to do great works.

Such self-perceptions can come to nothing if the individual's talents are negligible. Even with strong talents, there are no guarantees that achievement will follow, let alone that the end result will be for good rather than evil. Other factors enter into development. For one thing, leaders are like artists and other gifted people who often struggle with neuroses; their ability to function varies considerably even over the short run, and some potential leaders may lose the struggle altogether. Also, beyond early childhood, the patterns of development that affect managers and leaders involve the selective influence of particular people. Just as they appear flexible and evenly distributed in the types of talents available for development, managers form moderate and widely distributed attachments. Leaders, on the other hand, establish, and also break off, intensive one-to-one relationships.

It is a common observation that people with great talents are often only indifferent students. No one, for example, could have predicted Einstein's great achievements on the basis of his mediocre record in school. The reason for mediocrity is obviously not the absence of ability. It may result, instead, from self-absorption and the inability to pay attention to the ordinary tasks at hand. The only sure way an individual can interrupt reverie-like preoccupation and self-absorption is to form a deep attachment to a great teacher or other benevolent person who understands and has the ability to communicate with the gifted individual.

Whether gifted individuals find what they need in one-to-one relationships depends on the availability of sensitive and intuitive mentors who have a vocation in cultivating talent. Fortunately, when the generations do meet and the self-selections occur, we learn more about how to develop leaders and how talented people of different generations influence each other.

While apparently destined for a mediocre career, people who form important one-to-one relationships are able to accelerate and intensify their development through an apprenticeship. The background for such apprenticeships, or the psychological readiness of an individual to benefit from an intensive relationship, depends upon some experience in life that forces the individual to turn inward. A case example will make this point clearer. This example comes from the life of Dwight David Eisenhower, and illustrates the transformation of a career from competent to outstanding.[13]

Dwight Eisenhower's early career in the Army foreshadowed very little about his future development. During World War I, while some of his West Point classmates were already experiencing the war firsthand in France, Eisenhower felt "embedded in the monotony and unsought safety of the Zone of the Interior . . . that was intolerable punishment."[14]

Shortly after World War I, Eisenhower, then a young officer somewhat pessimistic about his career chances, asked for a transfer to Panama to work under General Fox Connor, a senior officer whom Eisenhower admired. The army turned down Eisenhower's request. This setback was very much on Eisenhower's mind when Ikey, his first-born son, succumbed to influenza. By some sense of responsibility for its own, the army transferred Eisenhower to Panama, where he took up his duties under General Connor with the shadow of his lost son very much upon him.

In a relationship with the kind of father he would have wanted to be, Eisenhower reverted to being the son he lost. In this highly charged situation, Eisenhower began to learn from his mentor. General Connor offered, and Eisenhower gladly took, a magnificent tutorial on the military. The effects of this relationship on Eisenhower cannot be measured quantitatively, but, in Eisenhower's own reflections and the unfolding of his career, one cannot overestimate its significance in the reintegration of a person shattered by grief.

As Eisenhower wrote later about Connor, "Life with General Connor was a sort of graduate school in military affairs and the humanities, leavened by a man who was experienced in his knowledge of men and their conduct. I can never adequately express my gratitude to this one gentleman. . . . In a lifetime of association with great and good men, he is the one more or less invisible figure to whom I owe an incalculable debt."[15]

Some time after his tour of duty with General Connor, Eisenhower's breakthrough occurred. He received orders to attend the Command and General Staff School at Fort Leavenworth, one of the most competitive schools in the army. It was a coveted appointment, and Eisenhower took advantage of the opportunity. Unlike his performance in high school and West Point, his work at the Command School was excellent; he was graduated first in his class.

Psychological biographies of gifted people repeatedly demonstrate the important part a mentor plays in developing an individual. Andrew Carnegie owed much to his senior, Thomas A. Scott. As head of the Western Division of the Pennsylvania Railroad, Scott recognized talent and the desire to learn in the young telegrapher assigned to him. By giving Carnegie increasing responsibility and by providing him with the opportunity to learn through close personal observation, Scott added to Carnegie's self-confidence and sense of achievement. Because of his own personal strength and achievement, Scott did not fear Carnegie's aggressiveness. Rather, he gave it full play in encouraging Carnegie's initiative.

Mentors take risks with people. They bet initially on talent they perceive in younger people. Mentors also risk emotional involvement in working closely with their juniors. The risks do not always pay off, but the willingness to take them appears crucial in developing leaders.

Can organizations develop leaders?

The examples I have given of how leaders develop suggest the importance of personal influence and the one-to-one relationship. For organizations to encourage consciously the development of leaders as compared with managers would mean developing one-to-one relationships between junior and senior executives and, more important, fostering a culture of individualism and possibly elitism. The elitism arises out of the desire to identify talent and other qualities suggestive of the ability to lead and not simply to manage.

The Jewel Companies Inc. enjoy a reputation for developing talented people. The chairman and chief executive officer, Donald S. Perkins, is perhaps a good example of a person brought along through the mentor approach. Franklin J. Lunding, who was Perkins's mentor, expressed the philosophy of taking risks with young people this way:

"Young people today want in on the action. They don't want to sit around for six months trimming lettuce." [16]

This statement runs counter to the culture that attaches primary importance to slow progression based on experience and proved competence. It is a high-risk philosophy, one that requires time for the attachment between senior and junior people to grow and be meaningful, and one that is bound to produce more failures than successes.

The elitism is an especially sensitive issue. At Jewel the MBA degree symbolized the elite. Lunding attracted Perkins to Jewel at a time when business school graduates had little interest in retailing in general, and food distribution in particular. Yet the elitism seemed to pay off: not only did Perkins become the president at age 37, but also under the leadership of young executives recruited into Jewel with the promise of opportunity for growth and advancement, Jewel managed to diversify into discount and drug chains and still remain strong in food retailing. By assigning each recruit to a vice president who acted as sponsor, Jewel evidently tried to build a structure around the mentor approach to developing leaders. To counteract the elitism implied in such an approach, the company also introduced an "equalizer" in what Perkins described as "the first assistant philosophy." Perkins stated:

"Being a good first assistant means that each management person thinks of himself not as the order-giving, domineering boss, but as the first assistant to those who 'report' to him in a more typical organizational sense. Thus we mentally turn our organizational charts upside-down and challenge ourselves to seek ways in which we can lead . . . by helping . . . by teaching . . . by listening . . . and by managing in the true democratic sense . . . that is, with the consent of the managed. Thus the satisfactions of leadership come from helping others to get things done and changed—and not from getting credit for doing and changing things ourselves." [17]

While this statement would seem to be more egalitarian than elitist, it does reinforce a youth-oriented culture since it defines the senior officer's job as primarily helping the junior person.

A myth about how people learn and develop that seems to have taken hold in the American culture also dominates thinking in business. The myth is that people learn best from their peers. Supposedly, the threat of evaluation and even humiliation recedes in peer relations because of the tendency for mutual identification and the social restraints on authoritarian behavior among equals. Peer training in organizations occurs in various forms. The use, for example, of task forces made up of peers from several interested occupational groups (sales, production, research, and finance) supposedly removes the restraints of authority on the individual's willingness to assert and exchange ideas. As a result, so the theory goes, people interact more freely, listen more objectively to criticism and other points of view and, finally, learn from this healthy interchange.

Another application of peer training exists in some large corporations, such as Philips, N.V. in Holland, where organization structure is built on the principle of joint responsibility of two peers, one representing the commercial end of the business and the other the technical. Formally, both hold equal responsibility for geographic operations or product groups, as the case may be. As a practical matter, it may turn out that one or the other of the peers dominates the management. Nevertheless, the main interaction is between two or more equals.

The principal question I would raise about such arrangements is whether they perpetuate the managerial orientation, and preclude the formation of one-to-one relationships between senior people and potential leaders.

Aware of the possible stifling effects of peer relationships on aggressiveness and individual initiative,

13. This example is included in Abraham Zaleznik and Manfred F.R. Kets de Vries, *Power and the Corporate Mind* (Boston: Houghton Mifflin, 1975).

14. Dwight D. Eisenhower, *At Ease: Stories I Tell to Friends* (New York: Doubleday, 1967), p. 136.

15. Ibid. p. 187.

16. "Jewel Lets Young Men Make Mistakes," *Business Week*, January 17, 1970, p. 90.

17. "What Makes Jewel Shine so Bright," *Progressive Grocer*, September, 1973, p. 76.

another company, much smaller than Philips, utilizes joint responsibility of peers for operating units, with one important difference. The chief executive of this company encourages competition and rivalry among peers, ultimately appointing the one who comes out on top for increased responsibility. These hybrid arrangements produce some unintended consequences that can be disastrous. There is no easy way to limit rivalry. Instead, it permeates all levels of the operation and opens the way for the formation of cliques in an atmosphere of intrigue.

A large, integrated oil company has accepted the importance of developing leaders through the direct influence of senior on junior executives. One chairman and chief executive officer regularly selected one talented university graduate whom he appointed his special assistant, and with whom he would work closely for a year. At the end of the year, the junior executive would become available for assignment to one of the operating divisions, where he would be assigned to a responsible post rather than a training position. The mentor relationship had acquainted the junior executive firsthand with the use of power, and with the important antidotes to the power disease called *hubris*—performance and integrity.

Working in one-to-one relationships, where there is a formal and recognized difference in the power of the actors, takes a great deal of tolerance for emotional interchange. This interchange, inevitable in close working arrangements, probably accounts for the reluctance of many executives to become involved in such relationships. *Fortune* carried an interesting story on the departure of a key executive, John W. Hanley, from the top management of Procter & Gamble, for the chief executive officer position at Monsanto.[18] According to this account, the chief executive and chairman of P&G passed over Hanley for appointment to the presidency and named another executive vice president to this post instead.

The chairman evidently felt he could not work well with Hanley who, by his own acknowledgement, was aggressive, eager to experiment and change practices, and constantly challenged his superior. A chief executive officer naturally has the right to select people with whom he feels congenial. But I wonder whether a greater capacity on the part of senior officers to tolerate the competitive impulses and behavior of their subordinates might not be healthy for corporations. At least a greater tolerance for interchange would not favor the managerial team player at the expense of the individual who might become a leader.

I am constantly surprised at the frequency with which chief executives feel threatened by open challenges to their ideas, as though the source of their authority, rather than their specific ideas, were at issue. In one case a chief executive officer, who was troubled by the aggressiveness and sometimes outright rudeness of one of his talented vice presidents, used various indirect methods such as group meetings and hints from outside directors to avoid dealing with his subordinate. I advised the executive to deal head-on with what irritated him. I suggested that by direct, face-to-face confrontation, both he and his subordinate would learn to validate the distinction between the authority to be preserved and the issues to be debated.

To confront is also to tolerate aggressive interchange, and has the net effect of stripping away the veils of ambiguity and signaling so characteristic of managerial cultures, as well as encouraging the emotional relationship leaders need if they are to survive.

Reprint 77312

18. "Jack Hanley Got There by Selling Harder," *Fortune*, November, 1976.

HBR Classic

Robert Tannenbaum and
Warren H. Schmidt

How to choose a leadership pattern

Should a manager be democratic or autocratic—or something in between?

Foreword

Since its publication in HBR's March-April 1958 issue, this article has had such impact and popularity as to warrant its choice as an "HBR Classic." Mr. Tannenbaum and Mr. Schmidt succeeded in capturing in a few succinct pages the main ideas involved in the question of how managers should lead their organizations. For this publication, the authors have written a commentary, in which they look at their article from a 15-year perspective (see page 9.) ◇ Mr. Tannenbaum is Professor of the Development of Human Systems at the Graduate School of Management, University of California, Los Angeles. He is also a Consulting Editor of the *Journal of Applied Behavioral Science* and coauthor (with Irving Weschler and Fred Massarik) of *Leadership and Organization: A Behavioral Science Approach* (New York, McGraw-Hill, 1961). Mr. Schmidt is also affiliated with the UCLA Graduate School of Management, where he is Senior Lecturer in Behavioral Science. Besides writing extensively in the fields of human relations and leadership and conference planning, Mr. Schmidt wrote the screenplay for a film, "Is It Always Right to be Right?" which won an Academcy Award in 1970.

> "I put most problems into my group's hands and leave it to them to carry the ball from there. I serve merely as a catalyst, mirroring back the people's thoughts and feelings so that they can better understand them."

> "It's foolish to make decisions oneself on matters that affect people. I always talk things over with my subordinates, but I make it clear to them that I'm the one who has to have the final say."

> "Once I have decided on a course of action, I do my best to sell my ideas to my employees."

> "I'm being paid to lead. If I let a lot of other people make the decisions I should be making, then I'm not worth my salt."

> "I believe in getting things done. I can't waste time calling meetings. Someone has to call the shots around here, and I think it should be me."

Each of these statements represents a point of view about "good leadership." Considerable experience, factual data, and theoretical principles could be cited to support each statement, even though they seem to be inconsistent when placed together. Such contradictions point up the dilemma in which modern managers frequently find themselves.

New problem

The problem of how modern managers can be "democratic" in their relations with subordinates and at the same time maintain the necessary authority and control in the organizations for which they are responsible has come into focus increasingly in recent years.

Earlier in the century this problem was not so acutely felt. The successful executive was generally pictured as possessing intelligence, imagination, initiative, the capacity to make rapid (and generally wise) decisions, and the ability to inspire subordinates. People tended to think of the world as being divided into "leaders" and "followers."

New focus: Gradually, however, from the social sciences emerged the concept of "group dynamics" with its focus on *members* of the group rather than solely on the leader. Research efforts of social scientists underscored the importance of employee involvement and participation in decision making.

Evidence began to challenge the efficiency of highly directive leadership, and increasing attention was paid to problems of motivation and human relations.

Through training laboratories in group development that sprang up across the country, many of the newer notions of leadership began to exert an impact. These training laboratories were carefully designed to give people a firsthand experience in full participation and decision making. The designated "leaders" deliberately attempted to reduce their own power and to make group members as responsible as possible for setting their own goals and methods within the laboratory experience.

It was perhaps inevitable that some of the people who attended the training laboratories regarded this kind of leadership as being truly "democratic" and went home with the determination to build fully participative decison making into their own organizations. Whenever their bosses made a decision without convening a staff meeting, they tended to perceive this as authoritarian behavior. The true symbol of democratic leadership to some was the meeting–and the less directed from the top, the more democratic it was.

Some of the more enthusiastic alumni of these training laboratories began to get the habit of categorizing leader behavior as "democratic" *or* "authoritarian." Bosses who made too many decisions themselves were thought of as authoritarian, and their directive behavior was often attributed solely to their personalities.

New need: The net result of the research findings and of the human relations training based upon them has been to call into question the stereotype of an effective leader. Consequently, modern managers often find themselves in an uncomfortable state of mind.

Often they are not quite sure how to behave; there are times when they are torn between exerting "strong" leadership and "permissive" leadership. Sometimes new knowledge pushes them in one direction ("I should really get the group to help make this decision"), but at the same time their experience pushes them in another direction ("I really understand the problem better than the group and therefore I should make the decision"). They are not sure when a group decision is really appropriate or when holding a staff meeting serves merely as a device for avoiding their own decision-making responsibility.

The purpose of our article is to suggest a framework which managers may find useful in grappling with this dilemma. First, we shall look at the different patterns of leadership behavior that managers can choose from in relating to their subordinates. Then, we shall turn to some of the questions suggested by this range of patterns. For instance, how important is it for managers' subordinates to know what type of leadership they are using in a situation? What factors should they consider in deciding on a leadership pattern? What difference do their long-run objectives make as compared to their immediate objectives?

Range of behavior

Exhibit I presents the continuum or range of possible leadership behavior available to managers. Each type of action is related to the degree of authority used by the boss and to the amount of freedom available to subordinates in reaching decisions. The actions seen on the extreme left characterize managers who maintain a high degree of control while those seen on the extreme right characterize managers who release a high degree of control. Neither extreme is absolute; authority and freedom are never without their limitations.

Now let us look more closely at each of the behavior points occurring along this continuum.

The manager makes the decision and announces it.

In this case the boss identifies a problem, considers alternative solutions, chooses one of them, and then reports this decision to the subordinates for implementation. The boss may or may not give consideration to what he or she believes the subordinates will think or feel about the decision; in any case, no opportunity is provided for them to participate directly in the decision-making process. Coercion may or may not be used or implied.

The manager "sells" the decision.

Here the manager, as before, takes responsibility for identifying the problem and arriving at a decision. However, rather than simply announcing it, he or she takes the additional step of persuading the subordinates to accept it. In doing so, the boss recognizes the possibility of some resistance among those who will be faced with the decision, and seeks to reduce this resistance by indicating, for example, what the employees have to gain from the decision.

The manager presents ideas, invites questions.

Here the boss who has arrived at a decision and who seeks acceptance of his or her ideas provides an opportunity for subordinates to get a fuller explanation of his or her thinking and intentions. After presenting the ideas, the manager invites questions so that the associates can better understand what he or she is trying to accomplish. This "give and take" also enables the manager and the subordinates to explore more fully the implications of the decision.

The manager presents a tentative decision subject to change.

This kind of behavior permits the subordinates to exert some influence on the decision. The initiative for identifying and diagnosing the problem remains with the boss. Before meeting with the staff, the manager has thought the problem through and arrived at a decision—but only a tentative one. Before finalizing it, he or she presents the proposed solution for the reaction of those who will be affected by it. He or she says in effect, "I'd like to hear what you have to say about this plan that I have developed. I'll appreciate your frank reactions but will reserve for myself the final decision."

The manager presents the problem, gets suggestions, and then makes the decision.

Up to this point the boss has come before the group with a solution of his or her own. Not so in this case. The subordinates now get the first chance to suggest solutions. The manager's initial role involves identifying the problem. He or she might, for example, say something of this sort: "We are faced with a number of complaints from newspapers and the general public on our service policy. What is wrong here? What ideas do you have for coming to grips with this problem?"

The function of the group becomes one of increasing the manager's repertory of possible solutions to the problem. The purpose is to capitalize on the knowledge and experience of those who are on the "firing line." From the expanded list of alternatives developed by the manager and the subordinates, the manager then selects the solution that he or she regards as most promising.[1]

The manager defines the limits and requests the group to make a decision.

At this point the manager passes to the group (possibly taking part as a member) the right to make decisions. Before doing so, however, he or she defines the problem to be solved and the boundaries within which the decision must be made.

An example might be the handling of a parking problem at a plant. The boss decides that this is something that should be worked on by the people involved, so they are called together. Pointing up the existence of the problem, the boss tells them:

"There is the open field just north of the main plant which has been designated for additional employee parking. We can build underground or surface multilevel facilities as long as the cost does not exceed $100,000. Within these limits we are free to work out whatever solution makes sense to us. After we decide on a specific plan, the company will spend the available money in whatever way we indicate."

The manager permits the group to make decisions within prescribed limits.

1. For a fuller explanation of this approach, see Leo Moore, "Too Much Management, Too Little Change," HBR January-February 1956, p. 41.

Exhibit I. Continuum of leadership behavior

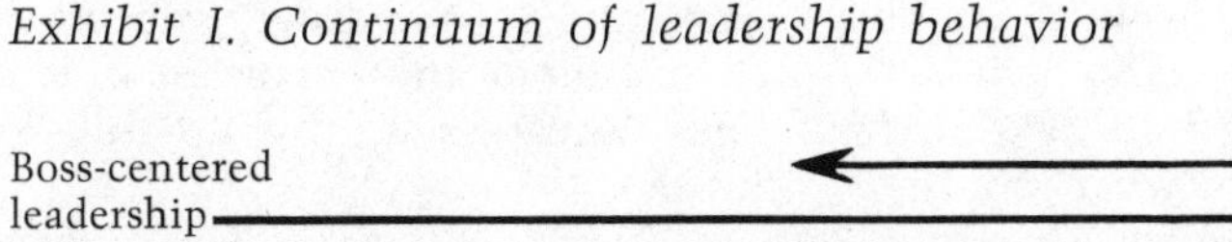

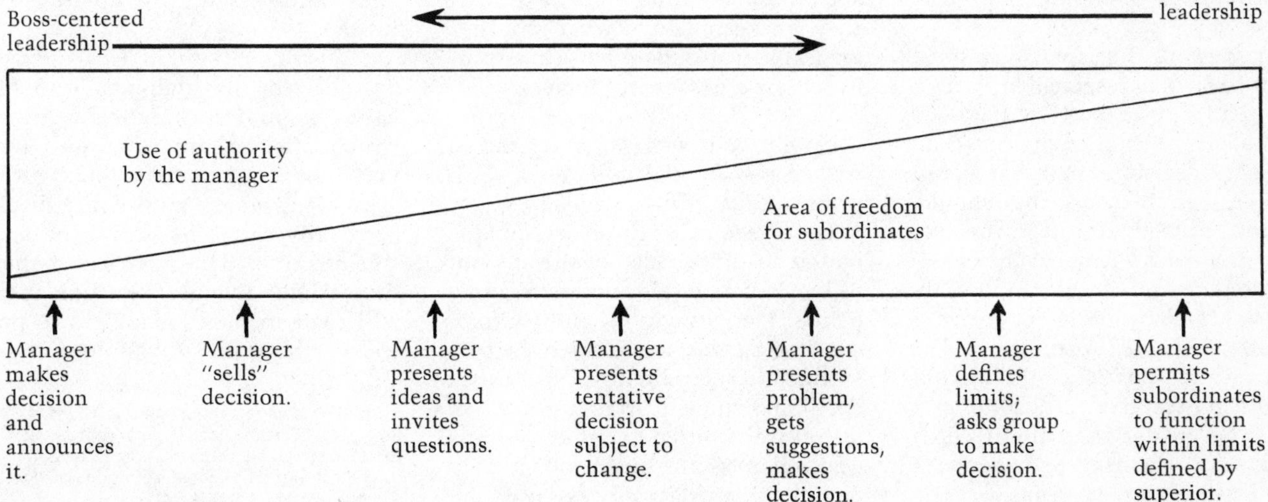

This represents an extreme degree of group freedom only occasionally encountered in formal organizations, as, for instance, in many research groups. Here the team of managers or engineers undertakes the identification and diagnosis of the problem, develops alternative procedures for solving it, and decides on one or more of these alternative solutions. The only limits directly imposed on the group by the organization are those specified by the superior of the team's boss. If the boss participates in the decision-making process, deciding in advance to assist in implementing whatever decision the group makes, he or she attempts to do so with no more authority than any other member of the group.

Key questions

As the continuum in *Exhibit I* demonstrates, there are a number of alternative ways in which managers can relate themselves to the group or individuals they are supervising. At the extreme left of the range, the emphasis is on the manager–on what *he* or *she* is interested in, how *he* or *she* sees things, how *he* or *she* feels about them. As we move toward the subordinate-centered end of the continuum, however, the focus is increasingly on the subordinates–on what *they* are interested in, how *they* look at things, how *they* feel about them.

When business leadership is regarded in this way, a number of questions arise. Let us take four of especial importance:

Can bosses ever relinquish their responsibility by delegating it to others?

Our view is that managers must expect to be held responsible by their superiors for the quality of the decisions made, even though operationally these decisions may have been made on a group basis. They should, therefore, be ready to accept whatever risk is involved whenever they delegate decision-making power to subordinates. Delegation is not a way of "passing the buck." Also, it should be emphasized that the amount of freedom bosses give to subordinates cannot be greater than the freedom which they themselves have been given by their own superiors.

Should the manager participate with subordinates once he or she has delegated responsibility to them?

Managers should carefully think over this question and decide on their role prior to involving the subordinate group. They should ask if their presence will inhibit or facilitate the problem-solving process. There may be some instances when they should leave the group to let it solve the problem for itself. Typically, however, the boss has useful ideas to contribute and should function as an additional member of the group. In the latter instance, it is important that he or she indicate clearly to the group that he or she is in a *member* role rather than an authority role.

How important is it for the group to recognize what kind of leadership behavior the boss is using?

It makes a great deal of difference. Many relationship problems between bosses and subordinates occur because the bosses fail to make clear how they plan to use their authority. If, for example, the boss actually intends to make a certain decision, but the subordinate group gets the impression that he or she has delegated this authority, considerable confusion and resentment are likely to follow. Problems may also occur when the boss uses a "democratic" facade to conceal the fact that he or she has already made a decision which he or she hopes the group will accept as its own. The attempt to "make them think it was their idea in the first place" is a risky one. We believe that it is highly important for managers to be honest and clear in describing what authority they are keeping and what role they are asking their subordinates to assume in solving a particular problem.

Can you tell how "democratic" a manager is by the number of decisions the subordinates make?

The sheer *number* of decisions is not an accurate index of the amount of freedom that a subordinate group enjoys. More important is the *significance* of the decisions which the boss entrusts to subordinates. Obviously a decision on how to arrange desks is of an entirely different order from a decision involving the introduction of new electronic data-processing equipment. Even though the widest possible limits are given in dealing with the first issue, the group will sense no particular degree of responsibility. For a boss to permit the group to decide equipment policy, even within rather narrow limits, would reflect a greater degree of confidence in them on his or her part.

Deciding how to lead

Now let us turn from the types of leadership which are possible in a company situation to the question of what types are *practical* and *desirable*. What factors or forces should a manager consider in deciding how to manage? Three are of particular importance:

> Forces in the manager.
> Forces in the subordinates.
> Forces in the situation.

We should like briefly to describe these elements and indicate how they might influence a manager's action in a decision-making situation.[2] The strength of each of them will, of course, vary from instance to instance, but managers who are sensitive to them can better assess the problems which face them and determine which mode of leadership behavior is most appropriate for them.

Forces in the manager: The manager's behavior in any given instance will be influenced greatly by the many forces operating within his or her own personality. Managers will, of course, perceive their leadership problems in a unique way on the basis of their background, knowledge, and experience. Among the important internal forces affecting them will be the following:

1. *Their value system.* How strongly do they feel that individuals should have a share in making the decisions which affect them? Or, how convinced are they that the official who is paid to assume responsibility should personally carry the burden of decision making? The strength of their convictions on questions like these will tend to move managers to one end or the other of the continuum

2. See also Robert Tannenbaum and Fred Massarik, "Participation by Subordinates in the Managerial Decision-Making Process," *Canadian Journal of Economics and Political Science*, August 1950, p. 413.

shown in *Exhibit I.* Their behavior will also be influenced by the relative importance that they attach to organizational efficiency, personal growth of subordinates, and company profits.[3]

2. *Their confidence in subordinates.* Managers differ greatly in the amount of trust they have in other people generally, and this carries over to the particular employees they supervise at a given time. In viewing his or her particular group of subordinates, the manager is likely to consider their knowledge and competence with respect to the problem. A central question managers might ask themselves is: "Who is best qualified to deal with this problem?" Often they may, justifiably or not, have more confidence in their own capabilities than in those of subordinates.

3. *Their own leadership inclinations.* There are some managers who seem to function more comfortably and naturally as highly directive leaders. Resolving problems and issuing orders come easily to them. Other managers seem to operate more comfortably in a team role, where they are continually sharing many of their functions with their subordinates.

4. *Their feelings of security in an uncertain situation.* Managers who release control over the decision-making process thereby reduce the predictability of the outcome. Some managers have a greater need than others for predictability and stability in their environment. This "tolerance for ambiguity" is being viewed increasingly by psychologists as a key variable in a person's manner of dealing with problems.

Managers bring these and other highly personal variables to each situation they face. If they can see them as forces which, consciously or unconsciously, influence their behavior, they can better understand what makes them prefer to act in a given way. And understanding this, they can often make themselves more effective.

Forces in the subordinate: Before deciding how to lead a certain group, managers will also want to consider a number of forces affecting their subordinates' behavior. They will want to remember that each employee, like themselves, is influenced by many personality variables. In addition, each subordinate has a set of expectations about how the boss should act in relation to him or her (the phrase "expected behavior" is one we hear more and more often these days at discussions of leadership and teaching). The better managers understand these factors, the more accurately they can determine what kind of behavior on their part will enable subordinates to act most effectively.

Generally speaking, managers can permit subordinates greater freedom if the following essential conditions exist:

> If the subordinates have relatively high needs for independence. (As we all know, people differ greatly in the amount of direction that they desire.)

> If the subordinates have a readiness to assume responsibility for decision making. (Some see additional responsibility as a tribute to their ability; others see it as "passing the buck.")

> If they have a relatively high tolerance for ambiguity. (Some employees prefer to have clear-cut directives given to them; others prefer a wider area of freedom.)

> If they are interested in the problem and feel that it is important.

> If they understand and identify with the goals of the organization.

> If they have the necessary knowledge and experience to deal with the problem.

> If they have learned to expect to share in decision making. (Persons who have come to expect strong leadership and are then suddenly confronted with the request to share more fully in decision making are often upset by this new experience. On the other hand, persons who have enjoyed a considerable amount of freedom resent bosses who begin to make all the decisions themselves.)

Managers will probably tend to make fuller use of their own authority if the above conditions do *not* exist; at times there may be no realistic alternative to running a "one-man show."

The restrictive effect of many of the forces will, of course, be greatly modified by the general feeling of confidence which subordinates have in the boss. Where they have learned to respect and trust the boss, he or she is free to vary his or her own behavior. The boss will feel certain that he or she will not be perceived as an authoritarian boss on those occasions when he or she makes decisions alone. Similarly, the boss will not be seen as using staff meetings to avoid decision-making responsibility. In a climate of mutual confidence and respect, people tend to feel less threatened by deviations from normal practice, which in turn makes possible a higher degree of flexibility in the whole relationship.

Forces in the situation: In addition to the forces which exist in managers themselves and in the subordinates, certain characteristics of the general situation will also affect managers' behavior. Among the more critical environmental pressures that surround them are those which stem from the organization, the work group, the nature of the problem, and the pressures of time. Let us look briefly at each of these:

Type of organization–Like individuals, organizations have values and traditions which inevitably influence the behavior of the people who work in them. Managers who are newcomers to a company quickly discover that certain kinds of behavior are approved while others are not. They also discover that to deviate radically from what is generally accepted is likely to create problems for them.

These values and traditions are communicated in numerous ways –through job descriptions, policy pronouncements, and public statements by top executives. Some organizations, for example, hold to the notion that the desirable executive is one who is dynamic, imaginative, decisive, and persuasive. Other organizations put more emphasis upon the importance of the executive's ability to work effectively with people–human relations skills. The fact that the person's superiors have a defined concept of what the good executive should be will very likely push the manager toward one end or the other of the behavioral range.

In addition to the above, the amount of employee participation is influ-

3. See Chris Argyris, "Top Management Dilemma: Company Needs vs. Individual Development," *Personnel*, September 1955, pp. 123-134.

enced by such variables as the size of the working units, their geographical distribution, and the degree of inter- and intra-organizational security required to attain company goals. For example, the wide geographical dispersion of an organization may preclude a practical system of participative decision making, even though this would otherwise be desirable. Similarly, the size of the working units or the need for keeping plans confidential may make it necessary for the boss to exercise more control than would otherwise be the case. Factors like these may limit considerably the manager's ability to function flexibly on the continuum.

Group effectiveness–Before turning decision-making responsibility over to a subordinate group, the boss should consider how effectively its members work together as a unit.

One of the relevant factors here is the experience the group has had in working together. It can generally be expected that a group which has functioned for some time will have developed habits of cooperation and thus be able to tackle a problem more effectively than a new group. It can also be expected that a group of people with similar backgrounds and interests will work more quickly and easily than people with dissimilar backgrounds, because the communication problems are likely to be less complex.

The degree of confidence that the members have in their ability to solve problems as a group is also a key consideration. Finally, such group variables as cohesiveness, permissiveness, mutual acceptance, and commonality of purpose will exert subtle but powerful influence on the group's functioning.

The problem itself–The nature of the problem may determine what degree of authority should be delegated by managers to their subordinates. Obviously, managers will ask themselves whether subordinates have the kind of knowledge which is needed. It is possible to do them a real disservice by assigning a problem that their experience does not equip them to handle.

Since the problems faced in large or growing industries increasingly require knowledge of specialists from many different fields, it might be inferred that the more complex a problem, the more anxious a manager will be to get some assistance in solving it. However, this is not always the case. There will be times when the very complexity of the problem calls for one person to work it out. For example, if the manager has most of the background and factual data relevant to a given issue, it may be easier for him or her to think it through than to take the time to fill in the staff on all the pertinent background information.

The key question to ask, of course, is: "Have I heard the ideas of everyone who has the necessary knowledge to make a significant contribution to the solution of this problem?"

The pressure of time–This is perhaps the most clearly felt pressure on managers (in spite of the fact that it may sometimes be imagined). The more that they feel the need for an immediate decision, the more difficult it is to involve other people. In organizations which are in a constant state of "crisis" and "crash programming" one is likely to find managers personally using a high degree of authority with relatively little delegation to subordinates. When the time pressure is less intense, however, it becomes much more possible to bring subordinates in on the decision-making process.

These, then, are the principal forces that impinge on managers in any given instance and that tend to determine their tactical behavior in relation to subordinates. In each case their behavior ideally will be that which makes possible the most effective attainment of their immediate goals within the limits facing them.

Long-run strategy

As managers work with their organizations on the problems that come up day to day, their choice of a leadership pattern is usually limited. They must take account of the forces just described and, within the restrictions those factors impose on them, do the best that they can. But as they look ahead months or even years, they can shift their thinking from tactics to large-scale strategy. No longer need they be fettered by all of the forces mentioned, for they can view many of them as variables over which they have some control. They can, for example, gain new insights or skills for themselves, supply training for individual subordinates, and provide participative experiences for their employee group.

In trying to bring about a change in these variables, however, they are faced with a challenging question: At which point along the continuum *should* they act?

Attaining objectives: The answer depends largely on what they want to accomplish. Let us suppose that they are interested in the same objectives that most modern managers seek to attain when they can shift their attention from the pressure of immediate assignments:

1. To raise the level of employee motivation.
2. To increase the readiness of subordinates to accept change.
3. To improve the quality of all managerial decisions.
4. To develop teamwork and morale.
5. To further the individual development of employees.

In recent years managers have been deluged with a flow of advice on how best to achieve these longer-run objectives. It is little wonder that they are often both bewildered and annoyed. However, there are some guidelines which they can usefully follow in making a decision.

Most research and much of the experience of recent years give a strong factual basis to the theory that a fairly high degree of subordinate-center behavior is associated with the accomplishment of the five purposes mentioned.[4] This does not mean that managers should always leave all decisions to their assistants. To provide the individual or the group with greater freedom than they are ready for at any given time may very well tend to generate anxieties and therefore inhibit rather than facilitate the attainment of desired objectives. But this should not keep managers from making a continuing effort to confront subordinates with the challenge of freedom.

4. For example, see Warren H. Schmidt and Paul C. Buchanan, *Techniques that Produce Teamwork* (New London, Arthur C. Croft Publications, 1954); and Morris S. Viteles, *Motivation and Morale in Industry* (New York, W.W. Norton & Company, Inc., 1953).

Conclusion

In summary, there are two implications in the basic thesis that we have been developing. The first is that successful leaders are those who are keenly aware of the forces which are most relevant to their behavior at any given time. They accurately understand themselves, the individuals and groups they are dealing with, and the company and broader social environment in which they operate. And certainly they are able to assess the present readiness for growth of their subordinates.

But this sensitivity or understanding is not enough, which brings us to the second implication. Successful leaders are those who are able to behave appropriately in the light of these perceptions. If direction is in order, they are able to direct; if considerable participative freedom is called for, they are able to provide such freedom.

Thus, successful managers of people can be primarily characterized neither as strong leaders nor as permissive ones. Rather, they are people who maintain a high batting average in accurately assessing the forces that determine what their most appropriate behavior at any given time should be and in actually being able to behave accordingly. Being both insightful and flexible, they are less likely to see the problems of leadership as a dilemma.

Retrospective commentary

Since this HBR Classic was first published in 1958, there have been many changes in organizations and in the world that have affected leadership patterns. While the article's continued popularity attests to its essential validity, we believe it can be reconsidered and updated to reflect subsequent societal changes and new management concepts.

The reasons for the article's continued relevance can be summarized briefly:

☐ The article contains insights and perspectives which mesh well with, and help clarify, the experiences of managers, other leaders, and students of leadership. Thus it is useful to individuals in a wide variety of organizations–industrial, governmental, educational, religious, and community.

☐ The concept of leadership the article defines is reflected in a continuum of leadership behavior (see *Exhibit I* in original article). Rather than offering a choice between two styles of leadership, democratic or authoritarian, it sanctions a range of behavior.

☐ The concept does not dictate to managers but helps them to analyze their own behavior. The continuum permits them to review their behavior within a context of other alternatives, without any style being labeled right or wrong.

(We have sometimes wondered if we have, perhaps, made it too easy for anyone to justify his or her style of leadership. It may be a small step between being nonjudgmental and giving the impression that all behavior is equally valid and useful. The latter was not our intention. Indeed, the thrust of our endorsement was for managers who are insightful in assessing relevant forces within themselves, others, and situations, and who can be flexible in responding to these forces.)

In recognizing that our article can be updated, we are acknowledging that organizations do not exist in a vacuum but are affected by changes that occur in society. Consider, for example, the implications for organizations of these recent social developments:

> The youth revolution that expresses distrust and even contempt for organizations identified with the establishment.

> The civil rights movement that demands all minority groups be given a greater opportunity for participation and influence in the organizational processes.

> The ecology and consumer movements that challenge the right of managers to make decisions without considering the interest of people outside the organization.

> The increasing national concern with the quality of working life and its relationship to worker productivity, participation, and satisfaction.

These and other societal changes make effective leadership in this decade a more challenging task, requiring even greater sensitivity and flexibility than was needed in the 1950's. Today's manager is more likely to deal with employees who resent being treated as subordinates, who may be highly critical of any organizational system, who expect to be consulted and to exert influence, and who often stand on the edge of alienation from the institution that needs their loyalty and commitment. In addition, the manager is frequently confronted by a highly turbulent, unpredictable environment.

In response to these social pressures, new concepts of management have emerged in organizations. Open-system theory, with its emphasis on subsystems' interdependency *and* on the interaction of an organization with its environment, has made a powerful impact on managers' approach to problems. Organization development has emerged as a new behavioral science approach to the improvement of individual, group, organizational, and interorganizational performance. New research has added to our understanding of motivation in the work situation. More and more executives have become concerned with social responsibility and

[Commentary continued on following page]

Exhibit II. Continuum of manager-nonmanager behavior

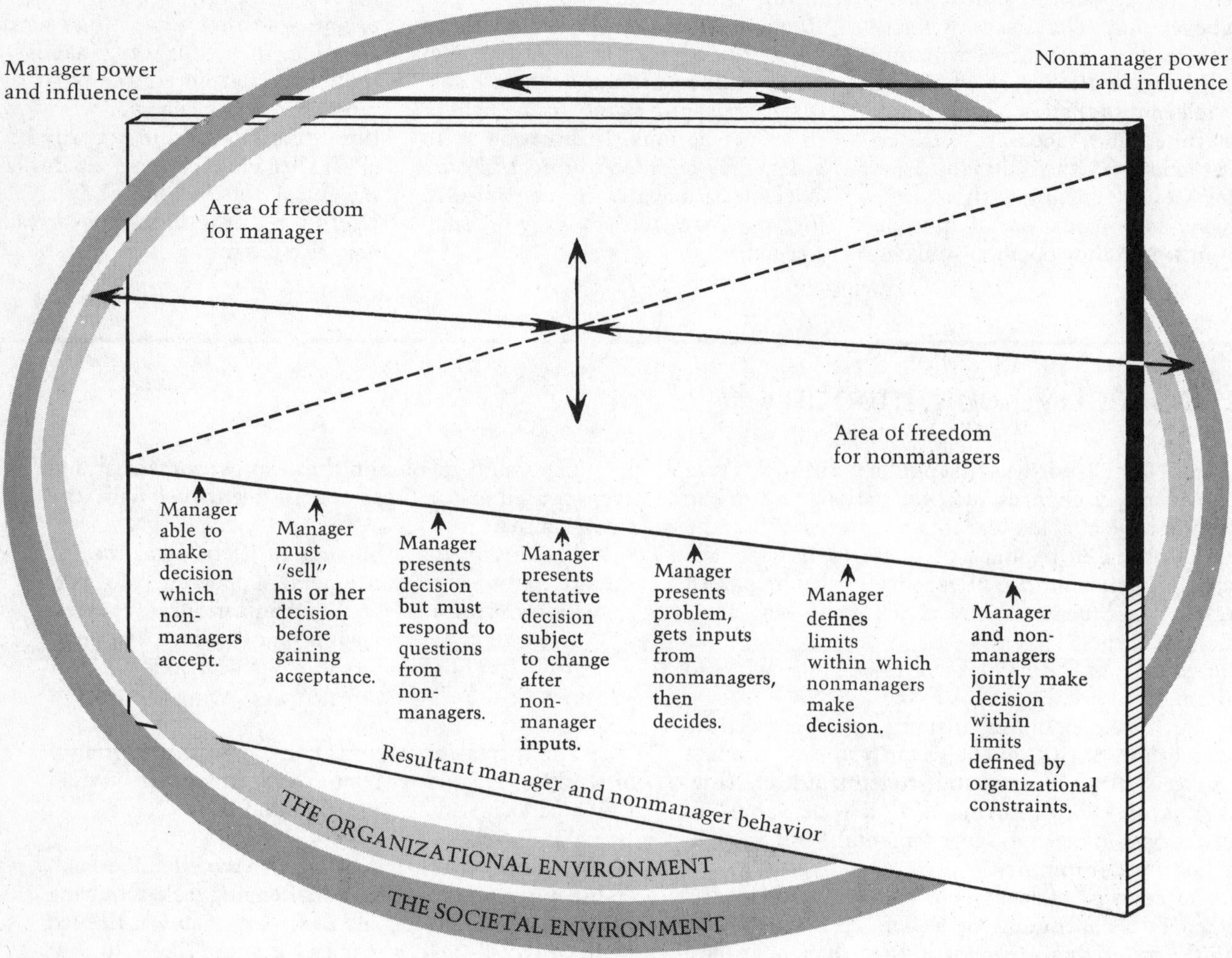

Manager power and influence

Nonmanager power and influence

Area of freedom for manager

Area of freedom for nonmanagers

Manager able to make decision which nonmanagers accept.

Manager must "sell" his or her decision before gaining acceptance.

Manager presents decision but must respond to questions from nonmanagers.

Manager presents tentative decision subject to change after nonmanager inputs.

Manager presents problem, gets inputs from nonmanagers, then decides.

Manager defines limits within which nonmanagers make decision.

Manager and nonmanagers jointly make decision within limits defined by organizational constraints.

Resultant manager and nonmanager behavior

THE ORGANIZATIONAL ENVIRONMENT

THE SOCIETAL ENVIRONMENT

have explored the feasibility of social audits. And a growing number of organizations, in Europe and in the United States, have conducted experiments in industrial democracy.

In light of these developments, we submit the following thoughts on how we would rewrite certain points in our original article.

The article described forces in the manager, subordinates, and the situation as givens, with the leadership pattern a result of these forces. We would now give more attention to the *interdependency* of these forces. For example, such interdependency occurs in: (a) the interplay between the manager's confidence in subordinates, their readiness to assume responsibility, and the level of group effectiveness; and (b) the impact of the behavior of the manager on that of subordinates, and vice versa.

In discussing the forces in the situation, we primarily identified organizational phenomena. We would now include forces lying outside the organization and would explore the relevant interdependencies between the organization and its environment.

In the original article, we presented the size of the rectangle in *Exhibit I* as a given, with its boundaries already determined by external forces–in effect, a closed system. We would now recognize the possibility of the manager and/or the subordinates taking the initiative to change those boundaries through interaction with relevant external forces–both within their own organization and in the larger society.

The article portrayed the manager as the principal and almost unilateral actor. He or she initiated and determined group functions, assumed responsibility, and exercised control. Subordinates made inputs and assumed power only at the will of the manager. Although the manager might have taken outside forces into account, it was *he* or *she* who decided where to operate on the continuum–that is, whether to announce a decision instead of trying to sell the idea to subordinates, whether to invite questions, to let subordinates decide an issue, and so on. While the manager has retained this clear prerogative in many organizations, it has been challenged in others. Even in situations where managers have retained it, however, the balance in the relationship between managers and subordinates at any given time is arrived at by interaction–direct or indirect–between the two parties.

Although power and its use by managers played a role in our article, we now realize that our concern with cooperation and collaboration, common goals, commitment, trust, and mutual caring limited our vision with respect to the realities of power. We did not attempt to deal with unions, other forms of joint worker action, or with individual workers' expressions of resistance. Today, we would recognize much more clearly the power available to *all* parties and the factors that underlie the interrelated decisions on whether to use it.

In the original article, we used the terms "manager" and "subordinate." We are now uncomfortable with "subordinate" because of its demeaning, dependency-laden connotations and prefer "nonmanager." The titles "manager" and "nonmanager" make the terminological difference functional rather than hierarchical.

We assumed fairly traditional organizational structures in our original article. Now we would alter our formulation to reflect newer organizational modes which are slowly emerging, such as industrial democracy, intentional communities, and "phenomenarchy."* These new modes are based on observations such as the following:

> Both manager and nonmanagers may be governing forces in their group's environment, contributing to the definition of the total area of freedom.

> A group can function without a manager, with managerial functions being shared by group members.

> A group, as a unit, can be delegated authority and can assume responsibility within a larger organizational context.

Our thoughts on the question of leadership have prompted us to design a new behavior continuum (see *Exhibit II*) in which the total area of freedom shared by manager and nonmanagers is constantly redefined by interactions between them and the forces in the environment.

The arrows in the exhibit indicate the continual flow of interdependent influence among systems and people. The points on the continuum designate the types of manager and nonmanager behavior that become possible with any given amount of freedom available to each. The new continuum is both more complex and more dynamic than the 1958 version, reflecting the organizational and societal realities of 1973.

*For a description of phenomenarchy, see Will McWhinney, "Phenomenarchy: A Suggestion for Social Redesign," *Journal of Applied Behavioral Science*, May 1973.

Reprint 73311

Harvard
Business Review

Abraham Zaleznik

Management of disappointment

Constructive introspection provides the key for closing the gap between what a leader wants to do and what he is able to accomplish

Foreword

While no one is immune to encounters with disappointment, men who want power and responsibility are especially vulnerable to episodes in which reality does not conform to their wishes or intentions. But, far from disappointment being a prelude to continued failure in their careers, these episodes may be occasions for accelerated personal growth and even the beginning of truly outstanding performance. The author discusses these immanent possibilities, illustrating his points with the reactions of well-known business and public leaders to the demands and stresses of responsibility. Mr. Zaleznik is Professor of Organizational Behavior, Harvard Business School; Affiliate Member and Research Fellow, Boston Psychoanalytic Society and Institute, Inc.; and author of *Human Dilemmas of Leadership* (Harper & Row, 1966).

A recent issue of *Life* magazine presented some unusually astute reflections on the leadership of President Johnson. Seen in the broadest possible perspective, these observations provoke a new set of questions about the motivation of leaders and, indirectly, fresh thinking about organizations, business as well as political.

The Editors of *Life* begin with the comment that President Johnson is not equally at home in each of the wide range of problems facing him. He would rather act on domestic problems than international issues; and if events force him to look beyond our borders, he would much prefer to deal with the new nations, the "have nots" in Asia, Africa, and Latin America as compared with the "haves" of the established industrial societies in Europe. In brief, President Johnson is propelled by an identification with the underdog and, if left to his own devices, would attack the problems of poverty, disease, education, and related concerns which seem at their core to cause human suffering. The thrust of his intentions to lead invariably aims at nurturing those for whom he feels strongly empathetic.

While these observations involve inevitably some oversimplification, they appear justified by the record of his Presidency thus far. The Editors of *Life* conclude with these comments:

"It can be argued—and is by many presidential scholars—that the man in the White House does not have a great deal of choice about the problems he gets or even how to deal with them. Perhaps that is so, but the Presidency still is a highly personal office. What pleases and placates, what intrigues and gratifies, what stimulates and flatters the man in the Oval Office subtly regulates the push and the priorities in the affairs of state that in the long run shape the era." [1]

Two points strike the reader of these editorial comments. The first is the rather tragic sense of leadership implied in the notion that events outside of one's control may not allow a man to do those things which he dearly wishes to do and for which his dispositions make him eminently suited. The second is the suggestion, even if only by inference, that we have here something more than a special situation or the idiosyncrasies of one man at one time and in one place.

We are not dealing with just the problems of political leaders, such as Johnson, although in many of the examples to follow I have used public figures, since their careers are well documented; if anything, we are more concerned with the problems of the head man of a business. For him, particularly, there may be some important generalizations about leadership in the idea that a man's inclinations, unknown to himself, channel him in a certain direction. A chief executive may therefore count himself lucky if he is able to utilize those tendencies with which he feels most comfortable, and over which in the end *he may have the least conscious control.* If we follow these leads, we soon delve into the borderland between personality and action in organizations.

It is my intention to take an excursion into this borderland, to leave the relatively safe, if somewhat arid, territory of organization theory which chooses to see management in terms divorced from the issues of personality. While, from a purely rational standpoint, a chief executive should be able to adjust the style and substance of his actions to the problems which press for solution, he is above all else a human being. The strategies and policies offered in his name, and the rationalistic terms with which they are advanced, often obscure the personal commitment in back of those formal programs. And, in fact, without the convictions drawn from personal commitment, the chief executive's attempts at persuasion and influence often leave others cold. On the other hand, while the conviction may be apparent, the direction of policy may appear so inconsistent and even unreal as to perplex subordinates and arouse wonder at the apparent displacement of personal concerns onto the business of the organization.

In effect, then, a corporate executive may face a paradoxical situation where he must live with himself and be himself while attempting to formulate realistic goals and means for implementing these goals.

Personal equation

Almost two decades ago, a young businessman exemplified some of the hazards involved in this paradox. Charles Luckman came to the presidency of Lever Brothers evidently intent on making a personal impact on the company and on the business community. His career ended abruptly when it became clear that his efforts at personal role building had far outstripped the sound development of business strategy and structure.[2]

In more recent times, the career of John Connor, former president of Merck & Co., Inc. and Secretary of Commerce, illustrated another aspect of this paradox: the gap between personal initiatives and the practical opportunities offered by the power structure for expressing these initiatives. As *Fortune* commented in "The Paradoxical Predicament of John Connor":

"Jack Connor took office with an ebullience he has been hard put to maintain. Within the Commerce Department, Connor is something

1. May 12, 1967, p. 46b.

2. See "The Case of Charles Luckman," *Fortune*, April 1950, p. 81.

less than the complete boss: his chief lieutenants are answerable less to him than to the President, who appointed them, has the power to promote, and holds their political loyalties. And despite his resounding Cabinet title, Connor finds he has a lot less influence on policy than he was once accustomed to."[3]

This gap between what a leader wants to do and the practical possibilities of action within the realities of power relationships poses a severe test for the individual. In Connor's case, according to *Fortune*, he endured the frustrations by a sense of optimism: "Putting the best possible face on what could have only been a severe disappointment, Connor made no complaint."[4] But there is a limit to any man's endurance, as indicated in Connor's later decision to resign his post and return to private enterprise.

For some executives, leadership is the conscious effort to suppress or subordinate their personal expression while meeting the standards and expectations others set. These executives usually do not provide remarkable case histories of business failure, but neither do they stand out as achievers. More significantly, they, along with a few intimates, measure the costs of unrealized hopes.

Where an individual expects, because of his ability, position, or wealth, to exert influence over events, there is no escape from the personal commitment to action. And, where such commitment is great, the potential for loss and disappointment is equally great. Consider:

☐ In the spring of 1966, Howard Hughes sold his holdings in Trans World Airlines. While he realized enormous monetary gains in this transaction, he endured high personal costs because he gave up his intention to influence, if not control outright, one of the major international airlines. The decision to end a battle for corporate control implied a personal reappraisal of the potential gains and losses in continuing a set of tactics. That it was no simple outcome of investment logics was reflected in the comments of Charles Tillinghast, President of TWA, who explained Hughes' actions this way: "Perhaps he is a proud personality and wanted to divest voluntarily."[5]

As these illustrations suggest, the executive career turns on the subtle capacity to take personal risks in making decisions and putting them into action. This personal view of the executive career can, by extension, provide the ideas for understanding better what actually goes on in organizations and in the exercise of leadership. Someday this personal view may also provide a theory which can be articulated and used in building organization structures. In the meantime, we need to know considerably more about the many sides of an individual's leadership style.

In studying effective executives, one usually asks: What were the man's experiences with success, and how did he build on them in his career? Psychological studies of creative people, including leaders, suggest that preoccupation with success may be less important than the role of disappointment in the evolution of a career.[6] Both the great strengths and weaknesses of gifted leaders often hinge on how they manage the disappointments which are inevitable in life.

The experience with disappointment is a catalytic psychological event that may foster growth or retardation in development. When the individual faces disappointment, he usually has to pull back his emotional investments in people and activities and reexamine them before reinvesting them in a new outward direction. The key idea, however, is in the *facing* of disappointment. If disappointment and the pains attendant on it are denied or otherwise hidden from view, the chances are great that the individual will founder on the unresolved conflicts at the center of his experience with disappointment.

Leadership style

In weighing ideas on the management of disappointment in the development of the executive career, we need to start with a clearer picture of the relationship between personality and leadership. This relationship involves the evolution of the individual's style of leadership. The concept of style refers to a widely noted observation that individuals who occupy the position of chief executive in similar organizations vary widely in the way they utilize the authority of their office.

The clearest illustration of this finding is offered in Richard E. Neustadt's study, *Presidential Power: The Politics of Leadership.*[7] In this

3. February 1966, p. 188.

4. Ibid., p. 152.

5. "Howard Hughes' Biggest Surprise," *Fortune*, July 1966, p. 119.

6. See Gregory Rochlin, *Griefs and Discontents* (Boston, Little, Brown and Company, 1965).

7. New York, John Wiley & Sons, Inc., 1960.

book Neustadt compares Roosevelt, Truman, and Eisenhower in their responses to the problem of power in executive relations. For Eisenhower, the use of power was a highly charged and ambivalent experience. His style, therefore, featured formalization of relationships within a staff system. The job of the staff, headed by Sherman Adams, was to screen and decide issues before they reached the personal level of the President. When top subordinates could not reach consensus, Eisenhower inadvertently allowed his power to be diffused and eroded through alternating responses which seemed to favor one side and then the other, as illustrated in the controversy over the 1957 budget.

In contrast to Eisenhower, who sought harmony, consensus, and tranquillity in the exercise of his responsibilities, Franklin D. Roosevelt was a man bent on taking the initiative. He was intent on making new departures, and he exploited every power base available to him to rally support for his decisions. Thus:

"The first task of an executive, as he [Roosevelt] evidently saw it, was to guarantee himself an effective flow of information and ideas. . . . Roosevelt's persistent effort therefore was to check and balance information acquired through official channels with information acquired through a myriad of private, informal, and unorthodox channels and espionage networks. At times he seemed almost to pit his personal sources against his public sources." [8]

In doing this, however, he not only checked and balanced the flow and validity of his information, but ensured for himself a position of the utmost centrality at every stage of the decision-making process. He could assess who wanted what and why he wanted it. He could establish his priorities and make his choices guided by clear indications as to where and at whom his power should be directed in order to secure support. At the same time, Roosevelt's style of leadership not only was that of an initiator, but involved the use of ambiguity in interpersonal relations. The use of ambiguity provided the means for maintaining his central position in the communications network and his flexibility in negotiation and decision making.

Similar observations about differences in style can be made about business leadership. Alfred P. Sloan, Jr. as head of General Motors functioned quite differently from his predecessor, William C. Durant.[9] Sloan was an organizer, while Durant was an entrepreneur. The entrepreneurial style of Durant was also quite different from the innovative pattern epitomized in the leadership of Henry Ford in the automotive industry. Ford's innovations depended on his ability to focus his goals, even to the point where they appeared to be fixations or obsessions. However much Ford operated with a one-track mind, he selected a profitable track that resulted in a major revolution in consumer behavior and industrial structure.

Differences in leadership style seem to revolve around differences in basic orientations to ideas, things, and people. Turning for help once again to Neustadt, we see how Roosevelt invested in ideas and political processes in a way that was free of conflicted attitudes toward people. For whatever reasons, Roosevelt was psychologically free to achieve his objectives through the use of all the bases of power available to him. He could *use* people. Consider:

"His [Roosevelt's] favorite technique was to keep grants of authority incomplete, jurisdictions uncertain, charters overlapping. The result of this competitive theory of administration was often confusion and exasperation on the operating level; but no other method could so reliably insure that in a large bureaucracy filled with ambitious men eager for power, the decisions and the power to make them would remain with the President." [10]

"Eisenhower's use of men tended to smother, not enhance, the competition roused by overlapping jurisdictions. Apparently this was intentional. . . . Eisenhower seemingly preferred to let subordinates proceed upon the lowest common denominators of agreement than to have their quarrels—and issues and details—pushed up to him." [11]

Patterns of investment in ideas, in things, and in people are relatively independent. An idea man may frequently experience personal conflict with people, but, as indicated in the case of Roosevelt, he may also be conflict-free in his relationships with others. A psychological study of Woodrow Wilson by Alexander and Juliette George [12] showed that Wilson's style of leader-

8. Neustadt, op. cit., p. 156.

9. See A. Chandler, *Strategy and Structure: Chapters in the History of Industrial Enterprises* (Cambridge, The M.I.T. Press, 1962).

10. A.M. Schlesinger, Jr., *The Age of Roosevelt, Vol. II: The Coming of the New Deal* (Boston, Houghton Mifflin Company, 1959). Quoted in Neustadt, op. cit., p. 157.

11. Neustadt, op.cit., p. 161.

12. *Woodrow Wilson and Colonel House: A Personality Study* (New York, Dover Publications, Inc., 1964).

ship reflected an emotional attachment to abstract ideals such as justice and democracy. But at an interpersonal level, Wilson had difficulty managing his competitive-aggressive strivings. He could work well with those few men, such as Colonel House, who flattered and openly adored him—or, interestingly enough, with those men who were his enemies. This polarization of relationships involving love and hate is more common than one would suppose and is found with considerable frequency among charismatic leaders.

Role of conflict

To achieve psychological understanding of the motives underlying a leadership style, one must be prepared to deal with the unexpected. In human affairs, relationships seldom persist for the simple reasons that appear on the surface. The central problem in the case of leadership styles is to grasp the meanings of the behavior and the multiple causes of action.

The concepts of *meaning* and *cause* when applied to human activities have at least two points of reference. The first is the relation of the leader's acts to some problem or tension in his environment. For example, Sloan's actions in establishing a rational formal organization can be analyzed in relation to the problems of constructing a balance between centralized and decentralized functions within a company made up of complex marketing, engineering, and production strategies. The second point of reference for behavior is the inner world of the actor. Here, we are concerned not only with the goals the individual seeks to achieve, but also with the nature of the stimuli that constantly threaten the individual's capacity to tolerate painful sensations and experiences.

Studying the external meanings of behavior requires a historical examination of institutions and their environments. The internal meanings also require a historical study, but of the individual and the legacies of his development. Leadership style is essentially the outcome of the developmental process and can be defined, following the psychoanalytic concept of "character," as *the patterned modes of behavior with which an individual relates himself to external reality and to his internal dispositions.*

One of the major contributions of psychoanalytic psychology has been to demonstrate the place of conflict in the development of the individual. Each stage in the life cycle involves personal conflict because the individual has the task of giving up one set of gratifications and searching for alternatives that take account simultaneously of biological, psychological, and social challenges. Failure to relinquish gratifications impedes development, while overly rapid learning establishes a gap between instinctual-emotional processes, on the one hand, and cognitive-rational capacities, on the other. This gap leads often to low tolerance for drives and emotions and to a highly rigid set of conditions for the exercise of competence.

Forrestal tragedy

The life and tragic death of James Forrestal is a case in point. Forrestal built a successful career on Wall Street and in government service. Toward the latter part of his service as the first Secretary of Defense, he developed a series of symptoms which later, when he left his post, took the form of manic-depressive psychosis with paranoid delusions. He took his life while under treatment, an end not uncommon in this type of illness.

Throughout his life, Forrestal, according to one biographer,[13] developed his capacity for work, but at the expense of achieving intimacy in his family. Forrestal broke with his parental family after completing college, in effect renouncing his past. Such breaks with the past do not usually occur apart from basic disappointments in the individual's experience with his development and his position in the family.

In Forrestal's case, while the data permit only reasoned speculations, they suggest the kinds of disappointments one finds in a harsh mother-child relationship. As the result of a complex psychological process, the individual renounces nurturance and other tender emotional exchanges, and substitutes instead a burning ambition and drive to achieve. If the individual has ability, as Forrestal clearly had in abundance, he may achieve leadership and success by any of the standards we use to evaluate performance. But the individual is vulnerable to continuing disappointment that may lead to breakdown. For Forrestal, the major disappointment in his career in government was probably his failure to achieve a power base independent of the President of the United States. He may even have harbored strong ambitions for the Presi-

13. A.A. Rogow, *James Forrestal: A Study of Personality, Politics, and Policy* (New York, The Macmillan Company, 1963).

dency–a position beyond his reach, given the political realities in our society.

Consequently, Forrestal's relationship with Truman became competitive and led to his replacement following the 1948 election. Forrestal fell ill immediately on the acceptance of his resignation and Louis Johnson's appointment as Secretary of Defense. As an active, ambitious man stripped of his power, he suffered a major deprivation with the severance of the channels formerly used in guiding his energies. Unfortunately, he had no alternative channels and no human relationship with which he could heal his wounds and rebuild his life.

Mastery process

The end need not have been tragic. Many great men work through their disappointments and emerge with greater strength and a heightened capacity for leadership. Winston Churchill must have suffered a similar disappointment during World War I. The disastrous campaign at Gallipoli became Churchill's responsibility and interrupted abruptly the career of this ambitious and powerful man. But he mastered this disappointment to become a leader during the supreme crisis of World War II.

The process of mastery must have demanded the kind of psychological work which usually occurs in psychoanalysis. Here, the individual withdraws and refocuses energy and attention from the outer world to himself. The outcome, if successful, is reorganization of personality based on insight, and then the renewal of active concern with the use of one's energy in work.

We know all too little about the self-curative processes which occur for "great men" in their struggle with disappointment.[14] But Churchill must have been aided immeasurably by his range of talents, not the least of which was writing. In other words, he did not have all his eggs in one basket. He also found strength in his relationship with his wife.

Similar processes must have occurred in the emergence of Franklin D. Roosevelt as a great leader. The injury he suffered, and I refer now to psychological injury as a result of the polio attack, was the critical episode in his career. But, again unlike Forrestal, he had the psychological resources and the relationships for performing the curative work necessary in a personal crisis.

Two final examples will clarify the complex way disappointment acts in the adult years as the developmental crisis of a career. Disappointment is not simply a condition where the outer evidences of success are absent or where the failure to realize ambitions is the critical event:

□ In his autobiographical writing John Stuart Mill described the onset of his late adolescent depression. He was reflecting on life and his ambitions, and asked himself this question: "Suppose that all your objects in life were realized; that all the changes in institutions and opinions which you were looking forward to could be completely effected at this very instant: would this be a great joy and happiness to you?" [15] His answer was negative, and the outcome of his personal honesty was an intense depression which lifted only after he was able to mourn and express the grief underlying the psychological loss connected with his disappointments in fantasy.

□ Henry Ford seems to have experienced a similar disappointment in fantasy on the success of the Model T. That great achievement marked a turning point in his career. Where formerly he could channel energies and direct others, he became increasingly rigid and unrealistic in his thinking. He entertained omnipotent and somewhat paranoid ideas, as evidenced by the ill-fated venture on the Peace Ship and his acceptance and support of the anti-Semitic campaigns of the newspaper, *The Dearborn Independent.*[16]

There are men who are spoiled by success and, as Sigmund Freud pointed out, develop symptoms only after major accomplishment.[17] To the naive observer, this consequence of achievement seems perverse or inexplicable. But it becomes comprehensible when analyzed in relation to the individual's investment in his fantasies. To produce a car, become president of a company, or make a great scientific discovery is not a simple dream.[18] Such dreams may also contain the

14. See, for example, Erik H. Erikson, *Young Man Luther* (New York, W.W. Norton & Company, Inc., 1958).

15. See John Stuart Mill, *Autobiography* (New York, The New American Library of World Literature, Inc., 1964), p. 107.

16. See Anne Jardim, *The First Henry Ford: A Study in Personality and Business Leadership* (unpublished doctoral dissertation, Harvard Business School, 1967); see also Allan Nevins and F.F. Hill, *Ford: The Times, the Man, and the Company; Ford: Expansion and Challenge;* and *Ford: Decline and Rebirth* (New York, Charles Scribner's Sons, 1954 [Vol. I], 1957 [Vol. II], 1963 [Vol. III]).

17. See Sigmund Freud, "Those Wrecked by Success," in *The Standard Edition of the Complete Psychological Works of Sigmund Freud,* edited by J. Strachey (London, The Hogarth Press, 1957), Vol. 14, pp. 316-331.

18. See Helen H. Tartakoff, "The Normal Personality in Our Culture and the Nobel Prize Complex," in *Psychoanalysis—A General Psychology, Essays in Honor of Heinz Hartman,* edited by R.M. Lowenstein, L.M. Newman, M. Schur,and A.J. Solnit (New York, International Universities Press, Inc., 1966).

hopes for restoring the individual to some state of happiness which he may have felt he once had and then lost. Or he may be enveloped by a sense of entitlement from which he views other persons as barriers to getting what he feels he justly deserves. These infantile wishes contained in the current actions of leaders are the most dangerous. Hell hath no fury like a woman scorned, or a man whose ambitions are frustrated because his dreams are incapable of realization no matter how hard he works or how tangible his achievements. Ambitions which contain hopes for changing the past and reversing the psychological disappointments encountered in development are self-defeating. The best that any of us can do is to understand the past. It cannot be changed.

Attachment to self

All human beings experience disappointment. If this hard fact of development were not so, it would be very difficult to explain the attractions of myth and legend. In myth we temporarily heal the wounds of disappointment and find ourselves restored to wishes once held and reluctantly abandoned in the interests of preserving attachment to reality and the objects we love. The psychology of the leader is therefore not different from that of other human beings in sharing an initial fate of injury and disappointment. But the psychology becomes different in the consequences of injury.

Most human beings accept disappointment and more or less content themselves with a collective engagement in which ritual and myth, along with work and human relationships, permit them to bear pain and loss. For creative people and those leaders endowed with special abilities, a sense of estrangement follows the early experiences with developmental conflicts. Like Narcissus, who caught his image in a reflecting pool and fell in love with this ideal self—in their childhood, leaders often direct their emotional investments inward. Their dreams and fantasies, translated as adults into ambitions, maintain their sense of being special. Very often these fantasies are part of an experience of destiny; their fate is to perform a great deed like Oedipus, who solved the riddle of the Sphinx, or the biblical Joseph, who interpreted the Pharaoh's dreams and predicted the famine.

The attachment to self leads to achievement, but only in conjunction with sharply developed talents. Without other qualities, such as the power to reason, to perceive the interplay of events in the environment, or to invent new solutions to old problems, the heightened sense of self would amount only to heightened frustration and, in the extreme, even madness. But the sense of self enters strongly into the personality of the leader and the ties others establish with him. What the leader does both with his abilities and with his investment in self is effectively the manifestation of what we call his style, with its special consequences for institutional management.

Resource or hazard?

The nature of policy and strategy in business organizations is a direct outcome of the actions of leaders. I do not believe it squares with reality to imagine that decisions are made in an impersonal way. They are made by men who think and act in relation to the influence of authority figures who themselves are, as I have tried to indicate, bound to a general process of human development.

In reaching decisions and charting a course for a corporation, considerable clarity of vision and accuracy in perception are necessary. The heightened sense of self that I have identified as a major factor in the psychology of leaders is both a resource and a hazard in corporate management and the fate of the individual. It is a resource in that the investment in self preserves the independence necessary to weigh opinions and advice of others. While it is good common sense to encourage subordinates to offer recommendations, in the final analysis a major policy cannot be advanced apart from the convictions of the chief executive. How does he achieve the conviction necessary to seal a decision? If he is dependent on others as a result of an impoverishment of self-confidence, it will be very difficult indeed for him to foster a position that will guide the destiny of the organization.

The problem of investment in self as a psychological quality of leadership is one of degree. Too little amounts to overdependence and often diffusion of purpose. The other extreme, overinvestment in self, poses problems as well, but in a more complex way than overdependence.

Freud, in his study "Group Psychology and the Analysis of the Ego,"[19] described the primal leader as an individual who loves no one but himself. This imagery suggests the autocrat who

19. See Sigmund Freud in Strachey, op. cit., Vol. 18, pp. 67-143.

keeps subordinates equidistant from himself and relatively deprived of independent action. This primal leader is not an archaic figure in business management. He is not idealized now as he was in the late nineteenth and early twentieth centuries; nevertheless, he still persists with all his strengths and weaknesses in small enterprises as well as in large corporations. The autocrat provides a direction, and if he selects a correct path, he usually manages a successful enterprise. As a leader, he tends to select subordinates in his own image, and they reflect all his virtues and vices.

The hazard facing the autocrat stems from the tendency for new ideas, information, and vision to find limited acceptance. Subordinates tell the primal leader only what he wants to hear, and the opportunities for communication are limited by his distance. If an incorrect or outdated strategy continues to direct the organization, then the future is in doubt. Precisely this set of conditions occurred in the Ford Motor Company, leading to its decline in the industry and to serious financial losses from the 1920's until World War II.

Balance & perspective: At a more personal level the problem the primal leader faces is maintaining balance and perspective through the inevitable disappointments when they occur—and especially those which he may experience at the height of his career. These disappointments may range from business setbacks to family problems—including the discovery that his sons and heirs are not made in his image and have distinct personalities and problems. The experience with these latter-day disappointments may produce a kind of psychic injury that reopens old wounds. The response may be rage and restitutive thought patterns that we recognize as a false sense of omnipotence and even delusions.

Evidently Harry Truman had some insight into the hazards of disappointment, particularly when a leader becomes aware of the limitations of his power to control events and actions of others. Neustadt describes Truman's sympathetic anticipation of Eisenhower's problems with the Presidency. Truman said, "He'll sit here and he'll say, 'Do this! Do that!' And nothing will happen. Poor Ike—it won't be a bit like the Army. He'll find it very frustrating."[20] What Truman evidently recognized is that no matter how powerful the leader's position, the issue of influence is still problematic. Whether things get done is beyond the magical thinking that equates authority with influence.

20. Neustadt, op. cit., p. 22.

The Narcissus-like leader who invests only in himself does not necessarily behave overtly like an autocrat, nor does he necessarily detach himself from others. Frequently one observes leaders who have close relationships with subordinates. We cannot conclude from superficial observation that the presence of these relationships indicates a balance between investment in self and others. Closer observation often shows that the ties are not in reality between two separate individuals who cooperate in a rational and purposive endeavor. Instead, the individuals position themselves around the leader as reflected images of himself taken from his infantile past. These executive structures then become dramatic reenactments of fantasies that existed to restore the self-esteem of the individual during his early experiences with disappointment.

The structure and dynamics of these relationships have a variety of unconscious meanings that are carried forward into major episodes of corporate life. While the relationships may have adaptive value, they may also become central to the outbreak of pathological processes within the leader and other key executives in the organization. And again I suggest that the pathologies involve the reexperience of disappointment and loss when the relationships shift or, under the influence of reality, fail as restitutive episodes.

While subordinates may be related to a leader in ways which become significant in the reenactment of fantasies, there is still room for modification. I am reminded of the tragedy of King Lear, who had to drive away those individuals who loved him most because he could not tolerate the intensity of his love for his youngest daughter, Cordelia. The only figure who remained close to Lear and who would tell him the truth was his fool. But the only way the fool could exist and speak the truth was to take the position of the castrated object who himself posed no threat to the power of the leader.

With this observation our problem shifts. Why would anyone give up his self-esteem to serve another, even though in a paradoxical way he performs noble work in helping the narcissistic leader maintain his fragile hold on reality? To be the king's fool strikes me as an excessive price to pay for another man's contributions to society. There is still another way, and that is to maintain one's integrity, to speak the truth, and to let the chips fall where they may. Subordinates to narcissistic leaders sometimes succumb to their own restitutive fantasies as a way of rationalizing their position. We can be sure that where a close relationship persists, there are more reasons than we know to account for the willingness of people to maintain object ties.

Self-examination need

Business managers, whether they know it or not, commit themselves to a career in which they have to work on themselves as a condition for effective working on and working with other people. This fact of the business career is so often neglected that we would do well to reexamine the implications of the need to work on oneself as a condition for the exercise of power.

The analysis presented in this article suggests that a significant area for the personal and inner work on oneself is the experience with disappointment. The question we now have to explore is: How does an executive make the management of disappointment a catalytic experience for personal growth? Here are some leads and suggestions.

Preventive aspects

First, as a preventive measure, examine carefully the personal goals in back of the decision to assume responsibility in a position. If the goals are themselves unrealistic, then major disappointment is inevitable.

A number of years ago, one man decided to change his career and take over a small enterprise. He told me that his reason for entering business was to put into practice the conceptions of good human relations in leadership to which he was personally dedicated. My question to him was this: How about going into business to manage a successful company and to make money? The intent of my question was not to insult his noble purposes but, rather, to suggest that the way one formulates his personal goals has something to do with the way he will practice his profession. In other words, a noble intention may enlighten work, but it is no substitute for competence. The investment in noble purposes may even prevent success and finally set the stage for the traumatic experience with disappointment.

McGregor's theories: A collection of essays by Douglas McGregor, published in 1966 following his death, offers by indirection some clues on how the clash between personal ideology and reality may obscure insight.[21]

McGregor, as you know, was the man who pointed out the difference between what he called *Theory X* and *Theory Y.* According to persuasive arguments, many managers of complex organizations are acting on the basis of an outmoded conception of human nature and institutions. This conception, Theory X, sees man as a stubborn, recalcitrant being who has to be motivated to work in directions consonant with organizational goals. Believing in this conception of man produces a self-fulfilling prophecy. That is, the type of leadership fostered by this "mechanical" man is apt to produce stubborn, recalcitrant individuals who sabotage the organization rather than contribute to its well-being.

In advocating the opposite view, Theory Y, throughout his essays, McGregor proposed that leaders should change their ideas about human nature. The content of this altered view is supported, according to McGregor, by the findings of behavioral science, particularly psychology. McGregor appealed to managers to adopt a philosophy of leadership based on the assumption that individuals want to be self-actualizing and want to participate in harmony with their environment. In this view the leader is an agronomist who cultivates the organizational environment in which this more optimistic picture of man will be fulfilled.

The message is powerful and at the root of McGregor's considerable stature as a management theorist. Its appeal lies in its humaneness and in the subtle way it addresses itself to the underlying guilt which plagues men who exercise power in modern organizations. All too often, leaders are uneasy about the power they have over men and decisions. The uneasiness is accompanied by a sense of guilt and a desire for reassurance, love, and approval from associates. It is as though leaders listen for the voices outside themselves which will testify to their humanity in opposition to the disquieting inner voices that disapprove, depreciate, and accuse. In short, McGregor's message was designed to deal as much with a bad conscience as with the realities of work, authority, and decisions in organizations.

21. *Leadership and Motivation* (Cambridge, The M.I.T. Press, 1966).

But how lasting and relevant are these external cures for a bad conscience? Whether in the name of religion or science, the cure is temporary as compared with the more arduous route of self-knowledge and mastery. Socrates' advice to "know thyself" is exceedingly relevant today for men of responsibility. Unfortunately, McGregor's theories avoid the inner conflicts and resolutions of leadership problems in their almost singular dedication to creating an ideal organization climate.

McGregor missed the point in the study of leadership because, while he was keen on talking to managers, he failed in a basic sense to identify with them. His identification was largely with subordinates; and in talking to managers, McGregor communicated the wish in all of us for benign and benevolent power figures. But to love and to be loved is not enough in the painful process of choice while exercising leadership.

McGregor did capture this idea in what must have been for him a period of intense stress. In his essay "On Leadership," written as he was about to leave the presidency of Antioch College, a position he held for six years, he said:

"Before coming to Antioch, I had observed and worked with top executives as an advisor in a number of organizations. I thought I knew how they felt about their responsibilities and what led them to behave as they did. I even thought I could create a role for myself that would enable me to avoid some of the difficulties they encountered. I was wrong! . . . I believed, for example, that a leader could operate successfully as a kind of advisor to his organization. I thought I could avoid being a 'boss.' Unconsciously, I suspect, I hoped to duck the unpleasant necessity of making difficult decisions, of taking responsibility for one course of action among many uncertain alternatives, of making mistakes and taking the consequences. I thought that maybe I could operate so that everyone would like me—that 'good human relations' would eliminate all discord and disappointment. I could not have been more wrong. . . ." [22]

The essay from which this quotation was taken appeared in May 1954. The subsequent essays, written while McGregor continued a distinguished career as Professor at M.I.T., suggest he had not assimilated the insight underlying his sense of disappointment. I suspect the insight got lost because McGregor was too hard on himself, as the brief quotation above suggests. In the later essays in this book, McGregor returns to the message through which he appealed to authority figures on behalf of subordinates.

Had he pursued the insight imbedded in the Antioch essay, he might have recognized that the essence of leadership is choice, a singularly individualistic act in which a man assumes responsibility for a commitment to direct an organization along a particular path. He might also have recognized that as much as a leader wishes to trust others, he has to judge the soundness and validity of the positions subordinates come to communicate. Otherwise, the leader is in danger of becoming a prisoner of the emotional commitments his subordinates demand, frequently at the expense of judging the correctness of policies and strategies.

McGregor's problem, I would suspect, developed out of his noble purposes. But nobility of purpose is not the first order of business in establishing one's position as chief executive of an organization. In the personal assessment of one's intention to lead, it is far better to assign the highest priority to discovering those things that need to be done, and then to devote oneself to engaging the commitments of others toward these goals. Of course, this does not rule out the possibility that historians can later look at this executive's work and discover the nobility which surrounded his leadership.

But no matter how hard one works on the preventive aspects, sooner or later disappointments occur, and the personal working through of these events then becomes the first order of business.

Facing issues

The second suggestion I shall make is to face the disappointment squarely. The temptation and the psychology of individual response to disappointment is to avoid the pain of self-examination. If an avoidance pattern sets in, the individual will pay dearly for it later. Usually, avoidance occurs because this mode of response is the individual's habitual way of dealing with disappointment from childhood days on. It also seems clear that those people who are lucky enough to have learned from childhood days how to face loss are best equipped to deal with the personal issues that arise during experiences with disappointment in the executive career. Consider:

22. Ibid., p. 67.

□ One line manager in a large corporation worked closely with a vice president, who in the course of events in business life came out second best in a rivalry. The vice president resigned, and his department was left in a vulnerable position, without a leader, and with a loss of status. The line manager, who was in his early forties, had spent his entire working career with this large corporation. He had an excellent reputation, and the senior executives were genuinely hopeful that he would remain with the company.

He thought the issue through and decided to resign, recognizing that his commitments to the deposed vice president were so strong that they would not permit him to reestablish ties with others and to work effectively without paying too high a personal price. He discovered that his experience and talents were indeed in high demand, and he made a successful transition to another corporation where, after demonstrating his competence, he became a vice president and senior executive in his own right.

The decision to remain or to leave was not the significant test of whether the line manager was actually facing the disappointment he had endured. Rather, the significant test came in his silent work of self-examination which he shared only with his wife, who matched his personal courage and willingness to take risks. In effect, this line manager learned to face events and to follow the principle of finance of writing off a loss and then setting forth on a new program.

Emotional awareness

The key factor in mastering disappointment is the capacity to experience the emotions connected with the personal career losses.[23] The flight from the work leading to mastery is usually connected with the individual's limited capacity to tolerate painful emotions. The third suggestion, therefore, is to become intimately acquainted with one's own emotional reactions.

An example of the issues implicit in attempting to face the emotional reactions following disappointment is poignantly described in Volume II of *The Diaries of Harold Nicolson*.[24] Nicolson, a member of Parliament, held the post of Parliamentary Secretary in the Ministry of Information during the early years of World War II. Churchill asked for his resignation in connection with a series of top-level changes in the ministry resulting from public criticism and charges of mismanagement. Nicolson resigned, and the following day (July 19, 1941) he noted this entry in his diary:

"I wake up feeling that something horrible has happened, and then remember that I have been sacked from the Government. Go to the Ministry and start clearing out some of my private possessions. Then attend the Duty Room, probably for the last time. I meet Gerald Campbell in the passage. 'I hear,' he says, 'that you have been thurtled?' [a] Everybody expresses dismay at my going.[b] I have a final drink in the Press Bar with Osbert Lancaster, and then lunch at the Travellers with Robin Maugham. He is as charming as he could be.

"But I mind more than I thought I should mind. It is mainly, I suppose, a sense of failure. I quite see that if the Labour leaders have been pressing to have my post, there is good cause why they should have it. But if I had more power and drive, I should have been offered Rab Butler's job at the Foreign Office,[c] which I should dearly have loved. As it is, I come back to the bench below the gangway having had my chance and failed to profit by it. Ever since I have been in the House I have been looked on as a might-be. Now I shall be a might-have-been. Always up till now I have been buoyed up by the hope of writing some good book or achieving a position of influence in politics. I now know that I shall never write a book better than I have written already, and that my political career is at an end. I shall merely get balder and fatter and more deaf as the years go by. This is an irritating thing. Success should come late in life in order to compensate for the loss of youth; I had youth and success together, and now I have old age and failure.[d] Apart from all this,

23. See Elizabeth R. Zetzel, "Depression and the Incapacity to Bear It," in *Drives, Affects, Behavior*, edited by Rudolph M. Loewenstein (New York, International Universities Press, Inc., Vol. II, 1965).

24. *The War Years, 1939-1945*, edited by Nigel Nicolson (New York, Atheneum Publishers, 1967).

a. Nicolson was replaced as Parliamentary Secretary by Ernest Thurtle, Labour M.P. for Shoreditch, who retained the office till the end of the war. Duff Cooper was succeeded as Minister by Brendan Bracken.

b. Duff Cooper wrote to him, "I think you have received very shabby treatment, and I find that everybody shares that view."

c. R.A. Butler, Under-Secretary of State for Foreign Affairs since 1938, was now appointed Minister of Education, and was succeeded at the Foreign Office by Richard Law.

d. Nicolson was then 54.

I mind leaving the Ministry where I did good work and had friends.

"This space indicates the end of my ambitions in life. 'Omnium consensu capax imperii nisi imperasset.'[e]"

According to the editor of the diaries, it took Nicolson some time before he could assimilate the disappointment and plunge anew into lesser responsibilities. But Nicolson's apparent honesty, and his gifts as an observer and recorder of events, evidently helped him during a difficult personal crisis.

Studies of individuals who get into trouble and present themselves for treatment to a psychoanalyst frequently show that the roots of their difficulties lie in a limited capacity to tolerate emotions, especially those connected with loss and disappointment. The business executive is especially vulnerable because he may have developed an unconscious strategy of forced activity or, more accurately, hyperactivity, as a defense against emotional awareness. The hyperactive executive is of course rewarded for his hyperactivity, since, in the conventional understanding of how an executive should behave, busyness is generally considered a good thing.

However good it is in some respects, it is also bad if busyness serves to build and maintain the wall between the inner worlds of thought and feeling. In the treatment of such individuals who are in trouble, the most positive indicator of progress is the appearance of sadness and depression. As the individual consciously assimilates the depression and relates it to his experiences with disappointment throughout his development, he becomes capable of undoing the ineffective patterns and of substituting more effective ways of dealing with the demands and stresses of responsibility.

Conclusion

No one is immune to encounters with disappointment. More significantly, individuals who want power and responsibility or seek creative expression are especially vulnerable to episodes in which reality does not conform to one's wishes or intentions. As I have indicated in this article, far from disappointment being a prelude to continued failure in career, these critical episodes may actually be occasions for accelerated growth and even the beginning of truly outstanding performance.

But much depends on the quality of the psychological work the individual accomplishes under the stress of the sense of loss and bewilderment which frequently accompanies disappointment. As in all matters of personal development, the outcome turns on the quality of the man, the measure of courage he can mobilize, the richness of his talents, and his ability for constructive introspection.

It is no easy task to examine one's own motivations. In fact, the necessity seldom arises for many people until they meet an impasse in life. At this juncture, they are confronted with two sets of personal concerns: those connected directly with the present disappointments and those related to the experiences with disappointment in the past. Usually a crisis in the present reopens problems from the past, and, in this sense, the individual experiences a telescoping of time in which the psychological past and present tend to merge.

But the degree of telescoping is critical in judging the intensity of stress involved in the management of disappointment. It is usually difficult enough to solve a current problem, with all its demands for accurate observation and realistic thought. The difficulty increases, however, when the route to solving current problems involves examination of one's history with loss or deprivation. Here the most effective step the individual can take is to seek competent help.

In the course of examining reactions to disappointment, a subtle change may take place in the individual's perspectives and attitudes. While he may come to recognize the impossible quality of certain goals and wishes, and be willing to relinquish their demands on his behavior, he may at the same time discover uncharted possibilities for productive work and pleasure. These immanent possibilities usually remain obscure so long as the individual is intent in his quest for restitutive rewards to make up for his felt losses of the past.

There is irony in all of human experience and no less in the solutions to the problem of disappointment. The deepest irony of all is to discover that one has been mourning losses that were never sustained, and yearning for a past that never existed, while ignoring one's own real capabilities for shaping the present.

e. Tacitus on the Emperor Galba. "Had he never been placed in authority, nobody would ever have doubted his capacity for it."

Reprint 67612

Ethical managers make their own rules

Ethics prize winner

Sir Adrian Cadbury

In 1900 Queen Victoria sent a decorative tin with a bar of chocolate inside to all of her soldiers who were serving in South Africa. These tins still turn up today, often complete with their contents, a tribute to the collecting instinct. At the time, the order faced my grandfather with an ethical dilemma. He owned and ran the second-largest chocolate company in Britain, so he was trying harder and the order meant additional work for the factory. Yet he was deeply and publicly opposed to the Anglo-Boer War. He resolved the dilemma by accepting the order, but carrying it out at cost. He therefore made no profit out of what he saw as an unjust war, his employees benefited from the additional work, the soldiers received their royal present, and I am still sent the tins.

My grandfather was able to resolve the conflict between the decision best for his business and his personal code of ethics because he and his family owned the firm which bore their name. Certainly his dilemma would have been more acute if he had had to take into account the interests of outside shareholders, many of whom would no doubt have been in favor both of the war and of profiting from it. But even so, not all my grandfather's ethical dilemmas could be as straightforwardly resolved.

So strongly did my grandfather feel about the South African War that he acquired and financed the only British newspaper which opposed it. He was also against gambling, however, and so he tried to run the paper without any references to horse racing. The effect on the newspaper's circulation was such that he had to choose between his ethical beliefs. He decided, in the end, that it was more important that the paper's voice be heard as widely as possible than that gambling should thereby receive some mild encouragement. The decision was doubtless a relief to those working on the paper and to its readers.

The way my grandfather settled these two clashes of principle brings out some practical points about ethics and business decisions. In the first place, the possibility that ethical and commercial considerations will conflict has always faced those who run companies. It is not a new problem. The difference now is that a more widespread and critical interest is being taken in our decisions and in the ethical judgments which lie behind them.

Secondly, as the newspaper example demonstrates, ethical signposts do not always point in the same direction. My grandfather had to choose between opposing a war and condoning gambling. The rule that it is best to tell the truth often runs up against the rule that we should not hurt people's feelings unnecessarily. There is no simple, universal formula for solving ethical problems. We have to choose from our own codes of conduct whichever rules are appropriate to the case in hand; the outcome of those choices makes us who we are.

Lastly, while it is hard enough to resolve dilemmas when our personal rules of conduct conflict, the real difficulties arise when we have to make decisions which affect the interests of others. We can work out what weighting to give to our own rules through trial and error. But business decisions require us to do the same for others by allocating weights to all the con-

George Adrian Hayhurst Cadbury is chairman of Cadbury Schweppes PLC. Readers who would like to know more about Sir Adrian's views on management practice and ethics can read "Cadbury Schweppes: More Than Chocolate and Tonic," an interview with HBR that appeared in January-February 1983.

The editors of Harvard Business Review *are glad to announce that "Ethical Managers Make Their Own Rules" has won* HBR's *1986 Ethics in Business Prize for the best original article written and submitted by a corporate manager on the ethical problems business executives face.*

flicting interests which may be involved. Frequently, for example, we must balance the interests of employees against those of shareholders. But even that sounds more straightforward than it really is, because there may well be differing views among the shareholders, and the interests of past, present, and future employees are unlikely to be identical.

Eliminating ethical considerations from business decisions would simplify the management task, and Milton Friedman has urged something of the kind in arguing that the interaction between business and society should be left to the political process. "Few trends could so thoroughly undermine the very foundation of our free society," he writes in *Capitalism and Freedom*, "as the acceptance by corporate officials of a social responsibility other than to make as much money for their shareholders as possible."

But the simplicity of this approach is deceptive. Business is part of the social system and we cannot isolate the economic elements of major decisions from their social consequences. So there are no simple rules. Those who make business decisions have to assess the economic and social consequences of their actions as best as they can and come to their conclusions on limited information and in a limited time.

We judge companies – and managers – by their actions, not their pious statements of intent.

As will already be apparent, I use the word ethics to mean the guidelines or rules of conduct by which we aim to live. It is, of course, foolhardy to write about ethics at all, because you lay yourself open to the charge of taking up a position of moral superiority, of failing to practice what you preach, or both. I am not in a position to preach nor am I promoting a specific code of conduct. I believe, however, that it is useful to all of us who are responsible for business decisions to acknowledge the part which ethics plays in those decisions and to encourage discussion of how best to combine commercial and ethical judgments. Most business decisions involve some degree of ethical judgment; few can be taken solely on the basis of arithmetic.

While we refer to a company as having a set of standards, that is a convenient shorthand. The people who make up the company are responsible for its conduct and it is their collective actions which determine the company's standards. The ethical standards of a company are judged by its actions, not by pious statements of intent put out in its name. This does not mean that those who head companies should not set down what they believe their companies stand for – hard though that is to do. The character of a company is a matter of importance to those in it, to those who do business with it, and to those who are considering joining it.

What matters most, however, is where we stand as individual managers and how we behave when faced with decisions which require us to combine ethical and commercial judgments. In approaching such decisions, I believe it is helpful to go through two steps. The first is to determine, as precisely as we can, what our personal rules of conduct are. This does not mean drawing up a list of virtuous notions, which will probably end up as a watered-down version of the Scriptures without their literary merit. It does mean looking back at decisions we have made and working out from there what our rules actually are. The aim is to avoid confusing ourselves and everyone else by declaring one set of principles and acting on another. Our ethics are expressed in our actions, which is why they are usually clearer to others than to ourselves.

Once we know where we stand personally we can move on to the second step, which is to think through who else will be affected by the decision and how we should weight their interest in it. Some interests will be represented by well-organized groups; others will have no one to put their case. If a factory manager is negotiating a wage claim with employee representatives, their remit is to look after the interests of those who are already employed. Yet the effect of the wage settlement on the factory's costs may well determine whether new employees are likely to be taken on. So the manager cannot ignore the interest of potential employees in the outcome of the negotiation, even though that interest is not represented at the bargaining table.

Black and white alternatives are a regrettable sign of the times.

The rise of organized interest groups makes it doubly important that managers consider the arguments of everyone with a legitimate interest in a decision's outcome. Interest groups seek publicity to promote their causes and they have the advantage of being single-minded: they are against building an airport on a certain site, for example, but take no responsibility for finding a better alternative. This narrow focus gives pressure groups a debating advantage against managements, which cannot evade the responsibility for taking decisions in the same way.

In *The Hard Problems of Management*, Mark Pastin has perceptively referred to this phenomenon as the ethical superiority of the uninvolved, and there is a good deal of it about. Pressure groups are skilled at seizing the high moral ground and arguing that our judgment as managers is at best biased and at worst influenced solely by private gain because we have a direct commercial interest in the outcome of our decisions. But as managers we are also responsible for arriving at business decisions which take account of all the interests concerned; the uninvolved are not.

At times the campaign to persuade companies to divest themselves of their South African subsidiaries has exemplified this kind of ethical high-handedness. Apartheid is abhorrent politically, socially, and morally. Those who argue that they can exert some influence on the direction of change by staying put believe this as sincerely as those who favor divestment. Yet many anti-apartheid campaigners reject the proposition that both sides have the same end in view. From their perspective it is self-evident that the only ethical course of action is for companies to wash their hands of the problems of South Africa by selling out.

Managers cannot be so self-assured. In deciding what weight to give to the arguments for and against divestment, we must consider who has what at stake in the outcome of the decision. The employees of a South African subsidiary have the most direct stake, as the decision affects their future; they are also the group whose voice is least likely to be heard outside South Africa. The shareholders have at stake any loss on divestment, against which must be balanced any gain in the value of their shares through severing the South African connection. The divestment lobby is the one group for whom the decision is costless either way.

What is clear even from this limited analysis is that there is no general answer to the question of whether companies should sell their South African subsidiaries or not. Pressure to reduce complicated issues to straightforward alternatives, one of which is right and the other wrong, is a regrettable sign of the times. But boards are rarely presented with two clearly opposed alternatives. Companies faced with the same issues will therefore properly come to different conclusions and their decisions may alter over time.

A less contentious divestment decision faced my own company when we decided to sell our foods division. Because the division was mainly a U.K. business with regional brands, it did not fit the company's strategy, which called for concentrating resources behind our confectionery and soft drinks brands internationally. But it was an attractive business in its own right and the decision to sell prompted both a management bid and external offers.

Employees working in the division strongly supported the management bid and made their views felt. In this instance, they were the best organized interest group and they had more information available to them to back their case than any of the other parties involved. What they had at stake was also very clear.

From the shareholders' point of view, the premium over asset value offered by the various bidders was a key aspect of the decision. They also had an interest in seeing the deal completed without regulatory delays and without diverting too much management attention from the ongoing business. In addition, the way in which the successful bidder would guard the brand name had to be considered, since the division would take with it products carrying the parent company's name.

In weighing the advantages and disadvantages of the various offers, the board considered all the groups, consumers among them, who would be affected by the sale. But our main task was to reconcile the interests of the employees and of the shareholders. (The more, of course, we can encourage employees to become shareholders, the closer together the interests of these two stakeholders will be brought.) The division's management upped its bid in the face of outside competition, and after due deliberation we decided to sell to the management team, believing that this choice best balanced the diverse interests at stake.

Actions are unethical if they won't stand scrutiny.

Companies whose activities are international face an additional complication in taking their decisions. They aim to work to the same standards of business conduct wherever they are and to behave as good corporate citizens of the countries in which they trade. But the two aims are not always compatible: promotion on merit may be the rule of the company and promotion by seniority the custom of the country. In addition, while the financial arithmetic on which companies base their decisions is generally accepted, what is considered ethical varies among cultures.

If what would be considered corruption in the company's home territory is an accepted business practice elsewhere, how are local managers expected to act? Companies could do business only in countries in which they feel ethically at home, provided always that their shareholders take the same view. But this approach could prove unduly restrictive, and there is also a certain arrogance in dismissing foreign codes of conduct without considering why they may be different. If companies find, for example, that they have to pay customs officers in another country just to do their job, it may be that the state is simply transferring its responsibilities to the private sector as an alternative to using taxation less efficiently to the same end.

Nevertheless, this example brings us to one of the most common ethical issues companies face – how far to go in buying business? What payments are legitimate for companies to make to win orders and, the reverse side of that coin, when do gifts to employees become bribes? I use two rules of thumb to test whether a payment is acceptable from the company's point of view: Is the payment on the face of the invoice? Would it embarrass the recipient to have the gift mentioned in the company newspaper?

The first test ensures that all payments, however unusual they may seem, are recorded and go through the books. The second is aimed at distinguishing bribes from gifts, a definition which depends on the size of the gift and the influence it is likely to have on the recipient. The value of a case of whiskey to me would be limited, because I only take it as medicine. We know ourselves whether a gift is acceptable or not and we know that others will know if they are aware of the nature of the gift.

As for payment on the face of the invoice, I have found it a useful general rule precisely because codes of conduct do vary round the world. It has legitimized some otherwise unlikely company payments, to the police in one country, for example, and to the official planning authorities in another, but all went through the books and were audited. Listing a payment on the face of the invoice may not be a sufficient ethical test, but it is a necessary one; payments outside the company's system are corrupt and corrupting.

The logic behind these rules of thumb is that openness and ethics go together and that actions are unethical if they will not stand scrutiny. Openness in arriving at decisions reflects the same logic. It gives those with an interest in a particular decision the chance to make their views known and opens to argument the basis on which the decision is finally taken. This in turn enables the decision makers to learn from experience and to improve their powers of judgment.

Openness is also, I believe, the best way to disarm outside suspicion of companies' motives and actions. Disclosure is not a panacea for improving the relations between business and society, but the willingness to operate an open system is the foundation of those relations. Business needs to be open to the views of society and open in return about its own activities; this is essential for the establishment of trust.

For the same reasons, as managers we need to be candid when making decisions about other people. Dr. Johnson reminds us that when it comes to lapidary inscriptions, "no man is upon oath." But what should be disclosed in references, in fairness to those looking for work and to those who are considering employing them?

The simplest rule would seem to be that we should write the kind of reference we would wish to read. Yet "do as you would be done by" says nothing about ethics. The actions which result from applying it could be ethical or unethical, depending on the standards of the initiator. The rule could be adapted to help managers determine their ethical standards, however, by reframing it as a question: If you did business with yourself, how ethical would you think you were?

Anonymous letters accusing an employee of doing something discreditable create another context in which candor is the wisest course. Such letters cannot by definition be answered, but they convey a message to those who receive them, however warped or unfair the message may be. I normally destroy these letters, but tell the person concerned what has been said. This conveys the disregard I attach to nameless allegation, but preserves the rule of openness. From a practical point of view, it serves as a warning if there is anything in the allegations; from an ethical point of view, the degree to which my judgment of the person may now be prejudiced is known between us.

Shelving hard decisions is the least ethical course.

The last aspect of ethics in business decisions I want to discuss concerns our responsibility for the level of employment; what can or should companies do about the provision of jobs? This issue is of immediate concern to European managers because unemployment is higher in Europe than it is in the United States and the net number of new jobs created has been much lower. It comes to the fore whenever companies face decisions which require a trade-off between increasing efficiency and reducing numbers employed.

If you believe, as I do, that the primary purpose of a company is to satisfy the needs of its customers and to do so profitably, the creation of jobs cannot be the company's goal as well. Satisfying customers requires companies to compete in the marketplace, and so we cannot opt out of introducing new technology, for example, to preserve jobs. To do so would be to deny consumers the benefits of progress, to shortchange the shareholders, and in the longer run to put the jobs of everyone in the company at risk. What destroys jobs certainly and permanently is the failure to be competitive.

Experience says that the introduction of new technology creates more jobs than it eliminates, in ways which cannot be forecast. It may do so, however, only after a time lag, and those displaced may not, through lack of skills, be able to take advantage of the new opportunities when they arise. Nevertheless, the company's prime responsibility to everyone who has a stake in it is to retain its competitive edge, even if this means a loss of jobs in the short run.

Where companies do have a social responsibility, however, is in how we manage that situation, how we smooth the path of technological change. Companies are responsible for the timing of such changes and we are in a position to involve those who will be affected by the way in which those changes are introduced. We also have a vital resource in our capacity to provide training, so that continuing employees can take advantage of change and those who may lose their jobs can more readily find new ones.

In the United Kingdom, an organization called Business in the Community has been established to encourage the formation of new enterprises. Companies have backed it with cash and with secondments. The secondment of able managers to worthwhile institutions is a particularly effective expression of concern, because the ability to manage is such a scarce resource. Through Business in the Community we can create jobs collectively, even if we cannot do so individually, and it is clearly in our interest to improve the economic and social climate in this way.

Throughout, I have been writing about the responsibilities of those who head companies and my emphasis has been on taking decisions, because that is what directors and managers are appointed to do. What concerns me is that too often the public pressures which are put on companies in the name of ethics encourage their boards to put off decisions or to wash their hands of problems. There may well be commercial reasons for those choices, but there are rarely ethical ones. The ethical bases on which decisions are arrived at will vary among companies, but shelving those decisions is likely to be the least ethical course.

The company which takes drastic action in order to survive is more likely to be criticized publicly than the one which fails to grasp the nettle and gradually but inexorably declines. There is always a temptation to postpone difficult decisions, but it is not in society's interests that hard choices should be evaded because of public clamor or the possibility of legal action. Companies need to be encouraged to take the decisions which face them; the responsibility for providing that encouragement rests with society as a whole.

Society sets the ethical framework within which those who run companies have to work out their own codes of conduct. Responsibility for decisions, therefore, runs both ways. Business has to take account of its responsibilities to society in coming to its decisions, but society has to accept its responsibilities for setting the standards against which those decisions are made.

Reprint 87502

How senior managers think

The higher you go in a company, the more important it is that you combine intuition and rationality, act while thinking, and see problems as interrelated

Daniel J. Isenberg

For the most part people view managers as rational, purposeful, and decisive. They see them as going through a series of stages of analysis before deciding what to do. The doing comes after the thinking. In his study of what senior managers think about and how they think, Daniel Isenberg found that this is only partly true. Most successful senior managers do not closely follow the classical rational model of first clarifying goals, assessing the situation, formulating options, estimating likelihoods of success, making their decision, and only then taking action to implement the decision. Nor do top managers select one problem at a time to solve, as the rational model implies.

Instead of having precise goals and objectives, successful senior executives have general overriding concerns and think more often about how to do things than about what is being accomplished. In addition to depending on their ability to analyze, they also rely heavily on a mix of intuition and disciplined analysis in their decision making and incorporate their action on a problem into their diagnosis of it. The author discusses some of the implications of his findings on how managers can exercise and use the skills that senior management positions call for.

Mr. Isenberg is assistant professor of business administration at the Harvard Graduate School of Business Administration. He is currently completing a study of the thinking processes used by 12 division heads in six corporations. Previous professional publications have focused on his research on how groups function.

Illustrations by Tom Briggs, Omnigraphics Inc.

"It is not enough to have a good mind. The main thing is to use it well."
René Descartes

Jim LeBlanc phoned Steve Baum, who formerly worked in his division, to ask about the CEO's new corporate task force on quality control that wanted to meet with Jim. Jim, the head of the industrial equipment division of Tanner Corporation, thought that Steve, now director of technology, could help him figure out why the task force wanted to meet with him in two weeks.

"It's because you're doing so damn well down there, boss!" Steve replied.

"Gee, thanks. By the way, Steve, what's the agenda for Singer's staff meeting for next week?" (Singer was the president and Jim's boss.)

"Well, we're going to talk about the reorganization and look at the overhead reduction figures for each division. Then Singer's going to report on last week's executive committee meeting and his trip to Japan."

"How did it go?"

"His telex from Osaka sounded enthusiastic, but he just got in last night and I haven't seen him yet."

"Well," said Jim, "I guess we'll just have to see, but if you hear something, call me right away because if Osaka comes through I'm going to have to hustle to get ready, and you know how Bernie hates to shake it. Now, about the task force..."

In the space of three minutes, Jim LeBlanc got a lot done. In addition to collecting critical information about a task force that the CEO, with un-

Author's note: Among the many people who have helped my research I want to single out Paul Lawrence and John Kotter. I also extend thanks to the corporate managers who have given freely of their time and ideas. Miriam Schustack made very helpful comments on a previous version of this article.

Research methodology

In studying these dozen executives, I conducted intensive interviews, observed them on the job, read documents, talked with their colleagues and, in some cases, subordinates, and engaged them in various exercises in which they recounted their thoughts as they did their work. I also reported my observations and inferences back to the managers to get feedback. I spent anywhere from 1 to 25 days studying each manager (the mode was two and a half days in field interviews and observation).

usual fanfare, had personally commissioned one month ago, he also began to plan his approach to the upcoming staff meeting. He decided *not* to try to get a presentation by his marketing people on opportunities in the Far East on the agenda. Sensing that Singer *was* optimistic about the Osaka trip, Jim decided that he should get his people ready for the possibility that the deal would materialize, which meant pulling engineers off another project for a while.

What were the thinking processes that allowed Jim to get so much done so pointedly and so rapidly? What was going on in his mind during his conversation with Steve? How, given the incomplete and uncertain information that Steve gave him, did Jim conclude that the Japan deal was imminent?

For the past two years I have studied the thought processes used by more than a dozen very senior managers while on the job. (See the insert on my research methodology.) The managers that I studied ranged in age from their lower 40s to their upper 50s, in managerial experience from 10 to 30 years, and in current job tenure from 4 months to 10 years. Their companies ranged from $1 billion divisions in *Fortune* "100" companies to $10 million entrepreneurial companies just beginning to take hold in the marketplace. Company products included low- and high-technology goods, and markets ranged from rapidly expanding to precipitately deteriorating. All but two of the executives were responsible for the overall performance of their business units. As all had been frequently promoted throughout their careers and were considered excellent performers across the board, they were a representative sample of today's successful business executives.

Two findings about how senior managers do *not* think stand out from the study. First, it is hard to pinpoint if or when they actually make decisions about major business or organizational issues on their own. And second, they seldom think in ways that one might simplistically view as "rational," i.e., they rarely systematically formulate goals, assess their worth, evaluate the probabilities of alternative ways of reaching them, and choose the path that maximizes expected return. Rather, managers frequently bypass rigorous, analytical planning altogether, particularly when they face difficult, novel, or extremely entangled problems. When they do use analysis for a prolonged time, it is always in conjunction with intuition.

Let me make myself clear. Obviously, decisions *do* get made in organizations and these *are* frequently justified by data and logic. In particular, when viewed retrospectively over a long time period, effective executives often appear quite rational. Yet when studying their concurrent thinking processes, being "rational" does not best describe what the manager presiding over the decision-making process thinks about nor *how* he or she thinks.

I have a fourfold purpose in this article. First, I want to present a more accurate and empirically grounded description of what goes on inside the minds of senior managers. (See the insert on the good and bad news about cognition.) Second, I hope to offer a more accurate description of managerial thinking that should help provide a beginning language for talking about these elusive mental phenomena. Third, I hope that this language will also help to relieve some managers of the inconsistency between their view of how they are "supposed to" think and the thinking processes that, through experience, they have learned are actually quite effective. Fourth, I want to take advantage of successful senior managers' experiences to explore the managerial implications of their thinking processes.

What senior managers think about

Senior managers tend to think about two kinds of problems: how to create effective organizational processes and how to deal with one or two overriding concerns, or very general goals. These two domains of thought underlie the two critical activities that John P. Kotter found general managers engaged in: developing and maintaining an extensive interpersonal network, and formulating an agenda.[1]

A focus on process

The primary focus of on-line managerial thinking is on organizational and interpersonal processes. By "process" I mean the ways managers bring people and groups together to handle problems and take action. Whether proposing a change in the execu-

Some good and bad news about cognition

Although the study of cognition is not new, in the past 30 years the popularity and practical importance of the "cognitive sciences" have increased dramatically, adding to our knowledge of the capabilities and limitations of the human mind. The news is both "good" and "bad" in terms of our accuracy as judges and decision makers.

Some good news The good news is that each of us possesses a wide range of cognitive capabilities, including many that even the most powerful computers cannot match. For all intents and purposes the long-term storage capacity of the human memory is unlimited, capable of storing perhaps trillions of bits of information. Furthermore, much of this memory is almost immediately accessible.

The human mind is also capable of performing very complicated simulations such as giving directions to someone on how to get to an office from an airport or rehearsing an upcoming meeting. We are also capable of making huge inferential leaps with rarely a hitch. Try interpreting the following sentences: "The manager prepared the forecast using an accepted inflation estimate. He knew that it was imprecise but figured that it was better than no projection at all." Who is "he"? What is "it"? What does "projection" refer to? We know what these sentences mean, yet to interpret them correctly required the reader to make a number of inferences, which he or she usually makes with unhesitating accuracy.

Finally, we are capable of using our unlimited memory, our rapid retrieval system, and our unconscious rules of inference to attain extremely high levels of skill, such as playing chess, analyzing stocks, conducting performance appraisals, or speaking a language. These skills do not come easily, requiring years of experience and many thousands of hours of practice. Nevertheless, when we use them we compress years of experience and learning into split seconds. This compression is one of the bases of what we call intuition as well as of the art of management.

Some bad news The same cognitive processes that underlie our greatest mental accomplishments also account for incorrigible flaws in our thinking. For instance, we easily believe that salient events occur more frequently than they really do: for example, despite the fact that dozens of examples exist where missed budgets did not lead to termination, managers interpret Sam's being fired for not making a budget as "There is a good chance that division heads who do not meet budgeted profit objectives will get axed."

A second family of flaws arises from our overconfidence in our own expertise at making complex judgments. Various cognitive biases such as the "hindsight bias," our retrospective confidence in judgments that we hesitated about making at the time ("I *knew* it wouldn't work when she first proposed it"), and our tendency to search for confirming but not for disconfirming evidence of our judgments, conspire to exaggerate that belief.

And finally, research has shown that when presented with data, we are not very good at assessing the degree of relationship among variables – even though this skill is critical for successful management. Unless the relationships are very obvious, we tend to rely on preconceptions and perceive illusory correlations.

A number of excellent books on human cognition are in print. For a nontechnical discussion of the good news, Morton Hunt's *The Universe Within* (Simon & Schuster, 1982), is a good starting place. A more technical discussion of human cognition is Stephen K. Reed's *Cognition: Theory and Applications* (Brooks/Cole, 1982). A somewhat technical but very comprehensive presentation of the bad news can be found in Daniel Kahneman, Paul Slovic, and Amos Tversky's edited volume, *Judgment Under Uncertainty: Heuristics and Biases* (Cambridge University Press, 1982).

---

tive compensation structure, establishing priorities for a diverse group of business units, consolidating redundant operations, or preparing for plant closings, a senior executive's conscious thoughts are foremost among the processes for accomplishing a change or implementing a decision: "Who are the key players here, and how can I get their support? Whom should I talk to first? Should I start by getting the production group's input? What kind of signal will that send to the marketing people? I can't afford to lose their commitment in the upcoming discussions on our market strategy."

During the first months of his tenure, one area general manager I studied asked all of his business unit management teams to evaluate their own units. Subsequently, the area manager and his staff spent a day or more with each team discussing the whole area, each business unit within it, and how the two interrelated. Although he was concerned with the substance of the business-unit priorities, uppermost in his mind was a series of process concerns: How could the review process help managers be increasingly committed to their goals? How could the process help

1 John P. Kotter, *The General Managers* (New York: Free Press, 1982).

managers to become increasingly aware of the interdependencies among business units? How did his business unit managers use their people in reviewing their business units? How much management depth existed in the units?

In addition to thinking about organizational processes, successful senior managers think a lot about interpersonal processes and the people they come in contact with. They try to understand the strengths and weaknesses of others, the relationships that are important to *them*, what *their* agendas and priorities are.

For example, the CEO of a small high-technology company spent over an hour with his personnel director, a woman he rated as having performed excellently so far and whom he saw as having great potential although still inexperienced. At the time of the discussion, the CEO was considering adopting a new top-management structure under which the personnel director would report to another staff member rather than directly to him.

The CEO explained the proposed change to the personnel director, pointing out that it was not definite and that he was soliciting her reactions. Managers' "maps" of people provide them with guides to action. In this case, because of his sense of the personnel director's needs, the CEO slowed the reorganizing process so that the people who reported to him could deal with the various issues that arose.

The CEO elaborately described to me his awareness of the personnel director's concern at being new and at being a woman, and her desire to be in direct contact with him. He also understood her worry that if she reported to someone lower than him, people would perceive that the new personnel function was not very important and she would lose power.

The overriding concern

The stereotypical senior executive pays a great deal of attention to the strategy of the business, carefully formulates goals, lays out quantified and clear objectives, and sets about to achieve these objectives in the most efficient way. Whereas senior executives certainly attend to specific strategies and objectives some of the time, in their day-to-day reality specific objectives lurk in the background, not in the forefront of their thoughts.

Approximately two-thirds of the senior managers I studied were preoccupied with a very limited number of quite general issues, each of which subsumed a large number of specific issues. This preoccupation persisted for anywhere from a month to several years and, when in effect, dominated the manager's attention and provided coherence to many of his or her chaotic and disorganized activities.

The general manager of one large division of an automotive company, for example, used the word "discipline" over a dozen times in the course of a two-hour interview. For him, this concept embodied his deep concern for creating order and predictability in a division that, in his view, had become too loose before he took it over. His concern for discipline appeared in a number of diverse actions–strongly discouraging his subordinates' fire-fighting mentality, criticizing their poor preparation for corporate reviews, introducing rigorous strategic planning, encouraging time management, putting out a yearly calendar with divisional and corporate meetings printed on it, publishing agendas for many of these meetings up to a year in advance, and, by keeping recent reports in the top drawer of his desk, forcing himself to review frequently the division's activities and performance.

Regardless of its substance, the overriding concern weaves its way in and out of all the manager's daily activities, at times achieving the dimensions of an all-consuming passion.

After his first 100 days in office, an area general manager described his experience turning around a subsidiary in these words:

"The personal cost of achieving our top priorities has been huge. I dropped all outside activities. Now I have a feeling of just having emerged, like a chap who's been taken by a surf wave and rolled. Suddenly he comes up and can look at daylight again. It has been like a single-minded rage or madness. At the end of the 100 days, somehow I have awakened. It was overwhelming."

Of course senior managers do think about the content of their businesses, particularly during crises and periodic business reviews. But this thinking is always in close conjunction with thinking about the process for getting *others* to think about the business. In other words, even very senior managers devote most of their attention to the tactics of implementation rather than the formulation of strategy.

How senior managers think

In making their day-by-day and minute-by-minute tactical maneuvers, senior executives tend to rely on several general thought processes such as using intuition; managing a network of interrelated problems; dealing with ambiguity, inconsistency, novelty, and surprise; and integrating action into the process of thinking.

Using intuition

Generations of writers on the art of management have recognized that practicing managers rely heavily on intuition.[2] In general, however, people have a poor grasp of what intuition is. Some see it as the opposite of rationality, others use it as an excuse for capriciousness, and currently some view it as the exclusive property of a particular side of the brain.

Senior managers use intuition in at least five distinct ways. First, they intuitively sense when a problem exists. The chief financial officer of a leading technical products company, for example, forecast a difficult year ahead for the company and, based on a vague gut feel that something was wrong, decided to analyze one business group. "The data on the group were inconsistent and unfocused," he said after doing the analysis. "I had the sense that they were talking about a future that just was not going to happen, and I turned out to be right."

Second, managers rely on intuition to perform well-learned behavior patterns rapidly. Early on, managerial action needs to be thought through carefully. Once the manager is "fluent" at performance, however, and the behavior is programmed, executives can execute programs without conscious effort. In the words of one general manager:

"It was very instinctive, almost like you have been drilled in close combat for years and now the big battle is on, and you really don't have time to think. It's as if your arms, your feet, and your body just move instinctively. You have a preoccupation with working capital, a preoccupation with capital expenditure, a preoccupation with people, and one with productivity, and all this goes so fast that you don't even know whether it's completely rational, or it's part rational, part intuitive."

Intuition here refers to the smooth automatic performance of learned behavior sequences. This intuition is not arbitrary or irrational, but is based on years of painstaking practice and hands-on experience that build skills. After a while a manager can perform a sequence of actions in a seamless fabric of action and reaction without being aware of the effort.

A third function of intuition is to synthesize isolated bits of data and experience into an integrated picture, often in an "aha!" experience. In the words of one manager: "Synergy is always nonrational because it takes you beyond the mere sum of the parts. It is a nonrational, nonlogical thinking perspective."

2 See, for example, Chester I. Barnard, *The Functions of the Executive* (Cambridge: Harvard University Press, 1938); also Henry Mintzberg, "Planning on the Left Side and Managing on the Right," HBR July-August 1976, p. 49.

Fourth, some managers use intuition as a check (a belt-and-suspenders approach) on the results of more rational analysis. Most senior executives are familiar with the formal decision analysis models and tools, and those that occasionally use such systematic methods for reaching decisions are leery of solutions that these methods suggest that run counter to their sense of the correct course of action.

Conversely, if managers completely trusted intuition, they'd have little need for rigorous and systematic analysis. In practice, executives work on an issue until they find a match between their "gut" and their "head." One manager explained to me, "Intuition leads me to seek out holes in the data. But I discount casual empiricism and don't act on it."

Fifth, managers can use intuition to bypass in-depth analysis and move rapidly to come up with a plausible solution. Used in this way, intuition is an almost instantaneous cognitive process in which a manager recognizes familiar patterns. In much the same way that people can immediately recognize faces that were familiar years ago, administrators have a repertoire of familiar problematic situations matched with the necessary responses. As one manager explained:

"My gut feel points me in a given direction. When I arrive there, then I can begin to sort out the issues. I do not do a deep analysis at first. I suppose the intuition comes from scar tissue, getting burned enough times. For example, while discussing the European budget with someone, suddenly I got the answer: it was hard for us to get the transfer prices. It rang a bell, then I ran some quick checks."

By now it should be clear that intuition is not the opposite of rationality, nor is it a random process of guessing. Rather, it is based on extensive experience both in analysis and problem solving and in implementation, and to the extent that the lessons of experience are logical and well-founded, then so is the intuition. Further, managers often combine gut feel with systematic analysis, quantified data, and thoughtfulness.

It should also be clear that executives use intuition during *all* phases of the problem-solving process: problem finding, problem defining, generating and choosing a solution, and implementing the solution. In fact, senior managers often ignore the implied linear progression of the rational decision-making model and jump opportunistically from phase to phase, allowing implementation concerns to affect the problem definition and perhaps even to limit the range of solutions generated.

Problem management

Managers at all levels work at understanding and solving the problems that arise in their jobs. One distinctive characteristic of top managers is that their thinking deals not with isolated and discrete items but with portfolios of problems, issues, and opportunities in which (1) many problems exist simultaneously, (2) these problems compete for some part of his or her immediate concern, and (3) the issues are interrelated.

The cognitive tasks in problem management are to find and define good problems, to "map" these into a network, and to manage their dynamically shifting priorities. For lack of a better term, I call this the process of problem management.

Defining the problem. After learning of a state health organization threat to exclude one of their major products from the list of drugs for which the state would reimburse buyers, top executives in a pharmaceutical company struggled to find a proper response. After some time, the managers discovered that the real problem was not the alleged drug abuse the availability of the drug on the street caused. Rather, the problem was budgetary: the health services department had to drastically reduce its budget and was doing so by trimming its list of reimbursable drugs. Once they redefined the problem, the pharmaceutical executives not only could work on a better, more real problem, but also had a chance to solve it – which they did.[3]

In another case, a division general manager discovered that, without his knowledge but with the approval of the division controller, one of his vice presidents had drawn a questionable personal loan from the company. The division manager told me how he defined the problem: "I could spend my time formulating rules to guide managers. But the real fundamental issue here was that I needed to expect and demand that my managers manage their resources effectively." Although he recognized the ethical components involved, he chose to define the problem as concerned with asset management rather than cheating. Because asset management was an issue the division frequently discussed, the manager felt that it was more legitimate and efficacious to define the problem in this way.

Making a network of problems. By forming problem categories, executives can see how individual problems interrelate. For instance, a bank CEO had a "network" of at least 19 related problems and issues that he was concerned about. Among these were: establishing credibility in international banking, strengthening the bank's role in corporate banking, increasing the range of financial services and products,

3 See my study, "Drugs and Drama: The Effects of Two Dramatic Events in a Pharmaceutical Company on Managers' Cognitions," Working Paper #83-55 (Boston: Harvard Business School, 1983).

being prepared to defensively introduce new products in response to competitors' innovations, developing systems to give product cost information, reducing operational costs, standardizing branch architecture, and utilizing space efficiently.

The bank CEO classified these problems in terms of broad issue categories. He found that many were related to the issue of expanding and broadening the bank's competence beyond consumer banking in which it was already firmly established. A second overarching issue was standardization of the bank's many branches with regard to architecture, physical layout, accounting systems, and so on.

Having an interrelated network of problems allows a manager to seize opportunities more flexibly and to use progress on one problem to achieve progress on another, related issue. The bank CEO likened himself to a frog on a lily pad waiting for the fly – the problem or issue – to buzz by. Having a mental network of problems helped him to realize the opportunities as they occurred.

Choosing which problem to work on. Although managers often decide to work on the problem that seems to offer the best opportunities for attack, determining which problems they ought to tackle can be hard. As one manager commented:

"I have to sort through so many issues at once. There are ten times too many. I use a number of defense mechanisms to deal with this overload – I use delaying actions, I deny the existence of problems, or I put problems in a mental queue of sorts. This is an uncomfortable process for me. My office and responsibility say I need to deal with all of these issues, so I create smoke or offer some grand theory as my only way to keep my own sanity. One of the frustrations is that I don't want to tell my people that their number one problems have lower priorities than they think they should get."

In my observations, how managers define and rank problems is heavily influenced by how easy the problems are to solve. Very shortly after perceiving that a problem exists, managers run a quick feasibility check to see if it is solvable. Only if they find it is solvable will they then invest further energy to understand its various ramifications and causes. In other words, managers tend not to think very much about a problem unless they sense that it is solvable. Contrary to some management doctrines, this finding suggests that a general concept of what is a possible solution often precedes and guides the process of conceptualizing a problem.

Thus, the two stages of problem analysis and problem solving are tightly linked and occur reiteratively rather than sequentially. By going back and forth between these two cognitive processes, managers define the array of problems facing them in terms that already incorporate key features of solutions and that thus make it easier for them to take action.

One outcome of this process is that managers have an organized mental map of all the problems and issues facing them. The map is neither static nor permanent; rather, managers continually test, correct, and revise it. In the words of one CEO, the executive "takes advantage of the best cartography at his command, but knows that that is not enough. He knows that along the way he will find things that change his maps or alter his perceptions of the terrain. He trains himself the best he can in the detective skills. He is endlessly sending out patrols to learn greater detail, overflying targets to get some sense of the general battlefield."

Tolerating ambiguity. The senior managers that I observed showed an ability to tolerate and even thrive on high degrees of ambiguity and apparent inconsistency. As one top executive said:

"I think ambiguity can be destroying, but it can be very helpful to an operation. Ambiguities come from the things you can't spell out exactly. They yield a certain freedom you need as a chief executive officer not to be nailed down on everything. Also, certain people thrive on ambiguity, so I leave certain things ambiguous. The fact is we tie ourselves too much to linear plans, to clear time scales. I like to fuzz up time scales completely."

Because demands on a manager become both stronger and more divergent as responsibility increases, the need to tolerate apparent ambiguity and inconsistency also increases. For example, the top manager has to deal with stakeholders who may have adversarial roles. By responding positively to one set of demands, the manager automatically will create other conflicting sets of demands.

The reason I have called the inconsistency "apparent" is that senior managers tend to have ways of thinking that make issues seem less inconsistent. For example, the president of a leading high-technology company was considering whether to exercise or forgo an option to lease land on which to build expensive warehouse space for one of the divisions at the same time as the division was laying off workers for the first time in its history. "To spend a half million dollars on keeping the land and building warehouse space while the plant is laying off people looks terrible and makes no sense," he said, "but if next year is a good year, we'll need to be in a position to make the product."

Perceiving and understanding novelty. The managers I observed dealt frequently with novel situations that were unexpected and, in many cases, were impossible to plan for in advance. For example, one division general manager found himself with the task of selling his division, which was still developing a marketable product. In response to its shareholders, the corporation had shifted its strategy and thus decided to divest the fledgling division. How should the general manager look for buyers? If buyers were not forthcoming, would the corporation retain a stake to reduce the risk to potential new partners? How should he manage his people in the process of selling? Should he himself look for a new position or commit himself to a new owner? These were some of the unique questions the division head faced while selling his own division, and there was no industry experience to give him clear answers.

In general, the human mind is conservative. Long after an assumption is outmoded, people tend to apply it to novel situations. One way in which some of the senior managers I studied counteract this conservative bent is by paying attention to their feelings of *surprise* when a particular fact does not fit their prior understanding, and then by highlighting rather than denying the novelty. Although surprise made them feel uncomfortable, it made them take the cause seriously and inquire into it–"What is behind the personal loan by my vice president of sales that appears on the books? How extensive a problem is it?" "Why did the management committee of the corporation spend over an hour of its valuable time discussing a problem three levels down in my division?" "Now that we've shown the health services department beyond a reasonable doubt that this drug is not involved in drug abuse, why don't they reinstate it on the list?"

Rather than deny, downplay, or ignore disconfirmation, successful senior managers often treat it as friendly and in a way cherish the discomfort surprise creates. As a result, these managers often perceive novel situations early on and in a frame of mind relatively undistorted by hidebound notions.

What to do about thinking

Having looked at the inner workings of the managerial mind, what insights can we derive from our observations? Literally hundreds of laboratory and field studies demonstrate that the human mind is imperfectly rational, and dozens of additional articles, offering arguments based on every field of study from psychology to economics, explain why.[4] The evidence that we should curtail our impractical and overly ambitious expectations of managerial rationality is compelling.

Yet abandoning the rational ideal leaves us with two glaring problems. First, whether managers think in a linear and systematic fashion or not, companies still need to strive toward rational action in the attainment of corporate goals, particularly in their use of resources. Second, we still need to spell out what kinds of thinking processes are attainable and helpful to senior managers.

Program rationality into the organization

Of course, rationality is desirable and should be manifest in the functioning of the company. One alternative to the vain task of trying to rationalize managers is to increase the rationality of organizational systems and processes. Although organizational behavior is never completely rational, managers can design and program processes and systems that will approach rationality in resource allocation and employment.

Decision support systems are one source of organizational rationality. These generally computerized routines perform many functions ranging from providing a broad and quantitative data base, to presenting that data base in easily understandable form, to modeling the impact of decisions on various financial and other criteria, to mimicking expert judgment such as in the diagnosis and repair of malfunctioning equipment or in oil field exploration.

Another rational process that many businesses employ is strategic planning. Nonrational or partly rational managers can devise, implement, and use a plan that systematically assesses a company's strengths and weaknesses, logically extrapolates a set of its competencies, proposes a quantitative assessment of environmental constraints and resources, and performs all these tasks in a time-sequenced, linear fashion.

Of course, companies have used rational systems for information gathering, strategic planning, budgeting, human resource planning, environmental

4 Some of Herbert A. Simon's classic work on bounded rationality and "satisficing" is collected in *Models of Thought* (New Haven: Yale University Press, 1979). More recently, Amos Tversky, Daniel Kahneman, and other psychologists have described the mechanisms producing imperfect judgment and nonrational choice. See, for example, Daniel Kahneman, Paul Slovic, and Amos Tversky, ed., *Judgment Under Uncertainty: Heuristics and Biases* (Cambridge, U.K.: Cambridge University Press, 1982).

5 Louis R. Goldberg, "Man vs. Model of Man: A Rationale, Plus Some Evidence, for a Method of Improving on Clinical Inferences," *Psychological Bulletin,* 1970, 73, p. 422.

6 Jon Elster, *Ulysses and the Sirens: Studies in Rationality and Irrationality* (Cambridge, Mass.: Cambridge University Press, 1979).

scanning, and so forth for a long time. But I see these systems not only as useful but also as a necessary complement to a manager's apparent inability to be very systematic or rational in thought.

But is it possible for imperfectly rational managers to design even more perfectly rational systems? The answer is a qualified yes. There is evidence, for example, that with help people can design systems that are better than they are themselves at making judgments.[5] Creating organizational systems to improve on their own behavior is not new to managers. In order to still hear the beautiful sirens yet prevent himself being seduced by the music and throwing himself into the sea, Ulysses ordered his men to block their own ears with wax, bind him to the mast, and to tighten his bindings if he ordered them to let him go. Although Ulysses begged his sailors to release him, they obeyed his original orders and Ulysses succeeded in both hearing the sirens and surviving their perilous allure.[6]

Programming rationality into the organizational functioning is important for another reason: rational systems free senior executives to tackle the ambiguous, ill-defined tasks that the human mind is uniquely capable of addressing. Many senior managers today face problems – developing new products for embryonic markets, creating new forms of manufacturing operations, conceiving of innovative human resource systems – that are new to them and new to their companies and that they can deal with only extemporaneously and with a nonprogrammable artistic sense. In fact, it may even seem paradoxical that managers need to create rational systems in order to creatively and incrementally tackle the nonrecurrent problems that defy systematic approaches.

Hone intellectual skills

In the literature on managerial behavior there is disagreement as to how much or how often senior managers engage in thoughtful reflection. Many executives that I studied do make time for in-depth thinking, sometimes while they are alone, sometimes with their peers or subordinates, and sometimes in active experimentation.

Furthermore, most senior managers I studied constantly maintain and sharpen their intellectual abilities in order to better analyze their current or past experiences. Rigorous thinking is a way of life for them, not a task they try to avoid or to expedite superficially.

These senior managers read books outside their fields, engage in enthusiastic discussions of political and economic affairs, attend academic lectures and management seminars, and tackle brain teasers such as word problems, chess, and crossword puzzles. One company president I studied is a regular theatergoer who can discuss Shakespearean and contemporary plays at great length, while another often immerses himself in classical music and allows ideas about difficult work-related issues to float around in his consciousness. These activities are valuable not only for their content but also for the thinking processes that they establish, develop, and refine. Whether managers indulge in such "blue sky" irrelevant activities at work or outside, they are developing critical mental resources that they can then apply to problems that arise in their jobs.

Think while doing

One of the implications of the intuitive nature of executive action is that "thinking" is inseparable from acting. Since managers often "know" what is right before they can analyze and explain it, they frequently act first and think later. Thinking is inextricably tied to action in what I call thinking/acting cycles, in which managers develop thoughts about their companies and organizations not by analyzing a problematic situation and then acting, but by thinking and acting in close concert. Many of the managers I studied were quite facile at using thinking to inform action and vice versa.

Given the great uncertainty of many of the management or business issues that they face, senior managers often instigate a course of action simply to learn more about an issue: "We bought that company because we wanted to learn about that business." They then use the results of the action to develop a more complete understanding of the issue. What may appear as action for action's sake is really the result of an intuitive understanding that analysis is only possible in the light of experience gained while attempting to solve the problem. Analysis is not a passive process but a dynamic, interactive series of activity and reflection.

One implication of acting/thinking cycles is that action is often part of defining the problem, not just of implementing the solution. Frequently, once they had begun to perceive the symptoms, but before they could articulate a problem, the managers I studied talked to a few people to collect more information and confirm what they already knew. The act of collecting more data more often than not changed the nature of the problem, in part because subordinates then realized that the problem was serious enough to warrant the boss's attention. Managers also often acted in the absence of clearly specified goals, allowing these to emerge from the process of clarifying the nature of the problem.

Yet how often do managers push their subordinates to spell out *their* goals clearly and specify *their* objectives? A creative subordinate will always be able to present a plausible and achievable goal when pressed, but in the early stages of a tough problem it is more helpful for managers to provide a receptive forum in which their people can play around with an issue, "noodle" it through, and experiment. Sometimes it will be necessary for managers to allow subordinates to act in the absence of goals to achieve a clearer comprehension of what is going on, and even at times to *discover* rather than achieve the organization's true goals.

Manage time by managing problems

All managers would like to accomplish more in less time. One of the implications of the process of mapping problems and issues is that when a manager addresses any particular problem, he or she calls a number of related problems or issues to mind at the same time. One by-product is that a manager can attain economies of effort.

For example, when working on a problem of poor product quality, a division manager might see a connection between poor quality and an inadequate production control system and tackle both problems together. To address the issues, she could form a cross-functional task force involving her marketing manager, who understands customers' tolerance for defects. (One reason for bringing him in might be to prepare him for promotion in two or three years.) She might intend the task force to reduce interdepartmental conflicts as well as prepare a report that she could present to corporate headquarters.

Managers can facilitate the process of creating a problem network in many ways. They can ask their staff to list short- and long-term issues that they think need to be addressed, consolidate these lists, and spend some time together mapping the interrelationships. Or they can ask themselves how an issue fits into other nonproblematic aspects of the company or business unit. How does product quality relate to marketing strategy? To capital expenditure guidelines? To the company's R&D center with a budget surplus? To the new performance appraisal system? To the company's recent efforts in affirmative action? To their own career plans? Managers should never deal with problems in isolation. They should always ask themselves what additional related issues they should be aware of while dealing with the problem at hand.[7]

Some suggestions

A number of suggestions on how managers can improve their thinking emerge from my study of senior managers' thought processes:

☐ Bolster intuition with rational thinking. Recognize that good intuition requires hard work, study, periods of concentrated thought, and rehearsal.

☐ Offset tendencies to be rational by stressing the importance of values and preferences, of using imagination, and of acting with an incomplete picture of the situation.

☐ Develop skills at mapping an unfamiliar territory by, for example, generalizing from facts and testing generalities by collecting more data.

☐ Pay attention to the simple rules of thumb–heuristics–that you have developed over the years. These can help you bypass many levels of painstaking analysis.

☐ Don't be afraid to act in the absence of complete understanding, but then cherish the feelings of surprise that you will necessarily experience.

☐ Spend time understanding what the problem or issue is.

☐ Look for the connections among the many diverse problems and issues facing you to see their underlying relationships with each other. By working on one problem you can make progress on others.

☐ Finally, recognize that your abilities to think are critical assets that you need to manage and develop in the same way that you manage other business assets. ▽

Reprint 84608

7 For an interesting application of these ideas to a different leadership setting, see my chapter "Some Hows and Whats of Managerial Thinking: Implications for Future Army Leaders" in *Military Leadership on the Future Battlefield* (New York: Pergamon Press, 1984).

HBR Classic

H. Edward Wrapp

Good managers don't make policy decisions

Rather, they give a sense of direction, and are masters at developing opportunities

This article was first published in the September-October 1967 issue. The editors have chosen it as an "HBR Classic" because it has passed the test of time with flying colors. Requests for reprints still come in at an impressive rate.

The article's continued success is all the more remarkable because in the 1960s its precepts of good management were heretical. The author's successful general manager is an opportunist and a muddler who does not spell out detailed company objectives or master plans, one who seldom makes forthright statements of policy, one who often gets personally involved in operating matters.

In a retrospective commentary, the author discusses putting his theories into practice, and points out the reasons why managers – even those who have tried to follow his precepts of good management – have been swept over the dam.

Mr. Wrapp retired in 1983 as professor of business policy at the Graduate School of Business, University of Chicago, a position he had held for 20 years. He also was director of the school's executive program and associate dean for management programs. He has served on the boards of numerous corporations.

The upper reaches of management are a land of mystery and intrigue. Very few people have ever been there, and the present inhabitants frequently send back messages that are incoherent both to other levels of management and to the world in general.

This absence of firsthand reports may account for the myths, illusions, and caricatures that permeate the literature of management – for example, such widely held notions as these:

> Life gets less complicated as a manager reaches the top of the pyramid.
>
> The manager at the top level knows everything that's going on in the organization, can command whatever resources he may need, and therefore can be more decisive.
>
> The general manager's day is taken up with making broad policy decisions and formulating precise objectives.
>
> The top executive's primary activity is conceptualizing long-range plans.
>
> In a large company, the top executive may be seen meditating about the role of his organization in society.

I suggest that none of these versions alone, or in combination, is an accurate portrayal of what a general manager does. Perhaps students of the management process have been overly eager to develop a theory and a discipline. As one executive I know puts it, "I guess I do some of the things described in the books and articles, but the descriptions are lifeless, and my job isn't."

What common characteristics, then, do successful executives exhibit in reality? I shall identify five skills or talents which, in my experience, seem especially significant. (For details on the method used in reaching these conclusions, see the insert.)

Keeping well informed

First, each of my heroes has a special talent for keeping himself informed about a wide range of operating decisions being made at different levels in the company. As he moves up the ladder, he develops a network of information sources in many different departments. He cultivates these sources and keeps them open no matter how high he climbs in the organization. When the need arises, he bypasses the lines on the organization chart to seek more than one version of a situation.

In some instances, especially when they suspect he would not be in total agreement with their decision, his subordinates will elect to inform him in advance, before they announce a decision. In these circumstances, he is in a position to defer the decision, or redirect it, or even block further action. However, he does not insist on this procedure. Ordinarily he leaves it up to the members of his organization to decide at what stage they inform him.

Top-level managers are frequently criticized by writers, consultants, and lower levels of management for continuing to enmesh themselves in operating problems, after promotion to the top, rather than withdrawing to the "big picture." Without any doubt, some managers do get lost in a welter of detail and insist on making too many decisions. Superficially, the good manager may seem to make the same mistake–but his purposes are different. He knows that only by keeping well informed about the decisions being made can he avoid the sterility so often found in those who isolate themselves from operations. If he follows the advice to free himself from operations, he may soon find himself subsisting on a diet of abstractions, leaving the choice of what he eats in the hands of his subordinates. As Kenneth Boulding puts it, "The very purpose of a hierarchy is to prevent information from reaching higher layers. It operates as an information filter, and there are little wastebaskets all along the way."[1]

What kinds of action does a successful executive take to keep his information live and accurate? One company president that I worked with, for example, sensed that his vice presidents were insulating him from some of the vital issues being discussed at lower levels. He accepted a proposal for a formal management development program primarily because it afforded him an opportunity to discuss company problems with middle managers several layers removed from him in the organization. By meeting with small groups of these men in an academic setting, he learned much about their preoccupations, and also about those of his vice presidents. And he accomplished his purposes without undermining the authority of line managers.

Focusing time & energy

The second skill of the good manager is that he knows how to save his energy and hours for those few particular issues, decisions, or problems to which he should give his personal attention. He knows the fine and subtle distinction between keeping fully informed about operating decisions and allowing the organization to force him into participating in these decisions or, even worse, making them. Recognizing that he can bring his special talents to bear on only a limited number of matters, he chooses those issues which he believes will have the greatest long-term impact on the company, and on which his special abilities can be most productive. Under ordinary circumstances, he will limit himself to three or four major objectives during any single period of sustained activity.

What about the situations he elects *not* to become involved in as a decision maker? He makes sure (using the skill first mentioned) that the organization keeps him informed about them at various stages; he does not want to be accused of indifference to such issues. He trains his subordinates not to bring the matters to him for a decision. The communication to him from below is essentially one of: "Here is our sizeup, and here's what we propose to do."

Reserving his hearty encouragement for those projects which hold superior promise of a contribution to total corporate strategy, he simply acknowledges receipt of information on other matters. When he sees a problem where the organization needs his help, he finds a way to transmit his know-how short of giving orders–usually by asking perceptive questions.

Playing the power game

To what extent do successful top executives push their ideas and proposals through the organization? The rather common notion that the "prime mover" continually creates and forces through new programs, like a powerful majority leader in a liberal Congress, is in my opinion very misleading.

The successful manager is sensitive to the power structure in the organization. In considering any major current proposal, he can plot the position of the various individuals and units in the organization on a scale ranging from complete, outspoken support down to determined, sometimes bitter, and oftentimes well-cloaked opposition. In the middle of the scale is an area of comparative indifference. Usually, several aspects of a proposal will fall into this area, and here is where he knows he can operate. He assesses the depth and nature of the blocks in the organization. His perception permits him to move through what I call corridors of comparative indifference. He seldom challenges when a corridor is blocked, preferring to pause until it has opened up.

Related to this particular skill is his ability to recognize the need for a few trial balloon launchers in the organization. He knows that the organization will tolerate only a certain number of proposals which emanate from the apex of the pyramid. No matter how sorely he may be tempted to stimulate the organization with a flow of his own ideas, he knows he must work through idea men in different parts of the organization. As he studies the reactions of key individuals and groups to the trial balloons these men send up, he is able to make a better assessment of how to limit the emasculation of the various proposals. For seldom does he find a proposal which is supported by all quarters of the organization. The emergence of strong support in certain quarters is almost sure to evoke strong opposition in others.

Sense of timing

Circumstances like these mean that a good sense of timing is a priceless asset for a top executive. For example, a vice president had for some time been convinced that his company lacked a sense of direction and needed a formal long-range planning activity to fill the void. Up to the time in question, his soft overtures to other top executives had been rebuffed. And then he spotted an opening.

A management development committee proposed a series of weekend meetings for second-level officers in the company. After extensive debate, but for reasons not announced, the president rejected this proposal. The members of the committee openly resented what seemed to them an arbitrary rejection.

The vice president, sensing a tense situation, suggested to the president that the same officers who were to have attended the weekend manage-

Editors' note: The editors ask that whenever you read the word "he," "him," or "his," you take it to mean "she," "her," or "hers" as well.

1 From a speech at a meeting sponsored by the Crowell Collier Institute of Continuing Education in New York, as reported in *Business Week*, February 18, 1967, p. 202.

Research

I have reached the conclusions outlined here after working closely with many managers in many different companies. In truth, the managers were not preselected with research in mind. Never did I tell the man that he was being studied, nor was I in fact studying his behavior. Research was not the purpose of our relationship. We were collaborating to solve some real problem.

Researching the management process when the manager is aware that he is being studied sometimes produces strange results. Rarely is a good executive able to think objectively about the management process as it is exemplified in his own methods. When he tries to explain to a researcher or writer, he tends to feel compelled to develop rational, systematic explanations of how he does his job – explanations that in my opinion are largely fictional.

A manager cannot be expected to describe his methods even if he understands them. They border on manipulation, and the stigma associated with manipulation can be fatal. If the organization ever identifies him as a manipulator, his job becomes more difficult. No one willingly submits to manipulation, and those around him organize to protect themselves. And yet every good manager does have to manipulate.

My definition of a good manager is a simple one: under competitive industry conditions, he is able to move his organization significantly toward the goals he has set, whether measured by higher return on investment, product improvement, development of management talent, faster growth in sales and earnings, or some other standard. Bear in mind that this definition does not refer to the administrator whose principal role is to maintain the status quo in a company or in a department. Keeping the wheels turning in a direction already set is a relatively simple task, compared to that of directing the introduction of a continuing flow of changes and innovations, and preventing the organization from flying apart under pressure.

ment development seminars be organized into a long-range planning committee. The timing of his suggestion was perfect. The president, looking for a bone to toss to the committee, acquiesced immediately, and the management development committee in its next meeting enthusiastically endorsed the idea.

This vice president had been conducting a kind of continuing market research to discover how to sell his long-range planning proposal. His previous probes of the "market" had told him that the president's earlier rejections of his proposal were not so final as to preclude an eventual shift in the corridors of attitude I have mentioned.

The vice president caught the committee in a conciliatory mood, and his proposal rode through with flying colors.

Cautious pressure

As a good manager stands at a point in time, he can identify a set of goals he is interested in, albeit the outline of them may be pretty hazy. His timetable, which is also pretty hazy, suggests that some must be accomplished sooner than others, and that some may be safely postponed for several months or years. He has a still hazier notion of how he can reach these goals. He assesses key individuals and groups. He knows that each has its own set of goals, some of which he understands rather thoroughly and others about which he can only speculate. He knows also that these individuals and groups represent blocks to certain programs or projects, and that these points of opposition must be taken into account. As the day-to-day operating decisions are made, and as proposals are responded to both by individuals and by groups, he perceives more clearly where the corridors of comparative indifference are. He takes action accordingly.

Appearing imprecise

The fourth skill of the successful manager is knowing how to satisfy the organization that it has a sense of direction without ever actually getting himself committed publicly to a specific set of objectives. This is not to say that he does not have objectives – personal and corporate, long-term and short-term. They are significant guides to his thinking, and he modifies them continually as he better understands the resources he is working with, the competition, and the changing market demands. But as the organization clamors for statements of objectives, these are samples of what it gets back from him:

"Our company aims to be number one in its industry."

"Our objective is growth with profit."

"We seek the maximum return on investment."

"Management's goal is to meet its responsibilities to stockholders, employees, and the public."

In my opinion, statements such as these provide almost no guidance to the various levels of management. Yet they are quite readily accepted as objectives by large numbers of intelligent people.

Maintain viability

Why does the good manager shy away from precise statements of his objectives for the organization? The main reason is that he finds it impossible to set down specific objectives which will be relevant for any reasonable period into the future. Conditions in business change continually and rapidly, and corporate strategy must be revised to take the changes into account. The more explicit the statement of strategy, the more difficult it becomes to persuade the organization to turn to different goals when needs and conditions shift.

The public and the stockholders, to be sure, must perceive the organization as having a well-defined set of objectives and a clear sense of direction. But in reality the good top manager is seldom so certain of the direction which should be taken. Better than anyone else, he senses the many, many threats to his company – threats which lie in the economy, in the actions of competitors, and, not least, within his own organization.

He also knows that it is impossible to state objectives clearly enough so that everyone in the organization understands what they mean. Objectives get communicated only over time by a consistency or pattern in operating decisions. Such decisions are more meaningful than words. In instances where precise objectives are spelled out, the organization tends to interpret them so they fit its own needs.

Subordinates who keep pressing for more precise objectives are in truth working against their own best interests. Each time the objectives are stated more specifically, a subordinate's range of possibilities for operating are reduced. The narrower field means less room to roam and to accommodate the flow of ideas coming up from his part of the organization.

Avoid policy straitjackets

The successful manager's reluctance to be precise extends into the area of policy decisions. He seldom makes a forthright statement of policy. He may be aware that in some companies there are executives who spend more time in arbitrating disputes caused by stated policies than in moving the company forward. The management textbooks contend that well-defined policies are the sine qua non of a well-managed company. My research does not bear out this contention.

For example, the president of one company with which I am familiar deliberately leaves the assignments of his top officers vague and refuses to define policies for them. He passes out new assignments with seemingly no pattern in mind and consciously sets up competitive ventures among his subordinates. His methods, though they would never be sanctioned by a classical organization planner, are deliberate – and, incidentally, quite effective.

Since able managers do not make policy decisions, does this mean that well-managed companies operate without policies? Certainly not. But the policies are those which evolve over time from an indescribable mix of operating decisions. From any single operating decision might have come a very minor dimension of the policy as the organization understands it; from a series of decisions comes a pattern of guidelines for various levels of the organization.

The skillful manager resists the urge to write a company creed or to compile a policy manual. Preoccupation with detailed statements of corporate objectives and departmental goals and with comprehensive organization charts and job descriptions – this is often the first symptom of an organization which is in the early stages of atrophy.

The "management by objectives" school, so widely heralded in recent years, suggests that detailed objectives be spelled out at all levels in the corporation. This method is feasible at lower levels of management, but it becomes unworkable at the upper levels. The top manager must think out objectives in detail, but ordinarily some of the objectives must be withheld, or at least communicated to the organization in modest doses. A conditioning process which may stretch over months or years is necessary in order to prepare the organization for radical departures from what it is currently striving to attain.

Suppose, for example, that a president is convinced his company must phase out of the principal business it has been in for 35 years. Although making this change of course is one of his objectives, he may well feel that he cannot disclose the idea even to his vice presidents, whose total know-how is in the present business. A blunt announcement that the company is changing horses would be too great a shock for most of them to bear. And so he begins moving toward this goal but without a full disclosure to his management group.

A detailed spelling out of objectives may only complicate the task of reaching them. Specific, detailed statements give the opposition an opportunity to organize its defenses.

Muddling with a purpose

The fifth, and most important, skill I shall describe bears little relation to the doctrine that management is (or should be) a comprehensive, systematic, logical, well-programmed science. Of all the heresies set forth here, this should strike doctrinaires as the rankest of all!

The successful manager, in my observation, recognizes the futility of trying to push total packages or programs through the organization. He is willing to take less than total acceptance in order to achieve modest progress toward his goals. Avoiding debates on principles, he tries to piece together particles that may appear to be incidentals into a program that moves at least part of the way toward his objectives. His attitude is based on optimism and persistence. Over and over he says to himself, "There must be some parts of this proposal on which we can capitalize."

Whenever he identifies relationships among the different proposals before him, he knows that they present opportunities for combination and restructuring. It follows that he is a man of wide-ranging interests and curiosity. The more things he knows about, the more opportunities he will have to discover parts which are related. This process does not require great intellectual brilliance or unusual creativity. The wider ranging his interests, the more likely that he will be able to tie together several unrelated proposals. He is skilled as an analyst, but even more talented as a conceptualizer.

If the manager has built or inherited a solid organization, it will be difficult for him to come up with an idea which no one in the company has ever thought of before. His most significant contribution may be that he can see relationships which no one else has seen.

A division manager, for example, had set as one of his objectives, at the start of a year, an improvement in product quality. At the end of the year, in reviewing his progress toward this objective, he could identify three significant events which had brought about a perceptible improvement.

First, the head of the quality control group, a veteran manager who was doing only an adequate job, asked early in the year for assignment to a new research group. This opportunity permitted the division manager to install a promising young engineer in this key spot.

A few months later, opportunity number two came along. The personnel department proposed a continuous program of checking the effectiveness of training methods for new employees. The proposal was acceptable to the manufacturing group. The division manager's only contribution was to suggest that the program should include a heavy emphasis on employees' attitudes toward quality.

Then a third opportunity arose when one of the division's best customers discovered that the wrong material had been used for a large lot of parts. The heat generated by this complaint made it possible to institute a completely new system of procedures for inspecting and testing raw materials.

As the division manager reviewed the year's progress on product quality, these were the three most important developments. None of them could have been predicted at the start of the year, but he was quick to see the potential in each as it popped up in the day-to-day operating routines.

Exploitation of change

The good manager can function effectively only in an environment of continual change. A *Saturday Review* cartoonist caught the idea when he pictured an executive seated at a massive desk instructing his secretary to "send in a deal; I feel like wheelin'." Only with many changes in the works can the manager discover new combinations of opportunities and open up new corridors of comparative indifference. His stimulation to creativity comes from trying to make something useful of the proposal or idea in front of him. He will try to make strategic change a way of life in the organization and continually review the strategy even though current results are good.

Charles Lindblom has written an article with an engaging title, "The Science of Muddling Through."[2] In this he describes what he calls "the rational comprehensive method" of decision making. The essence of this method is that the decision maker, for each of his problems, proceeds deliberately, one step at a time, to collect complete data; to analyze the data thoroughly; to study a wide range of alternatives, each with its own risks and consequences; and, finally, to formulate a detailed course of action. Lindblom immediately dismisses "the rational comprehensive method" in favor of what he calls "successive limited comparisons." He sees the decision maker as comparing the alternatives which are open to him in order to learn which most closely meets the objectives he has in mind. Since this is not so much a rational process as an opportunistic one, he sees the manager as a muddler, but a muddler with a purpose.

H. Igor Ansoff, in his book, *Corporate Strategy*, espouses a similar notion as he describes what he calls the "cascade approach."[3] In his view, possible decision rules are formulated in gross terms and are successively refined through several stages as the emergence of a solution proceeds. This process gives the appearance of solving the problem several times over, but with successively more precise results.

Both Lindblom and Ansoff are moving us closer to an understanding of how managers really think. The process is not highly abstract; rather, the manager searches for a means of drawing into a pattern the thousands of incidents which make up the day-to-day life of a growing company.

Contrasting pictures

It is interesting to note, in the writings of several students of management, the emergence of the concept that, rather than making decisions, the leader's principal task is maintaining operating conditions which permit the various decision-making systems to function effectively. The supporters of this theory, it seems to me, overlook the subtle turns of direction which the leader can provide. He cannot add purpose and structure to the balanced judgments of subordinates if he simply rubber-stamps their decisions. He must weigh the issues and reach his own decision.

Richard M. Cyert and James G. March contend that in real life managers do not consider all the possible courses of action, that their search ends once they have found a satisfactory alternative. In my sample, good managers are not guilty of such myopic thinking. Unless they mull over a wide range of possibilities, they cannot come up with the imaginative combinations of ideas which characterize their work.

Many of the articles about successful executives picture them as great thinkers who sit at their desks drafting master blueprints for their companies. The successful top executives I have seen at work do not operate this way. Rather than produce a full-grown decision tree, they start with a twig, help it grow, and ease themselves out on the limbs only after they have tested to see how much weight the limbs can stand.

In my picture, the general manager sits in the midst of a continuous stream of operating problems. His organization presents him with a flow of proposals to deal with the problems. Some of these proposals are contained in voluminous, well-documented, formal reports; some are as fleeting as the walk-in visit from a subordinate whose latest inspiration came during the morning's coffee break. Knowing how meaningless it is to say, "This is a finance problem," or, "That is a communications problem," the manager feels no compulsion to classify his problems. He is, in fact, undismayed by a problem that defies classification. As Gary Steiner, in one of his speeches, put it, "He has a high tolerance for ambiguity."

In considering each proposal, the general manager tests it against at least three criteria:

1 Will the total proposal – or, more often, will some part of the proposal – move the organization toward the objectives which he has in mind?

2 How will the whole or parts of the proposal be received by the various groups and subgroups in the organization? Where will the strongest opposition come from, which group will furnish the strongest support, and which group will be neutral or indifferent?

3 How does the proposal relate to programs already in process or currently proposed? Can some parts of the proposal under consideration be added on to a program already under way, or can they be combined with all or parts of other proposals in a package which can be steered through the organization?

The making of a decision

As another example of a general manager at work, let me describe the train of events which led to a parent company president's decision to

2 *Readings in Managerial Psychology*, ed. Harold J. Leavitt and Louis R. Pondy (Chicago: University of Chicago Press, 1964), p. 61.

3 New York: McGraw-Hill, 1965.

attempt to consolidate two of his divisions.

Let us call the executive Mr. Brown. One day the manager of Division A came to him with a proposal that his division acquire a certain company. That company's founder and president – let us call him Mr. Johansson – had a phenomenal record of inventing new products, but earnings in his company had been less than phenomenal. Johansson's asking price for his company was high when evaluated against the earnings record.

Not until Brown began to speculate on how Johansson might supply fresh vigor for new products in Division A did it appear that perhaps a premium price could be justified. For several years, Brown had been unsuccessful in stimulating the manager of that division to see that he must bring in new products to replace those which were losing their place in the market.

The next idea which came to Brown was that Johansson might invent not only for Division A but also for Division B. As Brown analyzed how this might be worked out organizationally, he began to think about the markets being served by Divisions A and B. Over the years, several basic but gradual changes in marketing patterns had occurred, with the result that the marketing considerations which had dictated the establishment of separate divisions no longer prevailed. Why should the company continue to support the duplicated overhead expenses in the two divisions?

As Brown weighed the issues, he concluded that by consolidating the two divisions he could also shift responsibilities in the management groups in ways that would strengthen them overall. If we were asked to evaluate Brown's capabilities, how would we respond? Putting aside the objection that the information is too sketchy, our tendency might be to criticize Brown. Why did he not identify the changing market patterns in his continuing review of company position? Why did he not force the issue when the division manager failed to do something about new product development? Such criticism would reflect "the rational comprehensive method" of decision making.

But, as I analyze the gyrations in Brown's thinking, one characteristic stands out. He kept searching for the follow-on opportunities which he could fashion out of the original proposal, opportunities which would stand up against the three criteria earlier mentioned. In my book, Brown would rate as an extremely skillful general manager.

Conclusion

To recapitulate, the general manager possesses five important skills. He knows how to:

1 **Keep open many pipelines of information.** No one will quarrel with the desirability of an early warning system which provides varied viewpoints on an issue. However, very few managers know how to practice this skill, and the books on management add precious little to our understanding of the techniques which make it practicable.

2 **Concentrate on a limited number of significant issues.** No matter how skillful the manager is in focusing his energies and talents, he is inevitably caught up in a number of inconsequential duties. Active leadership of an organization demands a high level of personal involvement, and personal involvement brings with it many time-consuming activities which have an infinitesimal impact on corporate strategy. Hence this second skill, while perhaps the most logical of the five, is by no means the easiest to apply.

3 **Identify the corridors of comparative indifference.** Are there inferences here that the good manager has no ideas of his own, that he stands by until his organization proposes solutions, that he never uses his authority to force a proposal through the organization? Such inferences are not intended. The message is that a good organization will tolerate only so much direction from the top; the good manager therefore is adept at sensing how hard he can push.

4 **Give the organization a sense of direction with open-ended objectives.** In assessing this skill, keep in mind that I am talking about top levels of management. At lower levels, the manager should be encouraged to write down his objectives, if for no other reason than to ascertain if they are consistent with corporate strategy.

5 **Spot opportunities and relationships in the stream of operating problems and decisions.** Lest it be concluded from the description of this skill that the good manager is more an improviser than a planner, let me emphasize that he is a planner and encourages planning by his subordinates. Interestingly, though, professional planners may be irritated by a good general manager. Most of them complain about his lack of vision. They devise a master plan, but the president (or other operating executive) seems to ignore it, or to give it minimum acknowledgment by borrowing bits and pieces for implementation. They seem to feel that the power of a good master plan will be obvious to everyone, and its implementation automatic. But the general manager knows that even if the plan is sound and imaginative, the job has only begun. The long, painful task of implementation will depend on his skill, not that of the planner.

If this analysis of how skillful general managers think and operate has validity, then it should help us see several problems in a better light. For instance, the investment community is giving increasing attention to sizing up the management of a company being appraised. Thus far, the analysts rely mainly on results or performance rather than on a probe of management skills. But current performance can be affected by many variables, both favorably and unfavorably, and is a dangerous base for predicting what the management of a company will produce in the future. Testing the key managers of a company against the five skills described holds promise for evaluating the caliber of a management group. The manager who is building his own company and the man who is moving up through the hierarchy of a larger organization require essentially the same capabilities for success.

In today's frenzy of acquisitions and mergers, why does a management usually prefer to acquire a company rather than to develop a new product and build an organization to make and sell it? One of the reasons can be found in the way a general manager thinks and operates. He finds it difficult to sit and speculate theoreti-

continued on page 70

Retrospective commentary: a muddler looks back

Selection of "Good Managers Don't Make Policy Decisions" as an HBR Classic is a posthumous honor for my strategy course at the University of Chicago. The article was an attempt to describe that course's philosophy of management over some 20 years and I probably would never have written it but for the insistence of George Shultz, then dean of the business school. After sitting in on several classes, he urged me to publish the conclusions drawn from the case discussions. I was reluctant, for it seemed to me that once the "answers" had been disclosed, future discussions of the cases would be perfunctory. But as it turned out, distributing the published article in my classes improved the quality of case discussions.

I remember that I gave an early draft to three friends for their comments. One, a widely read, successful CEO, called me the same day to say, "This is the first thing I have ever read that accurately describes what I do." The other two, respected academicians, were able to manage at best a pair of stifled yawns. This was to be the pattern of responses to the article over the years – widespread support from experienced general managers and a high level of skepticism from staff managers and teachers of management.

Since the article's publication in 1967, the pressures to establish financial goals, both short- and long-term, have increased manyfold, despite the difficulties of persuading organizations to rally around a cause defined in quantitative terms. This has made management's job more difficult, and has increased my conviction that successful organizations revolve around good general managers. As I noted in the mid-1970s:

"An organization is doomed to mediocrity unless it is guided by good general managers in key positions. A company can bumble along for years, but good general managers are the ingredient which will make it stand out from the pack. No matter how rich its other resources such as technical know-how, uniqueness of product, market monopoly, ample finances, or luck, an organization will not excel unless it is led by what are becoming increasingly rare individuals.

"Generally, it is a good general manager, not the staff specialist, who makes a company go, who turns an idea into a commercial success or converts a major disappointment into an opportunity which catches fire."[1]

Second thoughts

The heart of the HBR article was the following paragraph from the section "Muddling with a purpose":

"The good manager can function effectively only in an environment of continual change.... Only with many changes in the works can the manager discover new combinations of opportunities and open up new corridors of comparative indifference. His stimulation to creativity comes from trying to make something useful of the proposal or idea in front of him. He will try to make strategic change a way of life in the organization and continually review the strategy even though current results are good."

In retrospect, I feel that two points need qualification:

- The beneficial effect of "continual change" does not extend to frequent reorganizations of the management structure. These are among the most damaging abuses that so-called professional managers can inflict on a company. Unless executives' working relationships are reasonably stable, overall performance will suffer. The general manager who listens to organization planning staff views on such matters will almost certainly embark on a rash of ill-advised reorganizations.
- A continual review of strategy should go on only in the general manager's mind, for repeated questioning of strategy by subordinates would introduce too much uncertainty. The organization must stay the course long enough to demonstrate whether the strategy that it is attempting to implement will work. Only the general manager is continually on tenterhooks wondering whether to pause and reevaluate, or to forge ahead.

I would also like to add a qualification to the opening statement of a paragraph in the section, "Appearing imprecise," that "the fourth skill of the general manager is knowing how to satisfy the organization that it has a sense of direction without ever actually getting himself committed publicly to a specific set of objectives." The annual planning process is an exception to this generalization. Detailed and specific one-year plans can be useful to the general manager who is committed to the spirit of imprecision. As John J. Byrne, the CEO who took Geico Corporation from the verge of bankruptcy to a string of noteworthy successes, has observed, "In the annual plan, the organization needs to know where the goal line is. What does it take to make a touchdown?"

Proof of the pudding

The basic ideas of this article have been validated in several ways. Although selective perception may be at work, a procession of books and articles published since 1967 supports my findings on the skills of the general manager and the working environment in which he or she can thrive.

My personal sample of general managers has grown to include several dozen with different management styles and varying degrees of success. Some, managing in the mode of the article, have succeeded dramatically. But some have failed. Most companies' methods of selecting and grooming general managers continue to be woefully inadequate and the turnover in general management positions is frighteningly high. Many who tried to emulate my good manager have been swept over the dam, for one or a number of reasons:

Some took over businesses that had deteriorated beyond salvage.

Some drowned in a stream of operating decisions.

Some were sacked because they could not produce immediate profit turnarounds.

Some were immobilized by staff specialists.

Some kept searching for the right management consultant to tell them what to do.

Some simply lacked sufficient company and industry know-how to establish a credible sense of direction.

Some were too greedy.

Literally hundreds of students in advanced management programs have put the article to good test. Those who read it quickly invariably found themselves trapped by a superficial interpretation that collapsed in the face of challenges from fellow students. Even experienced managers did not easily understand its propositions. This simple diagram was helpful for many:

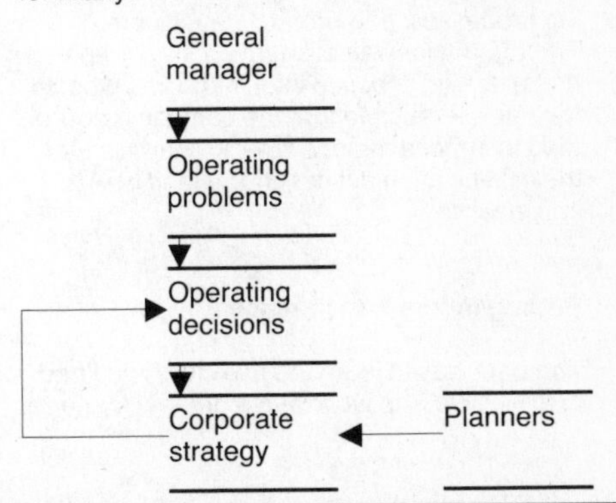

1 "Good General Managers Are Not Professional," Selected Paper 53, University of Chicago, Graduate School of Business, 1977.

cally about the future as he and his subordinates fashion a plan to exploit a new product. He is much more at home when taking over a going concern, even though he anticipates he will inherit many things he does not want. In the day-to-day operation of a going concern, he finds the milieu to maneuver and conceptualize.

Scarcely any manager in any business can escape the acutely painful responsibility to identify men with potential for growth in management and to devise methods for developing them for broader responsibilities. Few line managers or staff professionals have genuine confidence in the yardsticks and devices they use now. The five skills offer possibilities for raising an additional set of questions about management appraisal methods, job rotation practices, on-the-job development assignments, and the curricula of formal in-house management development programs.

One group of distinguished executives ignores with alarming regularity the implications of the five skills. These are the presidents of multidivision companies who "promote" successful division managers to the parent company level as staff officers. Does this recurring phenomenon cast doubt on the validity of my theory? I think not. To the contrary, strong supporting evidence for my thesis can be found in the results of such action. What happens is that line managers thus "promoted" often end up on the sidelines, out of the game for the rest of their careers. Removed from the tumult of operations, the environment which I contend is critical for their success, many of them just wither away in their high-status posts as senior counselors and never become effective. ⍒

Reprint 84416

The illustration is of a general manager involved in operating problems and therefore in a position to influence operating decisions. Over time, a corporate strategy, apparent to the organization, evolves from the patterns discernible in operating decisions. At this point, the general manager insists that those who are making current operating decisions ensure that they are consistent with the corporate strategy.

Simultaneously, a planning department may be churning out statements on corporate strategy. The general manager insists that these planners' statements are also compatible with what he or she wants to do.

Given such circumstances, two further conclusions emerge:

☐ The company whose general manager is involved in operating decisions is more likely to have a creative corporate strategy than the company whose general manager relies on formal planning techniques. Formal planning tends to produce conventional, pedestrian strategies.

☐ The skills required for effective implementation of a strategy are in shorter supply than those needed for formal planning.

Bill, a former outstanding student who is now a senior general manager of a large company, recently talked to me about his experiences with management skills. Reflecting on his personal growth, Bill recalled that it took at least two years after he read the article before he began to understand it.

A new group of managers took over his company, then near collapse, and they struggled for several years to return the company to its former preeminence. During this period, Bill was in a position to observe closely all the changes made and he found that they affirmed the precepts outlined in the article. He saw for himself how top managers with the patience to search out "the corridors of comparative indifference," and to build unanimity in the organization, successfully proceeded with major new marketing plans, manufacturing processes, and product development. Their behavior was in sharp contrast with that of the earlier, unsuccessful managers who, in their desperation to turn the company around, tried to impose major strategic changes that the organization did not understand how to implement.

Putting theory into practice

The best way to learn the five skills I outlined in my article is to work with a general manager who exercises them. The experience will be much more effectual than enrolling in a strategy course or reading books and articles. For reasons I do not confess to understand, I have found women quicker to master the subtle shadings of meaning so critical to effective application of management techniques.

The evidence suggests that a general manager can transfer management skills from one company to another, and that failure to duplicate earlier successes in a new company or industry is likely traceable to a lack of marketing or technical knowledge. The mismatched "creative placements" that plague the upper levels of some American companies could only be conceived in the minds of executive searchers.

The good management precepts for business executives are applicable, moreover, with minor modifications, to general managers in nonbusiness settings. Former students who find themselves managing a government facility or a hospital or a college remind me regularly that they too rely on the five skills. A few months ago, the rector of St. Vincent de Paul Seminary in Boynton Beach, Florida invited me to volunteer my services to develop a course in parish management. Writing cases about the pastors of parishes has been a refreshing exposure to another important general management area of our society. One pastor is adept at keeping informed; another is not. One saves himself for the critical things; another tries to respond to every demand. One is sensitive to the power structure; another points to his authority. One provides a good focus to parish activities; another is carried along by the tide of events. One is alert for opportunities; another complains about not having any. Familiar sounds from general managers in business?

Twenty years is an ephemeral test of endurability for a management philosophy. The rector of St. Vincent's loaned me a book on ancient Chinese philosophers. Their aphorisms and parables, recorded over two centuries ago, preserve counsels that are still relevant for today's general managers.

Much has been learned about general management during the past two decades, but we are still novices. As we try to learn more, we encounter severe limitations in the attempt to expand our knowledge by interviews, questionnaires, and even case writing. It's the unguarded moments when the general manager is not playing for the grandstand that often reveal the most about his or her skills, attitudes, and ways of thinking. Future probes of these deep pockets of ignorance will surely bring enlightenments that overshadow "present principles."

What effective general managers really do

They do not function in a crisply defined environment, or direct through formally delineated organizational channels, or systematically set and follow formal plans – in other words, they don't fit the stereotype

John P. Kotter

A rather large gap exists between the conventional wisdom on management functions, tools, and systems on the one hand and actual managerial behavior on the other. The former is usually discussed in terms of planning, controlling, staffing, organizing, and directing; the latter is characterized by long hours, fragmented episodes, and oral communication. Actual behavior, as a study of successful general managers shows, looks less systematic, more informal, less reflective, more reactive, less well organized, and more frivolous than a student of strategic planning systems, MIS, or organizational design would ever expect.

The gap is important and disturbing for many reasons. First of all, it raises serious questions about the kind of formal planning, performance appraisal, and other systems that are commonly in use today. In a similar way, it raises questions about management education, which usually relies heavily on management "theory" and which is currently producing more than 60,000 new MBAs each year. Furthermore, the gap makes it difficult for executives to coach younger managers and makes it hard for them to know how they might improve their own effectiveness.

The study was conducted by John P. Kotter, professor of organizational behavior at the Harvard Business School. This article, which is adapted from his book The General Managers *(Free Press, 1982), is his fourth in HBR. His last article, which he coauthored with John J. Gabarro, "Managing Your Boss," appeared in our January-February 1980 issue and won the McKinsey Award for the second best HBR article of that year.*

Here is a description of a reasonably typical day in the life of a successful executive. The individual in this case is Michael Richardson, the president of an investment management firm.

A.M. 7:35 He arrives at work after a short commute, unpacks his briefcase, gets some coffee, and begins a "to do" list for the day.

7:40 Jerry Bradshaw, a subordinate, arrives at his office, which is right next to Richardson's. One of Bradshaw's duties is to act as an assistant to Richardson.

7:45 Bradshaw and Richardson converse about a number of topics. Richardson shows Bradshaw some pictures he recently took at his summer home.

8:00 Bradshaw and Richardson talk about a schedule and priorities for the day. In the process, they touch on a dozen different subjects and issues relating to customers, and other subordinates.

8:20 Frank Wilson, another subordinate, drops in. He asks a few questions about a personnel problem and then joins in the ongoing discussion. The discussion is straightforward, rapid, and occasionally punctuated with humor.

Editor's note: All references are listed at the end of the article.

8:30 Fred Holly, the chairman of the firm and Richardson's "boss," stops in and joins in the conversation. He asks about an appointment scheduled for 11 o'clock and brings up a few other topics as well.

8:40 Richardson leaves to get more coffee. Bradshaw, Holly, and Wilson continue their conversation.

8:42 Richardson comes back. A subordinate of a subordinate stops in and says hello. The others leave.

8:43 Bradshaw drops off a report, hands Richardson instructions that go with it, and leaves.

8:45 Joan Swanson, Richardson's secretary, arrives. They discuss her new apartment and arrangements for a meeting later in the morning.

8:49 Richardson gets a phone call from a subordinate who is returning a call from the day before. They talk primarily about the subject of the report Richardson just received.

8:55 He leaves his office and goes to a regular morning meeting that one of his subordinates runs. There are about 30 people there. Richardson reads during the meeting.

9:09 The meeting is over. Richardson stops one of the people there and talks to him briefly.

9:15 He walks over to the office of one of his subordinates, who is corporate counsel. His boss, Holly, is there too. They discuss a phone call the lawyer just received. While standing, the three talk about possible responses to a problem. As before, the exchange is quick and includes some humor.

9:30 Richardson goes back to his office for a meeting with the vice chairman of another firm (a potential customer and supplier). One other person, a liaison with that firm and a subordinate's subordinate, also attends the meeting. The discussion is cordial. It covers many topics, from their products to U.S. foreign relations.

9:50 The visitor and the subordinate's subordinate leave. Richardson opens the adjoining door to Bradshaw's office and asks a question.

9:52 Richardson's secretary comes in with five items of business.

9:55 Bradshaw drops in, asks a question about a customer, and then leaves.

9:58 Frank Wilson and one of his people arrive. He gives Richardson a memo and then the three talk about the important legal problem. Wilson does not like a decision that Richardson has tentatively made and urges him to reconsider. The discussion goes back and forth for 20 minutes until they agree on the next action and schedule it for 9 o'clock the next day.

10:35 They leave. Richardson looks over papers on his desk, then picks one up and calls Holly's secretary regarding the minutes of the last board meeting. He asks her to make a few corrections.

10:41 His secretary comes in with a card for a friend who is sick. He writes a note to go with the card.

10:50 He gets a brief phone call, then goes back to the papers on his desk.

11:03 His boss stops in. Before Richardson and Holly can begin to talk, Richardson gets another call. After the call, he tells his secretary that someone didn't get a letter he sent and asks her to send another.

11:05 Holly brings up a couple of issues, and then Bradshaw comes in. The three start talking about Jerry Phillips, who has become a difficult problem. Bradshaw leads the conversation, telling the others what he has done during the last few days regarding this issue. Richardson and Holly ask questions. After a while, Richardson begins to take notes. The exchange, as before, is rapid and straightforward. They try to define the problem and outline possible alternative next steps. Richardson lets the discussion roam away from and back to the topic again and again. Finally, they agree on a next step.

P.M. 12:00 Richardson orders lunch for himself and Bradshaw. Bradshaw comes in and goes over a dozen items. Wilson stops by to say that he has already followed up on their earlier conversation.

12:10 A staff person stops by with some calculations Richardson had requested. He thanks her and has a brief, amicable conversation.

12:20 Lunch arrives. Richardson and Bradshaw go into the conference room to eat. Over lunch they pursue business and nonbusiness subjects. They laugh often at each other's humor. They end the lunch talking about a potential major customer.

1:15 Back in Richardson's office, they continue the discussion about the customer. Bradshaw gets a pad, and they go over in detail a presentation to the customer. Then Bradshaw leaves.

1:40 Working at his desk, Richardson looks over a new marketing brochure.

1:50 Bradshaw comes in again; he and Richardson go over another dozen details regarding the presentation to the potential customer. Bradshaw leaves.

1:55 Jerry Thomas comes in. He is a subordinate of Richardson, and he has scheduled for the afternoon some key performance appraisals, which he and Richardson will hold in Richardson's office. They talk briefly about how they will handle each appraisal.

2:00 Fred Jacobs (a subordinate of Thomas) joins Richardson and Thomas. Thomas runs the meeting. He goes over Jacobs's bonus for the year and the reason for it. Then the three of them talk about Jacobs's role in the upcoming year. They generally agree and Jacobs leaves.

2:30 Jane Kimble comes in. The appraisal follows the same format as for Fred Jacobs. Richardson asks a lot of questions and praises Kimble at times. The meeting ends on a friendly note of agreement.

3:00 George Houston comes in; the appraisal format is repeated again.

3:30 When Houston leaves, Richardson and Thomas talk briefly about how well they have accomplished their objectives in the meetings. Then they talk briefly about some of Thomas's other subordinates. Thomas leaves.

3:45 Richardson gets a short phone call. His secretary and Bradshaw come in with a list of requests.

3:50 Richardson receives a call from Jerry Phillips. He gets his notes from the 11 o'clock meeting about Phillips. They go back and forth on the phone talking about lost business, unhappy subordinates, who did what to whom, and what should be done now. It is a long, circular, and sometimes emotional conversation. Near the end, Phillips is agreeing with Richardson on the next step and thanking him.

4:55 Bradshaw, Wilson, and Holly all step in. Each is following up on different issues that were discussed earlier in the day. Richardson briefly tells them of his conversation with Phillips. Bradshaw and Holly leave.

5:10 Richardson and Wilson have a light conversation about three or four items.

5:20 Jerry Thomas stops in. He describes a new personnel problem and the three of them discuss it. More and more humor starts coming into the conversation. They agree on an action to take.

5:30 Richardson begins to pack his briefcase. Five people briefly stop by, one or two at a time.

5:45 He leaves the office.

In at least a dozen ways, Richardson's day is typical for a general manager. The daily behavior of the successful GMs I have studied generally conforms to these patterns (see the ruled insert for a description of the study):

1 They spend most of their time with others. The average GM spends only 25% of his working time alone, and this is spent largely at home, on airplanes, or while commuting. Few spend less than 70% of their time with others, and some spend up to 90% of their work time this way.

2 The people they spend time with include many in addition to their direct subordinates and boss. GMs regularly go around the formal chain of command. They also regularly see people who often appear to be unimportant outsiders.

3 The breadth of topics in these discussions is extremely wide. The GMs do not limit their focus to planning, business strategy, staffing, and other "top management concerns." They discuss virtually anything and everything even remotely associated with their businesses and organizations.

4 In these conversations, GMs typically ask a lot of questions. In a half-hour conversation, some will ask literally hundreds.

5 During these conversations, the GMs rarely seem to make "big" decisions.

6 These discussions usually contain a considerable amount of joking and kidding and concern non-work-related issues. The humor is often about others in the organization or industry. Nonwork discussions are usually about people's families, hobbies, or recent outside activities (e.g., golf scores).

7 In not a small number of these encounters, the substantive issue discussed is relatively unimportant to the business or organization. That is, GMs regularly engage in activities that even they regard as a waste of time.

8 In these encounters, the executives rarely give orders in a traditional sense. That is, they seldom "tell" people what to do.

9 Nevertheless, GMs frequently engage in attempts to influence others. However, instead of telling people what to do, they ask, request, cajole, persuade, and intimidate.

10 In allocating their time with others, GMs often react to others' initiatives. Much of the typical GM's day is unplanned. Even GMs who have a heavy schedule of planned meetings often end up spending a lot of time on topics that are not on the official agenda.

11 Most of their time with others is spent in short, disjointed conversations. Discussions of a single question or issue rarely last more than ten minutes. And it is not at all unusual for a GM to cover ten unrelated topics in a five-minute interaction.

12 They work long hours. The average person I have studied works just under 60 hours per week. Not many work fewer than 55 hours per week. Although some of their work is done at home, while commuting to work, or while traveling, they spend most of their time at their places of work.

These patterns in daily behavior, which Richardson's day illustrate, are basically consistent with other studies of managerial behavior,[1] especially those of high-level managers.[2] Nevertheless, as Henry Mintzberg has pointed out,[3] this behavior seems hard to reconcile, on the surface at least, with traditional notions of what top managers do (or should do). It is hard to fit the behavior into categories like "planning," "organizing," "controlling," "directing," "staffing," and so on.

And even if one tries, two conclusions surface: (1) The "planning" and "organizing" that these

Basis of the study

Conducted between 1976 and 1981, this study focused on a group of successful general managers in nine corporations. I examined what their jobs entailed, who they were, where they had come from, how they behaved, and how this all varied in different corporate and industry settings.

The participants all had some profit center and multifunctional responsibility. They were located in cities across the United States. They were involved in a broad range of industries, including banking, consulting, tire and rubber manufacture, TV, mechanical equipment manufacture, newspapers, copiers, investment management, consumer products, and still others. The businesses they were responsible for included some doing only $1 million to $10 million in sales, others in the $10 million to $50 million range, the $50 million to $100 million range, the $100 million to $1 billion range, and some doing $1 billion or more. On average, these executives were 47 years old. In 1978, they were paid (on average) about $150,000 (that is, well over $200,000 in 1982 dollars). And all, when selected, were believed to be performing well in their jobs.

Data collection involved three visits to each GM over 6 to 12 months. Each time I interviewed them for at least five hours, often more. I observed their daily routine for about 35 hours, and I interviewed for an hour each the dozen or so key people with whom each worked. The GMs filled out two questionnaires and gave me relevant documents, such as business plans, appointment diaries, and annual reports. From these various sources, I obtained information on the GMs' backgrounds, personalities, jobs, job contexts, behavior, and performance. Because data collection involved considerable effort for each individual, I had to limit the number of GMs selected for study to 15.

I measured the performance of the GMs by combining "hard" and "soft" indexes. The former included measures of revenue and profit growth, both in an absolute sense and compared with plans. The latter included opinions of people who worked with the GMs (including bosses, subordinates, and peers), as well as, when possible, industry analysts. Using this method, I judged most of the GMs to be doing a "very good" job. A few were rated "excellent" and a few "good/fair."

people do does not seem very systematically done; it seems rather hit or miss, rather sloppy. (2) A lot of behavior ends up being classified as "none of the above." The implication is that these are things that top managers should not be doing. Nevertheless, hit or miss is precisely how planning and organizing manifest themselves in the daily behavior of effective executives, and for perfectly understandable reasons.

How effective executives approach their jobs

To understand why effective GMs behave as they do, it is essential first to recognize the types of challenges and dilemmas found in most of their jobs, the two most fundamental of which are:

Figuring out what to do despite uncertainty, great diversity, and an enormous amount of potentially relevant information.

Getting things done through a large and diverse set of people despite having little direct control over most of them.

The severity of these challenges in complex organizations is much greater than most nonexecutives would suspect. And the implications of these job demands for the traditional management functions of planning, staffing, organizing, directing, and controlling are very powerful.

Exhibit I suggests that the very nature of executive jobs requires a complex and subtle approach to planning, organizing, staffing, and so forth. The approach needs to take into account the uncertainty involved, as well as the diversity and volume of potentially relevant information. It must also come to grips with the difficult human environment; it must somehow help executives get things done despite their dependency on a large number of people, many of whom are not their subordinates.

An examination of effective general managers suggests that they have found just such an approach, a central part of which might be usefully thought of as "agenda setting" and "network building."

Exhibit I **Behavioral implications, given the nature of GM jobs, for the traditional management functions**

Implications for traditional management functions	**Dilemmas inherent in the job**	
	Figuring out what to do despite great uncertainty, great diversity, and an enormous quantity of potentially relevant information.	**Getting things done** through a large and diverse group of people despite having little direct control over most of them.
Planning	Planning is very difficult to do well in such a context. It requires a lot of time and attention, not just a series of meetings once a year. It requires some good information systems to sort out the noise and focus on essential data.	Planning must be done in a way that does not exacerbate the already very difficult human environment. One must therefore be very careful regarding what is put on paper or said to others.
Staffing and organizing	Some type of sound plan or map is essential, because without it there is no rational basis for "staffing" and "organizing."	The resources one needs to get the job done include many people besides direct subordinates. Hence, some form of "staffing" and "organizing" activity must be aimed at many others and this activity will have to rely mainly on methods other than formal staffing and organizing procedures.
Directing and controlling	Some type of sound plan or map is essential, because without it, it is impossible to know where to direct one's attention among the infinite possibilities. Without it, one cannot know what to direct or control.	A fairly strong set of cooperative relationships to those resources on which one is dependent is essential, or one simply will not be able to "direct" and "control."

Agenda setting

During their first six months to a year in a new job, GMs usually spend considerable time establishing their agendas. Later, they continue to update them but in a less time-consuming process.

Effective executives develop agendas that are made up of loosely connected goals and plans that address their long-, medium-, and short-term responsibilities. The agendas usually address a broad range of financial, product/market, and organizational issues. They include both vague and specific items. *Exhibit II* summarizes the contents of a typical GM's agenda.

Although most corporations today have formal planning processes that produce written plans, GMs' agendas always include goals, priorities, strategies, and plans that are not in these documents. This is not to say that formal plans and the GMs' agendas are incompatible. Generally they are very consistent, but they differ in at least three important ways:

☐ First, the formal plans tend to be written mostly in terms of detailed financial numbers. GMs' agendas tend to be less detailed in financial objectives and more detailed in strategies and plans for the business or the organization.

☐ Second, formal plans usually focus entirely on the short and moderate run (3 months to 5 years), while GMs' agendas tend to focus on a broader time frame, which includes the immediate future (1 to 30 days) and the longer run (5 to 20 years).

☐ Finally, the formal plans tend to be more explicit, rigorous, and logical, especially regarding how various financial items fit together. GMs' agendas often contain lists of goals or plans that are not as explicitly connected.

Executives begin the process of developing these agendas immediately after starting their jobs, if not before. They use their knowledge of the businesses and organizations involved along with new information received each day to quickly develop a rough agenda – typically, this contains a very loosely connected and incomplete set of objectives, along with a few specific strategies and plans. Then over time, as more and more information is gathered, they incrementally (one step at a time) make the agendas more complete and more tightly connected.

In gathering information to set their agendas, effective GMs rely more on discussions with others than on books, magazines, or reports. These people tend to be individuals with whom they have relationships, not necessarily people in the "appropriate" job or function (e.g., such as a person in the planning function). In this way, they obtain information continuously, day after day, not just at planning meetings. And they do so by using their current knowledge of the business and organization and of management in general to help them direct their questioning, not by asking broad or general questions. In other words, they find ways within the flow of their workdays to ask a few critical questions and to receive in return some information that would be useful for agenda-setting purposes.

With this information, GMs make agenda-setting decisions both consciously (or analytically) and unconsciously (or intuitively) in a process that is largely internal to their minds. Indeed, important agenda-setting decisions are often not observable. In selecting specific activities to include in their agendas, GMs look for those that accomplish multiple goals, that are consistent with all other goals and plans, and that are within their power to implement. Projects and programs that seem important and logical but do not meet these criteria tend to be discarded or are at least resisted.

Almost all effective GMs seem to use this type of agenda-setting process, but the best performers do so to a greater degree and with more skill. For example, the "excellent" performers I have studied develop agendas based on more explicit business strategies that address longer time frames and that include a wider range of business issues. They do so by more aggressively seeking information from others (including "bad news"), by more skillfully asking questions, and by more successfully seeking out programs and projects that can help accomplish multiple objectives at once.[4]

Exhibit II **A GM's typical agenda**

Time frame	**Key issues**		
	Financial	**Business** product/ market	**Organizational** people
Long run 5 to 20 years	A vague notion of revenues or ROI desired in 10 to 20 years.	Only a vague notion of what kind of business (products and markets) the GM wants to develop.	Vague; sometimes includes a notion about the type of company the GM wants and the caliber of management that will be needed.
Medium run 1 to 5 years	A fairly specific set of goals for sales and income and ROI for the next five years.	Some goals and plans for growing the business, such as: (a) introduce three new products before 1985, and (b) explore acquisition possibilities in the communications industry.	A short list of items, such as: (a) by 1983 we will need a major reorganization, and (b) find a replacement for Corey by 1984.
Short run zero to 12 months	A very detailed list of financial objectives for the quarter and the year in all financial areas: sales, expenses, income, ROI, and so on.	A set of general objectives and plans aimed at such things as: (a) the market share for various products, and (b) the inventory levels of various lines.	A list of items, such as: (a) find a replacement for Smith soon, and (b) get Jones to commit himself to a more aggressive set of five-year objectives.

Network building

In addition to setting agendas, effective GMs allocate significant time and effort when they first take their jobs to developing a network of cooperative relationships among those people they feel are needed to satisfy their emerging agendas. Even after the first six months, this activity still takes up considerable time; but generally, it is most intense during the first months in a job. After that, their attention shifts toward using the networks to both implement and help in updating the agendas.

This network-building activity, as I have observed it and had it described to me, is aimed at much more than just direct subordinates. GMs develop cooperative relationships with and among peers, outsiders, their bosses' boss, and their subordinates' subordinates. Indeed, they develop relationships with (and sometimes among) any and all of the hundreds or even

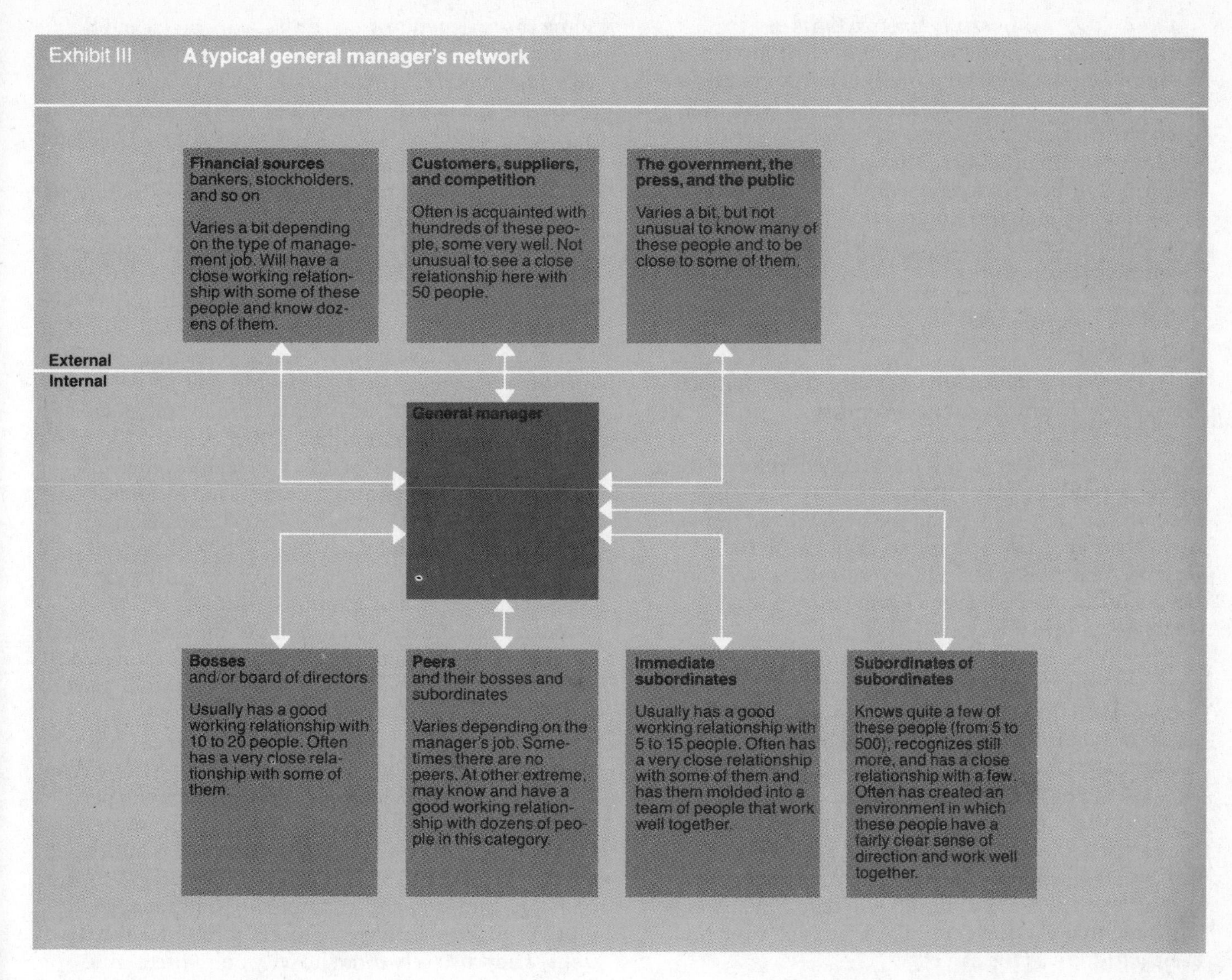

thousands of people on whom they feel dependent because of their jobs. That is, just as they create an agenda that is different from, although generally consistent with, formal plans, they also create a network that is different from, but generally consistent with, the formal organization structure (see *Exhibit III* for a typical GM's network).

In these large networks, the nature of the relationships varies significantly in intensity and in type; some relationships are much stronger than others, some much more personal than others, and so on. Indeed, to some degree, every relationship in a network is different because it has a unique history, it is between unique people, and so forth.

GMs develop these networks of cooperative relationships using a wide variety of face-to-face methods. They try to make others feel legitimately obliged to them by doing favors or by stressing their formal relationships. They act in ways to encourage others to identify with them. They carefully nurture their professional reputations in the eyes of others. They even maneuver to make others feel that they are particularly dependent on the GMs for resources, or career advancement, or other support.

In addition to developing relationships with existing personnel, effective GMs also often develop their networks by moving, hiring, and firing subordinates. Generally, they do so to strengthen their ability to get things done. In a similar way, they also change suppliers or bankers, lobby to get different people into peer positions, and even restructure their boards to improve their relationship with a needed resource.

Furthermore, they also sometimes shape their networks by trying to create certain types of relationships *among* the people in various parts of the network. That is, they try to create the appropriate "environment" (norms and values) they feel is necessary to implement their agendas. Typically this is an environment in which people are willing to work hard on the GM's agenda and cooperate for the greater good. Although executives sometimes try to create such an environment among peers, bosses, or outsiders, they do so most often among their subordinates.

Almost all effective GMs use this network-building process, but the best performers do so more aggressively and more skillfully. "Excellent" performers, for example, create networks with many talented people in them and with strong ties to and among their subordinates. They do so by using a wide variety of methods with great skill. The "good/fair" performers tend to use fewer network-building methods, employ them less aggressively, and in the process, create weaker networks.[5]

Execution: getting networks to implement agendas

After they have largely developed their networks and agendas, effective GMs tend to shift their attention toward using the networks to implement their agendas. In doing so, they marshal their interpersonal skills, budgetary resources, and information to influence people and events in a variety of direct and indirect ways.

In implementing their agendas, GMs often call on virtually their entire network of relationships to help them. They do not limit their assistance to direct subordinates and a boss; when necessary, they use any and all of their relationships. During my time with GMs, I have seen some of them call on peers, corporate staff people, subordinates reporting three or four levels below them, bosses reporting two or three levels above them, suppliers or customers, even competitors, to help them get something done. There is no category of people that was never used. And in each case, the basic pattern was the same:

> The GM was trying to get some action on items in his agenda that he felt would not be accomplished without intervention on his part.
>
> The people he approached could be of help, often uniquely so.
>
> The people he approached were part of his network.
>
> The GM chose people and an approach with an eye toward achieving multiple objectives at once and doing so without inadvertently disturbing important relationships in the network.

Having approached people, GMs often influence them by simply asking or suggesting that they do something, knowing that because of their relationship with the person, he or she will comply. In some cases, depending on the issue involved and the nature of the relationship, they also use their knowledge and information to help persuade these people. Under other circumstances, they will use resources available to them to negotiate a trade. And occasionally, they even resort to intimidation and coercion.

Effective GMs also often use their networks to exert indirect influence on people, including people who are not a part of that network. In some cases, GMs will convince one person who is in their network to get a second, who is not, to take some needed action. More indirectly still, GMs will sometimes approach a number of different people, requesting them to take actions that would then shape events that influence other individuals. Perhaps the most common example of indirect influence involves staging an event of some sort. In a typical case, the GM would set up a meeting or meetings and influence others through the selection of participants, the choice of an agenda, and often by his own participation.

Unlike the case of direct influence, GMs achieve much of their more indirect influence through symbolic methods. That is, they use meetings, architecture, language, stories about the organization, time, and space as symbols in order to get some message across indirectly.

All effective GMs seem to get things done this way, but the best performers do so more than others and with greater skill. That is, the better performers tend to mobilize more people to get more things done, and do so using a wider range of influence tactics. "Excellent" performers ask, encourage, cajole, praise, reward, demand, manipulate, and generally motivate others with great skill in face-to-face situations. They also rely more heavily on indirect influence than the "good" managers, who tend to rely on a more narrow range of influence techniques and apply them with less finesse.[6]

How the job determines behavior

Most of the visible patterns in daily behavior seem to be direct consequences of the way GMs approach their job, and thus consequences of the nature of the job itself and the type of people involved. More specifically, some of these patterns seem to derive from the approach taken to agenda setting, others from network building, others from how they tend to use networks to implement agendas, and still others from the approach in general.

Spending most of the time with others (pattern 1) seems to be a natural consequence of the GM's overall approach to the job and the central role the network of relationships plays. As we saw earlier, GMs develop a network of relationships with those the job makes them dependent on and then use that network to help create, implement, and update an organizational agenda. As such, the whole approach to the job involves interacting with people. Hence it should not be surprising to find that on a daily basis, GMs spend most of their time with others.

Likewise, because the network tends to include all those the GM is dependent on, it is hardly surprising to find the GM spending time with many besides a boss and direct subordinates (pattern 2). And because the agenda tends to include items related to all the long-, medium-, and short-run responsibilities associated with the job, it is to be expected that the breadth of topics covered in daily conversations might be very wide (pattern 3).

A few of the other patterns seem to be a direct consequence of the agenda-setting approach employed by GMs. As we saw earlier, agenda setting involves gathering information on a continuous basis from network members, usually by asking questions. That GMs ask a lot of questions (pattern 4) follows directly. With the information in hand, we saw that GMs create largely unwritten agendas. Hence, major agenda-setting decisions are often invisible; they occur in the GM's mind (pattern 5).

We also saw that network building involves the use of a wide range of interpersonal tactics. Since humor and nonwork discussions can be used as effective tools for building relationships and maintaining them under stressful conditions, we should not be surprised to find these tools used often (as we do—pattern 6). Since maintaining relationships requires that one deal with issues that other people feel are important (regardless of their centrality to the business), it is also not surprising to find the GMs spending time on substantive issues that seem unimportant to us and them (pattern 7).

As I indicated earlier, after the initial period on the job the thrust of the GMs' approach is to use their networks to implement their agendas. They do so using a wide variety of direct and indirect influence methods. Ordering is only one of many methods. Under these circumstances, one would expect to find them rarely ordering others (pattern 8) but spending a lot of time trying to influence others (pattern 9).

The efficiency of seemingly inefficient behavior

Of all the patterns visible in daily behavior, perhaps the most difficult to understand, or at least appreciate, are that the executives do not plan their days in advance in much detail but instead react (pattern 10) and that conversations are short and disjointed (pattern 11). On the surface at least, behaving this way seems particularly unmanagerial. Yet these patterns are possibly the most important and efficient of all.

The following is a typical example of the effectiveness and efficiency of "reactive" behavior. On his way to a meeting, a GM bumped into a staff member who did not report to him. Using this opportunity, in a two-minute conversation he: (a) asked two questions and received the information he needed; (b) reinforced their good relationship by sincerely complimenting the staff member on something he had recently done; and (c) got the staff member to agree to do something that the GM needed done.

The agenda in his mind guided the executive through this encounter, prompting him to ask important questions and to request an important action. And his relationship with this member of his network allowed him to get the cooperation he needed to do all this very quickly. Had he tried to plan this encounter in advance, he would have had to set up and attend a meeting, which would have taken at least 15 to 30 minutes, or 750% to 1,500% more time than the chance encounter. And if he had not already had a good relationship with the person, the meeting may have taken even longer or been ineffective.

In a similar way, agendas and networks allow GMs to engage in short and disjointed conversations, which can be extremely efficient. The following set of very short discussions, taken from a day in the life of John Thompson, a division manager in a financial services corporation, is typical in this regard. The conversation occurred one morning in Thompson's office. With him were two of his subordinates, Phil Dodge and Jud Smith:

Thompson: "What about Potter?"

Dodge: "He's OK."

Smith: "Don't forget about Chicago."

Dodge: "Oh yeah." [Makes a note to himself.]

Thompson: "OK. Then what about next week?"

Dodge: "We're set."

Thompson: "Good. By the way, how is Ted doing?"

Smith: "Better. He got back from the hospital on Tuesday. Phyllis says he looks good."

Thompson: "That's good to hear. I hope he doesn't have a relapse."

Dodge: "I'll see you this afternoon." [Leaves the room.]

Thompson: "OK. [To Smith.] Are we all set for now?"

Smith: "Yeah." [He gets up and starts to leave.]

Lawrence: [Steps into the doorway from the hall and speaks to Thompson.] "Have you seen the April numbers yet?"

Thompson: "No, have you?"

Lawrence: "Yes, five minutes ago. They're good except for CD, which is off by 5%."

Thompson: "That's better than I expected."

Smith: "I bet George is happy."

Thompson: [Laughing.] "If he is, he won't be after I talk to him."

[Turner, Thompson's secretary, sticks her head through the doorway and tells him Bill Larson is on the phone.]

Thompson: "I'll take it. Will you ask George to stop by later? [Others leave and Thompson picks up the phone.] Bill, good morning, how are you?...Yeah....Is that right?...No, don't worry about it.... I think about a million and a half.... Yeah....OK....Yeah, Sally enjoyed the other night too. Thanks again.... OK....Bye."

Lawrence: [Steps back into the office.] "What do you think about the Gerald proposal?"

Thompson: "I don't like it. It doesn't fit with what we've promised Corporate or Hines."

Lawrence: "Yeah, that's what I thought too. What is Jerry going to do about it?"

Thompson: "I haven't talked to him yet. [He turns to the phone and dials.] Let's see if he's in."

This dialogue may seem chaotic to an outsider, but that's only because an outsider does not share the business or organizational knowledge these managers have and does not know Thompson's agenda. That is, an outsider would not know who Potter, Ted, Phyllis, Bill Larson, Sally, Hines, or Jerry are, or what exactly "Chicago," "April numbers," "CD," or the "Gerald proposal" refer to. Nor would an outsider know what role Potter or Hines plays in Thompson's agenda. But to someone with that knowledge, the conversations make sense.

But more important, beyond being "not chaotic," these conversations are in fact amazingly efficient. In less than two minutes Thompson accomplished all of the following:

1 He learned that Mike Potter agreed to help on a particular problem loan. That problem, if not resolved successfully, could have seriously hurt Thompson's plan to increase the division's business in a certain area.

2 He reminded one of his managers to call someone in Chicago in reference to that loan.

3 He found out that the plans for the next week, about that loan, were all set. These included two internal meetings and a talk with the client.

4 He learned that Ted Jenkins was feeling better after an operation. Ted worked for Thompson and was an important part of Thompson's plans for the direction of the division over the next two years.

5 He found out that division income for April was on budget except in one area, which reduced pressures on him to focus on monthly income and to divert attention away from an effort to build revenues in one area.

6 He initiated a meeting with George Masolia to talk about the April figures. Thompson had been considering various future alternatives for the CD product line, which he felt must get on budget to support his overall thrust for the division.

7 He provided some information (as a favor) to Bill Larson, a peer in another part of the bank. Larson had been very helpful to Thompson in the past and was in a position to be very helpful in the future.

8 He initiated a call to Jerry Wilkins, one of his subordinates, to find out his reaction to a proposal from another division that would affect Thompson's division. He was concerned that the proposal could interfere with the division's five-year revenue goals.

In a general sense, John Thompson and most of the other effective GMs I have known are, as one HBR author recently put it, "adept at grasping and taking advantage of each item in the random succession of time and issue fragments that crowd [their] day[s]."[7] This seems to be particularly true for the best performers. And central to their ability to do so are their networks and agendas. The agendas allow the GMs to react in an opportunistic (and highly efficient) way to the flow of events around them, yet knowing that they are doing so within some broader and more rational framework. The networks allow terse (and very efficient) conversations to happen; without them, such short yet meaningful conversations would be impossible. Together, the agenda and networks allow the GMs to achieve the efficiency they need to cope with very demanding jobs in fewer than 60 hours per week (pattern 12), through daily behavior patterns that on the surface can look "unmanagerial."

What should top managers do?

Some of the most important implications of all this include the following:

1 At the start, putting someone in a GM job who does not know the business or the people involved, because he is a successful "professional manager," is probably very risky. Unless the business is easy to learn, it would be very difficult for an individual to learn enough, fast enough, to develop a good agenda. And unless it is a small situation with few people involved, it would be difficult to build a strong network fast enough to implement the agenda.

Especially for large and complex businesses, this condition suggests that "growing" one's own executives should have a high priority. Many companies today say that developing their own executives is important, but in light of the booming executive search business, one has to conclude that either they are not trying very hard or that their efforts simply are not succeeding.

2 Management training courses, both in universities and in corporations, probably overemphasize formal tools, unambiguous problems, and situations that deal simplistically with human relationships.

Some of the time-management programs, currently in vogue, are a good example of the problem here. Based on simplistic conceptions about the nature of managerial work, these programs instruct managers to stop letting people and problems "interrupt" their daily work. They often tell potential executives that short and disjointed conversations are ineffective. They advise that one should discipline oneself not to let "irrelevant" people and topics get on one's schedule. In other words, they advise people to behave differently from the effective executives in this study. Seminars on "How to Run Meetings" are probably just as bad.

Another example of inappropriate courses is university-based executive training programs that emphasize formal quantitative tools. These programs are based, at least implicitly, on the assumption that such tools are central to effective performance. All evidence suggests that while they are sometimes relevant, they are hardly central.

3 People who are new in general management jobs can probably be gotten up to speed more effectively than is the norm today. Initially, a new GM usually needs to spend considerable time collecting information, establishing relationships, selecting a basic direction for his or her area of responsibilities, and developing a supporting organization. During the first three to six months, demands from superiors to accomplish specific tasks, or to work on pet projects, can often be counterproductive. Indeed, anything that significantly diverts attention away from agenda setting and network building can prove to be counterproductive.

In a more positive sense, those who oversee GMs can probably be most helpful initially if they are sensitive to where the new executive is likely to have problems and help him or her in those areas. Such areas are often quite predictable. For example, if people have spent their careers going up the ladder in one function and have been promoted into the general manager's job in an autonomous division (a common occurrence, especially in manufacturing organizations), they will probably have problems with agenda setting because of a lack of detailed knowledge about the other functions in the division.

On the other hand, if people have spent most of their early careers in professional, staff, or assistant-to jobs and are promoted into a GM's job where they suddenly have responsibility for hundreds or thousands of people (not an unusual occurrence in professional organizations), they will probably have great difficulty at first building a network. They don't have many relationships to begin with and they are not used to spending time developing a large network.

In either case, a GM's boss can be a helpful coach and can arrange activities that foster instead of retard the types of actions the new executive should be taking.

4 Finally, the formal planning systems within which many GMs must operate probably hinder effective performance.

A good planning system should help a GM create an intelligent agenda and a strong network that can implement it. That is, it should encourage the GM to think strategically, to consider both the long and short term, and, regardless of the time frame, to take into account financial, product/market, and organizational issues. Furthermore, it should be a flexible tool that the executive can use to help build a network. It should give the GM leeway and options, so that, depending on what kind of environment among subordinates is desired, he or she can use the planning system to help achieve the goals.

Unfortunately, many of the planning systems used by corporations do nothing of the sort. Instead, they impose a rigid "number crunching" requirement on GMs that often does not require much strategic or long-range thinking in agenda setting and which can make network building and maintenance needlessly difficult by creating unnecessary stress among people. Indeed, some systems seem to do nothing but generate paper, often a lot of it, and distract executives from doing those things that are really important. ∇

Reprint 82609

References

1 Such as Sune Carlson, *Executive Behavior: A Study of the Work Load and the Working Methods of Managing Directors* (Stockholm, Sweden: Strombergs, 1951); Thomas Burns, "Management in Action," *Operational Research Quarterly,* vol. 8, 1957; Rosemary Stewart, "To Understand the Manager's Job: Consider Demands, Constraints, Choices," *Organizational Dynamics,* Spring 1976, p. 22; Michael Cohen and James March, *Leadership and Ambiguity* (New York: McGraw-Hill, 1974); R. Dubin and S.L. Spray, "Executive Behavior and Interaction," *Industrial Relations,* 1964, vol. 3, p. 99; and E. Brewer and J.W.C. Tomlinson, "The Manager's Working Day," *Journal of Industrial Economics,* 1964, vol. 12, p. 191.

2 See Morgan McCall, Ann Morrison, and Robert Hannan, "Studies of Managerial Work: Results and Methods," Technical Report No. 9, (Greensboro, N.C.: Center for Creative Leadership, 1978). This excellent report summarizes dozens of different studies ranging from Sune Carlson's groundbreaking work in 1951 to recent work by Mintzberg, Stewart, and others.

3 See "The Manager's Job: Folklore or Fact," HBR July-August 1975, p. 49.

4 Although these patterns are not widely recognized in today's conventional wisdom on management, there is evidence from other studies that GMs and other top managers do use such a process. See, for example, James Brian Quinn, *Strategies for Change: Logical Incrementalism* (Homewood, Ill.: Richard D. Irwin, 1980); Henry Mintzberg, *The Nature of Managerial Work* (New York: Harper & Row, 1973); H. Edward Wrapp, "Good Managers Don't Make Policy Decisions," HBR September-October 1967, p. 91; Charles Lindblom, "The Science of 'Muddling Through,'" *Public Administration Review,* vol. 19, 1959, p. 79; James March and Herbert Simon, *Organizations* (New York: John Wiley, 1958); Chester Barnard, *The Functions of the Executive* (Cambridge: Harvard University Press, 1939); Rosemary Stewart, "Managerial Agendas – Reactive or Proactive," *Organizational Dynamics,* Autumn 1979, p. 34; Frank Aguilar, *Scanning the Business Environment* (New York: Macmillan, 1967); and Michael McCaskey, "A Contingency Approach to Planning: Planning with Goals and Planning without Goals," *Academy of Management Journal,* June 1974, p. 91.

5 Although there is not a great deal of supporting evidence elsewhere, some does exist that is consistent with these findings. See, for example, John F. Gabarro, "Socialization at the Top – How CEOs and Their Subordinates Evolve Interpersonal Contacts," *Organizational Dynamics,* Winter 1979, p. 2; Jeffrey Pfeffer and Jerry Salancik, "Who Gets Power and How They Hold on to It," *Organizational Dynamics,* Winter 1977, p. 2; my article, "Power, Dependence, and Effective Management," HBR July-August 1977, p. 125; Melville Dalton, *Men Who Manage* (New York: John Wiley, 1959); and Richard Tanner Pascale and Anthony G. Athos, *The Art of Japanese Management* (New York: Simon & Schuster, 1981).

6 Once again, this type of behavior has been recognized and discussed in some management literature, but not in a great deal of it. See recent work by Thomas J. Peters and Jeffrey Pfeffer, in particular. For example, see Thomas J. Peters, "Symbols, Patterns, and Settings: An Optimistic Case for Getting Things Done," *Organizational Dynamics,* Autumn 1978; and Jeffrey Pfeffer, "Management as Symbolic Action," in *Research in Organizational Behavior,* vol. 3, L.L. Cummings and Barry M. Staw, ed. (Greenwich, Conn.: JAI Press, 1980). Also, see M. Andrew Pettigrew, *The Politics of Organizational Decision Making* (London: Tavistock Publications, 1973); and my article, "Power, Dependence, and Effective Management," HBR July-August 1977, p. 125.

7 Thomas J. Peters, "Leadership: Sad Facts and Silver Linings," HBR November-December 1979, p. 164.

Not all corporate success is due to leadership...

In Praise of Followers

by Robert E. Kelley

We are convinced that corporations succeed or fail, compete or crumble, on the basis of how well they are led. So we study great leaders of the past and present and spend vast quantities of time and money looking for leaders to hire and trying to cultivate leadership in the employees we already have.

I have no argument with this enthusiasm. Leaders matter greatly. But in searching so zealously for better leaders we tend to lose sight of the people these leaders will lead. Without his armies, after all, Napoleon was just a man with grandiose ambitions. Organizations stand or fall partly on the basis of how well their leaders lead, but partly also on the basis of how well their followers follow.

In 1987, declining profitability and intensified competition for corporate clients forced a large commercial bank on the east coast to reorganize its operations and cut its work force. Its most seasoned managers had to spend most of their time in the field working with corporate customers. Time and energies were stretched so thin that one department head decided he had no choice but to delegate the responsibility for reorganization to his staff people, who had recently had training in self-management.

Despite grave doubts, the department head set them up as a unit without a leader, responsible to one another and to the bank as a whole for writing their own job descriptions, designing a training program, determining criteria for performance evaluations, planning for operational needs, and helping to achieve overall organizational objectives.

They pulled it off. The bank's officers were delighted and frankly amazed that rank-and-file employees could assume so much responsibility so successfully. In fact, the department's capacity to control and direct itself virtually without leadership saved the organization months of turmoil, and as the bank struggled to remain a major player in its region, valuable management time was freed up to put out other fires.

Robert E. Kelley teaches at the Graduate School of Industrial Administration, Carnegie Mellon University. He is the author of Gold-Collar Worker: Harnessing the Brainpower of the New Work Force *(Addison-Wesley, 1985) and* Consulting: The Complete Guide to a Profitable Career *(Scribner, rev.ed., 1986). The material in this article is drawn from a book in progress,* Followership–Leadership–Partnership. *This is his second article for HBR.*

What was it these singular employees did? Given a goal and parameters, they went where most departments could only have gone under the hands-on guidance of an effective leader. But these employees accepted the delegation of authority and went there alone. They thought for themselves, sharpened their skills, focused their efforts, put on a fine display of grit and spunk and self-control. They followed effectively.

To encourage this kind of effective following in other organizations, we need to understand the nature of the follower's role. To cultivate good followers, we need to understand the human qualities that allow effective followership to occur.

The Role of Follower

Bosses are not necessarily good leaders; subordinates are not necessarily effective followers. Many bosses couldn't lead a horse to water. Many subordinates couldn't follow a parade. Some people avoid either role. Others accept the role thrust upon them and perform it badly.

At different points in their careers, even at different times of the working day, most managers play both roles, though seldom equally well. After all, the leadership role has the glamour and attention. We take courses to learn it, and when we play it well we get applause and recognition. But the reality is that most of us are more often followers than leaders. Even when we have subordinates, we still have bosses. For every committee we chair, we sit as a member on several others.

So followership dominates our lives and organizations, but not our thinking, because our preoccupation with leadership keeps us from considering the nature and the importance of the follower.

DRAWINGS BY MICHAEL WITTE

What distinguishes an effective from an ineffective follower is enthusiastic, intelligent, and self-reliant participation – without star billing – in the pursuit of an organizational goal. Effective followers differ in their motivations for following and in their perceptions of the role. Some choose followership as their primary role at work and serve as team players who take satisfaction in helping to further a cause, an idea, a product, a service, or, more rarely, a person. Others are leaders in some situations but choose the follower role in a particular context. Both these groups view the role of follower as legitimate, inherently valuable, even virtuous.

Some potentially effective followers derive motivation from ambition. By proving themselves in the follower's role, they hope to win the confidence of peers and superiors and move up the corporate ladder. These people do not see followership as attractive in itself. All the same, they can become good followers if they accept the value of learning the role, studying leaders from a subordinate's perspective, and polishing the followership skills that will always stand them in good stead.

Understanding motivations and perceptions is not enough, however. Since followers with different motivations can perform equally well, I examined the behavior that leads to effective and less effective following among people committed to the organization and came up with two underlying behavioral dimensions that help to explain the difference.

One dimension measures to what degree followers exercise independent, critical thinking. The other ranks them on a passive/active scale. The resulting diagram identifies five followership patterns.

Sheep are passive and uncritical, lacking in initiative and sense of responsibility. They perform the tasks given them and stop. Yes People are a livelier but equally unenterprising group. Dependent on a leader for inspiration, they can be aggressively deferential, even servile. Bosses weak in judgment and self-confidence tend to like them and to form alliances with them that can stultify the organization.

Alienated Followers are critical and independent in their thinking but passive in carrying out their role. Somehow, sometime, something turned them off. Often cynical, they tend to sink gradually into disgruntled acquiescence, seldom openly opposing a leader's efforts. In the very center of the diagram we have Survivors, who perpetually sample the wind and live by the slogan "better safe than sorry." They are adept at surviving change.

In the upper right-hand corner, finally, we have Effective Followers, who think for themselves and carry out their duties and assignments with energy and assertiveness. Because they are risk takers, self-starters, and independent problem solvers, they get consistently high ratings from peers and many superiors. Followership of this kind can be a positive and acceptable choice for parts or all of our lives—a source of pride and fulfillment.

Effective followers are well-balanced and responsible adults who can succeed without strong leadership. Many followers believe they offer as much value to the organization as leaders do, especially in project or task-force situations. In an organization of effective followers, a leader tends to be more an overseer of change and progress than a hero. As organizational structures flatten, the quality of those who follow will become more and more important. As Chester I. Barnard wrote 50 years ago in *The Functions of the Executive*, "The decision as to whether an order has authority or not lies with the person to whom it is addressed, and does not reside in 'persons of authority' or those who issue orders."

The Qualities of Followers

Effective followers share a number of essential qualities:

1. They manage themselves well.
2. They are committed to the organization and to a purpose, principle, or person outside themselves.
3. They build their competence and focus their efforts for maximum impact.
4. They are courageous, honest, and credible.

Self-Management. Paradoxically, the key to being an effective follower is the ability to think for oneself—to exercise control and independence and to work without close supervision. Good followers are people to whom a leader can safely delegate responsibility, people who anticipate needs at their own level of competence and authority.

Another aspect of this paradox is that effective followers see themselves—except in terms of line responsibility—as the equals of the leaders they follow. They are more apt to openly and unapologetically disagree with leadership and less likely to be intimidated by hierarchy and organizational structure. At the same time, they can see that the people they follow are, in turn, following the lead of others, and they try to appreciate the goals and needs of the team and the organization. Ineffective followers, on the other hand, buy into the hierarchy and, seeing themselves as subservient, vacillate between despair over their seeming powerlessness and attempts to manipulate leaders for their own purposes. Either their fear of powerlessness becomes a self-fulfilling prophecy—for themselves and often for their work units as well—or their resentment leads them to undermine the team's goals.

Self-managed followers give their organizations a significant cost advantage because they eliminate much of the need for elaborate supervisory control systems that, in any case, often lower morale. In 1985, a large midwestern bank redesigned its personnel selection system to attract self-managed workers. Those conducting interviews began to look for particular types of experience and capacities—initiative, teamwork, independent thinking of all kinds—and the bank revamped its orientation program to emphasize self-management. At the executive level, role playing was introduced into the interview process: how you disagree with your boss, how you prioritize your in-basket after a vacation. In the three years since, employee turnover has dropped dramatically, the need for supervisors has decreased, and administrative costs have gone down.

Of course not all leaders and managers like having self-managing subordinates. Some would rather have sheep or yes people. The best that good followers can do in this situation is to protect themselves with a little career self-management—that is, to stay attractive in the marketplace. The qualities that make a good follower are too much in demand to go begging for long.

Commitment. Effective followers are committed to something—a cause, a product, an organization, an idea—in addition to the care of their own lives and careers. Some leaders misinterpret this commitment. Seeing their authority acknowledged, they mistake loyalty to a goal for loyalty to themselves. But the fact is that many effective followers see leaders merely as coadventurers on a worthy crusade, and if they suspect their leader of flagging commitment or conflicting motives they may just withdraw their support, either by changing jobs or by contriving to change leaders.

Self-confident followers see colleagues as allies and leaders as equals.

The opportunities and the dangers posed by this kind of commitment are not hard to see. On the one hand, commitment is contagious. Most people like working with colleagues whose hearts are in their work. Morale stays high. Workers who begin to wander from their purpose are jostled back into line. Projects stay on track and on time. In addition, an ap-

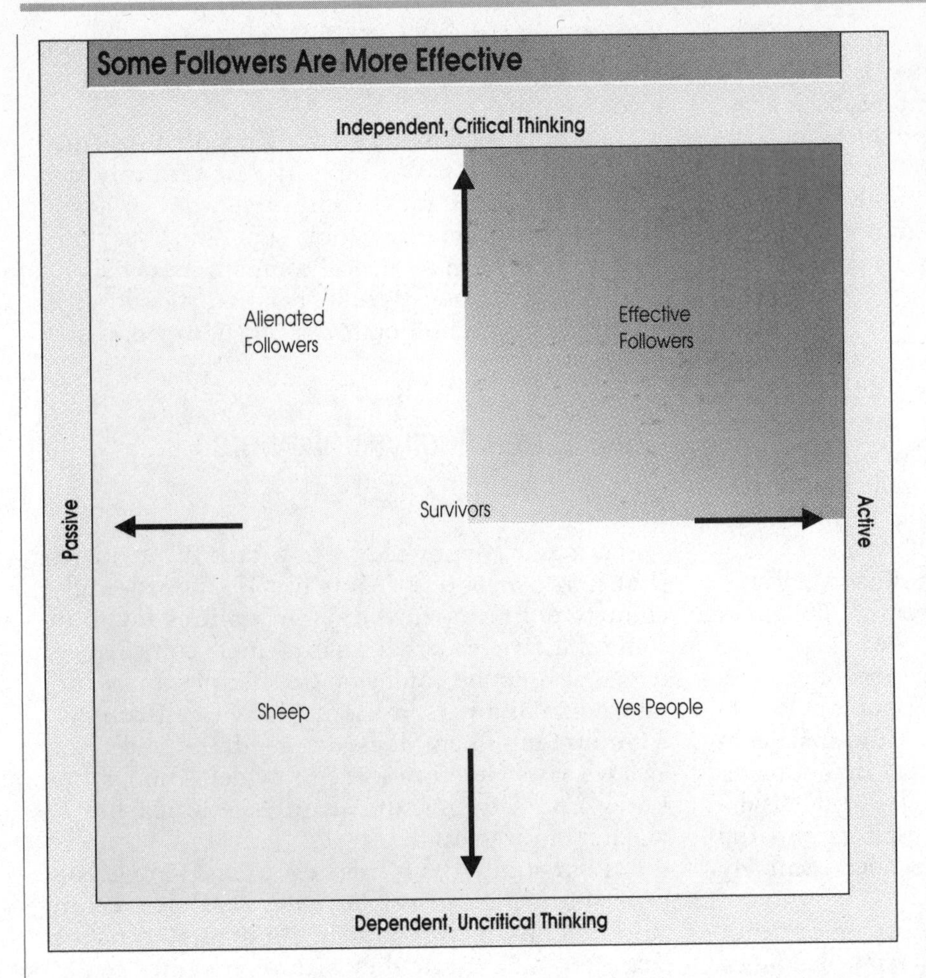

preciation of commitment and the way it works can give managers an extra tool with which to understand and channel the energies and loyalties of their subordinates.

On the other hand, followers who are strongly committed to goals not consistent with the goals of their companies can produce destructive results. Leaders having such followers can even lose control of their organizations.

A scientist at a computer company cared deeply about making computer technology available to the masses, and her work was outstanding. Since her goal was in line with the company's goals, she had few problems with top management. Yet she saw her department leaders essentially as facilitators of her dream, and when managers worked at cross-purposes to that vision, she exercised all of her considerable political skills to their detriment. Her immediate supervisors saw her as a thorn in the side, but she was quite effective in furthering her cause because she saw eye to eye with company leaders. But what if her vision and the company's vision had differed?

Effective followers temper their loyalties to satisfy organizational needs–or they find new organizations. Effective leaders know how to channel the energies of strong commitment in ways that will satisfy corporate goals as well as a follower's personal needs.

Competence and Focus. On the grounds that committed incompetence is still incompetence, effective followers master skills that will be useful to their organizations. They generally hold higher performance standards than the work environment requires, and continuing education is second nature to them, a staple in their professional development.

Less effective followers expect training and development to come to them. The only education they acquire is force-fed. If not sent to a seminar, they don't go. Their competence deteriorates unless some leader gives them parental care and attention.

Good followers take on extra work gladly, but first they do a superb job on their core responsibilities. They are good judges of their own strengths and weaknesses, and they contribute well to teams. Asked to perform in areas where they are poorly qualified, they speak up. Like athletes stretching their capacities, they don't mind chancing failure if they know they can succeed, but they are careful to spare the company wasted energy, lost time, and poor performance by accepting challenges that coworkers are better prepared to meet. Good followers see coworkers as colleagues rather than competitors.

At the same time, effective followers often search for overlooked problems. A woman on a new product development team discovered that no one was responsible for coordinating engineering, marketing, and manufacturing. She worked out an interdepartmental review schedule that identified the people who should be involved at each stage of development. Instead of burdening her boss with yet another problem, this woman took the initiative to present the issue along with a solution.

Another woman I interviewed described her efforts to fill a dangerous void in the company she cared about. Young managerial talent in this manufacturing corporation had traditionally made careers in production. Convinced that foreign competition would alter the shape of the industry, she realized that marketing was a neglected area. She took classes, attended seminars, and read widely. More important, she visited customers to get feedback about her company's and competitors' products, and she soon knew more about the product's customer appeal and market position than any of her peers. The extra competence did wonders for her own career, but it also helped her company weather a storm it had not seen coming.

Courage. Effective followers are credible, honest, and courageous. They establish themselves as independent, critical thinkers whose knowledge and judgment can be trusted. They give credit where credit is due, admitting mistakes and sharing successes. They form their own views and ethical standards and stand up for what they believe in.

Insightful, candid, and fearless, they can keep leaders and colleagues honest and informed. The other side of the coin of course is that they can also cause great trouble for a leader with questionable ethics.

Jerome LiCari, the former R&D director at Beech-Nut, suspected for several years that the apple concentrate Beech-Nut was buying from a new supplier at 20% below market price was adulterated. His department suggested switching suppliers, but top management at the financially strapped company put the burden of proof on R&D.

By 1981, LiCari had accumulated strong evidence of adulteration and issued a memo recommending a change of supplier. When he got no response, he went

> Courageous followers can keep a leader honest—and out of trouble.

to see his boss, the head of operations. According to LiCari, he was threatened with dismissal for lack of team spirit. LiCari then went to the president of Beech-Nut, and when that, too, produced no results, he gave up his three-year good-soldier effort, followed his conscience, and resigned. His last performance evaluation praised his expertise and loyalty, but said his judgment was "colored by naiveté and impractical ideals."

In 1986, Beech-Nut and LiCari's two bosses were indicted on several hundred counts of conspiracy to commit fraud by distributing adulterated apple juice. In November 1987, the company pleaded guilty and agreed to a fine of $2 million. In February of this year, the two executives were found guilty on a majority of the charges. The episode cost Beech-Nut an estimated $25 million and a 20% loss of market share. Asked during the trial if he had been naive, LiCari said, "I guess I was. I thought apple juice should be made from apples."

Is LiCari a good follower? Well, no, not to his dishonest bosses. But yes, he is almost certainly the kind of employee most companies want to have: loyal, honest, candid with his superiors, and thoroughly credible. In an ethical company involved unintentionally in questionable practices, this kind of follower can head off embarrassment, expense, and litigation.

Cultivating Effective Followers

You may have noticed by now that the qualities that make effective followers are, confusingly enough, pretty much the same qualities found in some effective leaders. This is no mere coincidence, of course. But the confusion underscores an important point. If a person has initiative, self-control, commitment, talent, honesty, credibility, and courage, we say, "Here is a leader!" By definition, a follower cannot exhibit the qualities of leadership. It violates our stereotype.

But our stereotype is ungenerous and wrong. Followership is not a person but a role, and what distinguishes followers from leaders is not intelligence or character but the role they play. As I pointed out at the beginning of this article, effective followers and effective leaders are often the same people playing different parts at different hours of the day.

In many companies, the leadership track is the only road to career success. In almost all companies, leadership is taught and encouraged while followership is not. Yet effective followership is a prerequisite for organizational success. Your organization can take four steps to cultivate effective followers in your work force.

1. *Redefining Followership and Leadership.* Our stereotyped but unarticulated definitions of leadership and followership shape our expectations when we occupy either position. If a leader is defined as responsible for motivating followers, he or she will likely act toward followers as if they needed motivation. If we agree that a leader's job is to transform followers, then it must be a follower's job to provide the clay. If followers fail to need transformation, the leader looks ineffective. The way we define the roles clearly influences the outcome of the interaction.

Instead of seeing the leadership role as superior to and more active than the role of the follower, we can think of them as equal but different activities. The operative definitions are roughly these: people who are effective in the leader role have the vision to set corporate goals and strategies, the interpersonal skills to achieve consensus, the verbal capacity to communicate enthusiasm to large and diverse groups of individuals, the organizational talent to coordinate disparate efforts, and, above all, the desire to lead.

People who are effective in the follower role have the vision to see both the forest and the trees, the social capacity to work well with others, the strength of character to flourish without heroic status, the moral and psychological balance to pursue personal and corporate goals at no cost to either, and, above all, the desire to participate in a team effort for the accomplishment of some greater common purpose.

This view of leadership and followership can be conveyed to employees directly and indirectly–in training and by example. The qualities that make good followers and the value the company places on effective followership can be articulated in explicit follower training. Perhaps the best way to convey this message, however, is by example. Since each of us plays a follower's part at least from time to time, it is essential that we play it well, that we contribute our competence to the achievement of team goals, that we support the team leader with candor and self-control, that we do our best to appreciate and enjoy the role of quiet contribution to a larger, common cause.

2. *Honing Followership Skills.* Most organizations assume that leadership has to be taught but that everyone knows how to follow. This assumption is based on three faulty premises: (1) that leaders are more important than followers, (2) that following is simply doing what you are told to do, and (3) that followers inevitably draw their energy and aims, even their talent, from the leader. A program of follower training can correct this misapprehension by focusing on topics like:

Good leaders know how to follow–and they set an example for others.

Improving independent, critical thinking.
Self-management.
Disagreeing agreeably.
Building credibility.
Aligning personal and organizational goals and commitments.
Acting responsibly toward the organization, the leader, coworkers, and oneself.
Similarities and differences between leadership and followership roles.
Moving between the two roles with ease.

3. *Performance Evaluation and Feedback.* Most performance evaluations include a section on leadership skills. Followership evaluation would include items like the ones I have discussed. Instead of rating employees on leadership qualities such as self-management, independent thinking, originality, courage, competence, and credibility, we can rate them on these same qualities in both the leadership and followership roles and then evaluate each individual's ability to shift easily from the one role to the other. A variety of performance perspectives will help most people understand better how well they play their various organizational roles.

Moreover, evaluations can come from peers, subordinates, and self as well as from supervisors. The process is simple enough: peers and subordinates who come into regular or significant contact with another employee fill in brief, periodic questionnaires where they rate the individual on followership qualities. Findings are then summarized and given to the employee being rated.

4. *Organizational Structures That Encourage Followership.* Unless the value of good following is somehow built into the fabric of the organization, it is likely to remain a pleasant conceit to which everyone pays occasional lip service but no dues.

> Groups with many leaders can be chaos. Groups with none can be very productive.

Here are four good ways to incorporate the concept into your corporate culture:

In leaderless groups, all members assume equal responsibility for achieving goals. These are usually small task forces of people who can work together under their own supervision. However hard it is to imagine a group with more than one leader, groups with none at all can be highly productive if their members have the qualities of effective followers.

Groups with temporary and rotating leadership are another possibility. Again, such groups are probably best kept small and the rotation fairly frequent, although the notion might certainly be extended to include the administration of a small department for, say, six-month terms. Some of these temporary leaders will be less effective than others, of course, and some may be weak indeed, which is why critics maintain that this structure is inefficient. Why not let the best leader lead? Why suffer through the tenure of less effective leaders? There are two reasons. First, experience of the leadership role is essential to the education of effective followers. Second, followers learn that they must compensate for ineffective leadership by exercising their skill as good followers. Rotating leader or not, they are bound to be faced with ineffective leadership more than once in their careers.

Delegation to the lowest level is a third technique for cultivating good followers. Nordstrom's, the Seattle-based department store chain, gives each sales clerk responsibility for servicing and satisfying the customer, including the authority to make refunds without supervisory approval. This kind of delegation makes even people at the lowest levels responsible for their own decisions and for thinking independently about their work.

Finally, companies can use rewards to underline the importance of good followership. This is not as easy as it sounds. Managers dependent on yes people and sheep for ego gratification will not leap at the idea of extra rewards for the people who make them most uncomfortable. In my research, I have found that effective followers get mixed treatment. About half the time, their contributions lead to substantial rewards. The other half of the time they are punished by their superiors for exercising judgment, taking risks, and failing to conform. Many managers insist that they want independent subordinates who can think for themselves. In practice, followers who challenge their bosses run the risk of getting fired.

In today's flatter, leaner organization, companies will not succeed without the kind of people who take pride and satisfaction in the role of supporting player, doing the less glorious work without fanfare. Organizations that want the benefits of effective followers must find ways of rewarding them, ways of bringing them into full partnership in the enterprise. Think of the thousands of companies that achieve adequate performance and lackluster profits with employees they treat like second-class citizens. Then imagine for a moment the power of an organization blessed with fully engaged, fully energized, fully appreciated followers.

Author's note: I am indebted to Pat Chew for her contributions to this article. I also want to thank Janet Nordin, Howard Seckler, Paul Brophy, Stuart Mechlin, Ellen Mechlin, and Syed Shariq for their critical input.

Reprint 88606

Leaders Reflect on Leadership

"Insecure managers create complexity. Real leaders don't need clutter."

Speed, Simplicity, Self-Confidence: An Interview with Jack Welch

by Noel Tichy and Ram Charan

John F. Welch, Jr., chairman and CEO of General Electric, leads one of the world's largest corporations. It is a very different corporation from the one he inherited in 1981. GE is now built around 14 distinct businesses – including aircraft engines, medical systems, engineering plastics, major appliances, NBC television, and financial services. They reflect the aggressive strategic redirection Welch unveiled soon after he became CEO.

By now the story of GE's business transformation is familiar. In 1981, Welch declared that the company would focus its operations on three "strategic circles" – core manufacturing units such as lighting and locomotives, technology-intensive businesses, and services – and that each of its businesses would rank first or second in its global market. GE has achieved world market-share leadership in nearly all of its 14 businesses. In 1988, its 300,000 employees generated revenues of more than $50 billion and net income of $3.4 billion.

GE's strategic redirection had essentially taken shape by the end of 1986. Since then, Welch has embarked on a more imposing challenge: building a revitalized "human engine" to animate GE's formidable "business engine."

His program has two central objectives. First, he is championing a companywide drive to identify and eliminate unproductive work in order to energize GE's employees. It is neither realistic nor useful, Welch argues, to expect employees of a decidedly leaner corporation to complete all the reports, reviews, forecasts, and budgets that were standard operating procedure in more forgiving times. He is developing procedures to speed decision cycles, move information through the organization, provide quick and effective feedback, and evaluate and reward managers on qualities such as openness, candor, and self-confidence.

Second, and perhaps of even greater significance, Welch is leading a transformation of attitudes at GE – struggling, in his words, to release "emotional energy" at all levels of the organization and encourage creativity and feelings of ownership and self-worth. His ultimate goal is to create an enterprise that can tap the benefits of global scale and diversity without the stifling costs of bureaucratic controls and hierarchical authority and without a managerial focus on personal power and self-perpetuation. This requires a transformation not only of systems and procedures, he argues, but also of people themselves.

This interview was conducted at Welch's office in Fairfield, Connecticut by Noel Tichy and Ram Charan. Mr. Tichy was manager of GE's Management Education Operation from 1985 through 1987. He is a professor at the University of Michigan's School of Business Administration, director of its Global Leadership Program, and coauthor of The Transformational Leader *(John Wiley & Sons, 1986). Mr. Charan is a Dallas-based consultant who advises companies in the United States, Europe, and Asia on implementing global strategies.*

HBR: *What makes a good manager?*

Jack Welch: I prefer the term business leader. Good business leaders create a vision, articulate the vision, passionately own the vision, and relentlessly drive it to completion. Above all else, though, good leaders are open. They go up, down, and around their organization to reach people. They don't stick to the established channels. They're informal. They're straight with people. They make a religion out of being accessible. They never get bored telling their story.

Real communication takes countless hours of eyeball to eyeball, back and forth. It means more listening than talking. It's not pronouncements on a videotape, it's not announcements in a newspaper. It is human beings coming to see and accept things through a constant interactive process aimed at consensus. And it must be absolutely relentless. That's a real challenge for us. There's still not enough candor in this company.

What do you mean by "candor"?

I mean facing reality, seeing the world as it is rather than as you wish it were. We've seen over and over again that businesses facing market downturns, tougher competition, and more demanding customers inevitably make forecasts that are much too optimistic. This means they don't take advantage of the opportunities change usually offers. Change in the marketplace isn't something to fear; it's an enormous opportunity to shuffle the deck, to replay the game. Candid managers – leaders – don't get paralyzed about the "fragility" of the organization. They tell people the truth. That doesn't scare them because they realize their people know the truth anyway.

We've had managers at GE who couldn't change, who kept telling us to leave them alone. They wanted to sit back, to keep things the way they were. And that's just what they did – until they and most of their staffs had to go. That's the lousy part of this job. What's worse is that we still don't understand why so many people are incapable of facing reality, of being candid with themselves and others.

But we are clearly making progress in facing reality, even if the progress is painfully slow. Take our locomotive business. That team was the only one we've ever had that took a business whose forecasts and plans were headed straight up, and whose market began to head straight down, a virtual collapse, and managed to change the tires while the car was moving. It's the team that forecast the great locomotive boom, convinced us to invest $300 million to renovate its plant in Erie, and then the market went boom all right – right into a crater. But when it did, that team turned on a dime. It reoriented the business.

Several of our other businesses in the same situation said, "Give it time, the market will come back." Locomotive didn't wait. And today, now that the market *is* coming back, the business looks great. The point is, what determines your destiny is not the

DRAWING BY ANATOLY

hand you're dealt; it's how you play the hand. And the best way to play your hand is to face reality–see the world the way it is–and act accordingly.

What makes an effective organization?

For a large organization to be effective, it must be simple. For a large organization to be simple, its people must have self-confidence and intellectual self-assurance. Insecure managers create complexity. Frightened, nervous managers use thick, convoluted planning books and busy slides filled with everything they've known since childhood. Real leaders don't need clutter. People must have the self-confidence to be clear, precise, to be sure that every person in their organization–highest to lowest–understands what the business is trying to achieve. But it's not easy. You can't believe how hard it is for people to be simple, how much they fear being simple. They worry that if they're simple, people will think they're simple-minded. In reality, of course, it's just the reverse. Clear, tough-minded people are the most simple.

> "Change in the marketplace isn't something to fear; it's an opportunity to shuffle the deck."

Soon after you became CEO, you articulated GE's now-famous strategy of "number one or number two globally." Was that an exercise in the power of simplicity?

Yes. In 1981, when we first defined our business strategy, the real focus was Japan. The entire organization had to understand that GE was in a tougher, more competitive world, with Japan as the cutting edge of the new competition. Nine years later, that competitive toughness has increased by a factor of five or ten. We face a revitalized Japan that's migrated around the world–to Thailand, Malaysia, Mexico, the United States–and responded successfully to a massive yen change. Europe is a different game today. There are great European businesspeople, dynamic leaders, people who are changing things. Plus you've got all the other Asian successes.

So being number one or number two globally is more important than ever. But scale alone is not enough. You have to combine financial strength, market position, and technology leadership with an organizational focus on speed, agility, and simplicity. The world moves so much faster today. You can be driving through Seoul, talking to France on the phone and making a deal, and have a fax waiting for you when you get back to the United States with the deal in good technical shape. Paolo Fresco, senior vice president of GE International, has been negotiating around-the-clock for the past two days on a deal in England. Last night I was talking with Larry Bossidy, one of our vice chairmen, who was in West Germany doing another deal. We never used to do business this way. So you can be the biggest, but if you're not flexible enough to handle rapid change and make quick decisions, you won't win.

How have you implemented your commitment to simplicity at the highest levels of GE, where you can have the most direct impact on what happens?

First, we took out management layers. Layers hide weaknesses. Layers mask mediocrity. I firmly believe that an overburdened, overstretched executive is the best executive because he or she doesn't have the time to meddle, to deal in trivia, to bother people. Remember the theory that a manager should have no more than 6 or 7 direct reports? I say the right number is closer to 10 or 15. This way you have no choice but to let people flex their muscles, let them grow and mature. With 10 or 15 reports, a leader can focus only on the big important issues, not on minutiae.

We also reduced the corporate staff. Headquarters can be the bane of corporate America. It can strangle, choke, delay, and create insecurity. If you're going to have simplicity in the field, you can't have a big staff at home. We don't need the questioners and the checkers, the nitpickers who bog down the process, people whose only role is to second-guess and kibitz, the people who clog communication inside the company. Today people at headquarters are experts in taxes, finance, or some other key area that can help people in the field. Our corporate staff no longer just challenges and questions; it assists. This is a mindset change: staff essentially reports to the field rather than the other way around.

> "An overburdened, overstretched executive is the best executive. He doesn't have time to meddle, to deal in trivia."

So many CEOs disparage staff and middle management–you know, "If only those bureaucrats would buy into my vision." When you talk about "nitpickers" and "kibitzers," are you talking about lousy people or about good people forced into lousy jobs?

People are not lousy, period. Leaders have to find a better fit between their organization's needs and their people's capabilities. Staff people, whom I prefer to call individual contributors, can be tremendous sources of added value in an organization. But each staff person has to ask, "How do I add value? How do I help make people on the line more effective and more competitive?" In the past, many staff functions were driven by control rather than adding value. Staffs with that focus have to be eliminated. They sap emotional energy in the organization. As for middle managers, they can be the stronghold of the organization. But their jobs have to be redefined. They have to see their roles as a combination of teacher, cheerleader, and liberator, not controller.

You've dismantled GE's groups and sectors, the top levels of the corporate organization to which individual strategic business units once reported. That certainly makes the organization chart more simple–you now have 14 separate businesses reporting directly to you or your two vice chairmen. How does the new structure simplify how GE operates on a day-to-day basis?

Cutting the groups and sectors eliminated communications filters. Today there is direct communication between the CEO and the leaders of the 14 businesses. We have very short cycle times for decisions and little interference by corporate staff. A major investment decision that used to take a year can now be made in a matter of days.

We also run a Corporate Executive Council, the CEC. For two days every quarter, we meet with the leaders of the 14 businesses and our top staff people. These aren't stuffy, formal strategic reviews. We share ideas and information candidly and openly, including programs that have failed. The important thing is that at the end of those two days everyone in the CEC has seen and discussed the same information. The CEC creates a sense of trust, a sense of personal familiarity and mutual obligation at the top of the company. We consider the CEC a piece of organizational technology that is very important for our future success.

Still, how can it be "simple" to run a $50 billion enterprise? Doesn't a corporation as vast as GE need management layers, extensive review systems, and formal procedures–if for no other reason than to keep the business under control?

People always overestimate how complex business is. This isn't rocket science; we've chosen one of the world's more simple professions. Most global businesses have three or four critical competitors, and you know who they are. And there aren't that many things you can do with a business. It's not as if you're choosing among 2,000 options.

You mentioned review systems. At our 1986 officers' meeting, which involves the top 100 or so executives at GE, we asked the 14 business leaders to present reports on the competitive dynamics in their businesses. How'd we do it? We had them each prepare one-page answers to five questions: What are your market dynamics globally today, and where are they going over the next several years? What actions have your competitors taken in the last three years to upset those global dynamics? What have you done in the last three years to affect those dynamics? What are the most dangerous things your competitor could do in the next three years to upset those dynamics? What are the most effective things you could do to bring your desired impact on those dynamics?

> "People overestimate how complex business is. We've chosen one of the world's more simple professions."

Five simple charts. After those initial reviews, which we update regularly, we could assume that everyone at the top knew the plays and had the same playbook. It doesn't take a genius. Fourteen businesses each with a playbook of five charts. So when Larry Bossidy is with a potential partner in Europe, or I'm with a company in the Far East, we're always there with a competitive understanding based on our playbooks. We know exactly what makes sense; we don't need a big staff to do endless analysis. That means we should be able to act with speed.

Probably the most important thing we promise our business leaders is fast action. Their job is to create and grow new global businesses. Our job in the executive office is to facilitate, to go out and negotiate a deal, to make the acquisition, or get our businesses the partners they need. When our business leaders call, they don't expect studies–they expect answers.

Take the deal with Thomson, where we swapped our consumer electronics business for their medical equipment business. We were presented with an opportunity, a great solution to a serious strategic problem, and we were able to act quickly. We didn't need to go back to headquarters for a strategic analysis and a bunch of reports. Conceptually, it took us about 30 minutes to decide that the deal made sense and then a meeting of maybe two hours with the Thomson people to work out the basic terms. We signed a letter of intent in five days. We had to close it with the usual legal details, of course, so from beginning to end it took five months. Thomson had the same clear view of where it wanted to go – so it worked perfectly for both sides.

Another of our jobs is to transfer best practices across all the businesses, with lightning speed. Staff often put people all over the place to do this. But they aren't effective lightning rods to transfer best practice; they don't have the stature in the organization. Business leaders do. That's why every CEC meeting deals in part with a generic business issue – a new pay plan, a drug-testing program, stock options. Every business is free to propose its own plan or program and present it at the CEC, and we put it through a central screen at corporate, strictly to make sure it's within the bounds of good sense. We don't approve the details. But we want to know what the details are so we can see which programs are working and immediately alert the other businesses to the successful ones.

You make it sound so easy.

Simple *doesn't* mean easy, especially as you try to move this approach down through the organization. When you take out layers, you change the exposure of the managers who remain. They sit right in the sun. Some of them blotch immediately; they can't stand the exposure of leadership.

We now have leaders in each of the businesses who *own* those businesses. Eight years ago, we had to sell the idea of ownership. Today the challenge is to move that sense of ownership, that commitment to relentless personal interaction and immediate sharing of information, down through the organization. We're very early in this, and it's going to be anything but easy. But it's something we have to do.

From an organizational point of view, how are the 14 businesses changing? Are they going through a delayering process? Are their top people communicating as the CEC does?

In addition to locomotives, which I've already discussed, we've had major delayering and streamlining in almost all of our businesses, and they have made significant improvements in total cost productivity.

The CEC concept is flowing down as well. For example, each of the businesses has created its own executive committee to meet on policy questions. These committees meet weekly or monthly and include the top staff and line people from the businesses. Everyone in the same room, everyone with the same information, everyone buying into the targets. Each business also has an operations committee. This is a bigger group of maybe 30 people for each business: 5 staffers, 7 people from manufacturing, 6 from engineering, 8 from marketing, and so on. They get together every quarter for a day and a half to thrash out problems, to get people talking across functions, to communicate with each other about their prospects and programs. That's 30 people in 14 businesses, more than 400 people all together, in a process of instant communication about their businesses and the company.

You see, I operate on a very simple belief about business. If there are six of us in a room, and we all get the same facts, in most cases, the six of us will reach roughly the same conclusion. And once we all accept that conclusion, we can force our energy into it and put it into action. The problem is, we don't get the same information. We each get different pieces. Business isn't complicated. The complications arise when people are cut off from information they need. That's what we're trying to change.

> "When our business leaders call, they don't expect studies – they expect answers."

That brings us to Work-Out, which you've been championing inside GE since early this year. Why are you pushing it so hard?

Work-Out is absolutely fundamental to our becoming the kind of company we must become. That's why I'm so passionate about it. We're not going to succeed if people end up doing the same work they've always done, if they don't feel any psychic or financial impact from the way the organization is changing. The ultimate objective of Work-Out is so clear. We want 300,000 people with different career objectives, different family aspirations, different financial goals, to share directly in this company's vision, the information, the decision-making process, and the rewards. We want to build a more stimulating environment, a more creative environment, a freer work atmosphere, with incentives tied directly to what people do.

Now, the business leaders aren't particularly thrilled that we're so passionate about Work-Out. In 1989, the CEO is going to every business in this company to sit in on a Work-Out session. That's a little

Work-Out: A Case Study

GE Medical Systems (GEMS) is the world leader in medical diagnostic imaging equipment, including CT scanners, magnetic resonance equipment, and X-ray mammography. Its more than 15,000 employees face formidable international competition. Despite positive financial results, GEMS is working to transform its human organization. Work-Out is designed to identify sources of frustration and bureaucratic inefficiency, eliminate unnecessary and unproductive work, and overhaul how managers are evaluated and rewarded.

Work-Out began last fall when some 50 GEMS employees attended a five-day offsite session in Lake Lawn, Wisconsin. The participants included senior vice president and group executive John Trani, his staff, six employee relations managers, and informal leaders from technology, finance, sales, service, marketing, and manufacturing. Trani selected these informal leaders for their willingness to take business risks, challenge the status quo, and contribute in other key ways to GEMS. We participated as Work-Out faculty members and have participated in follow-up sessions that will run beyond 1989.

The Lake Lawn session took place after two important preliminary steps. First, we conducted in-depth interviews with managers at all levels of GEMS. Our interviews uncovered many objections to and criticisms of existing procedures, including measurement systems (too many, not focused enough on customers, cross-functional conflicts); pay and reward systems (lack of work goals, inconsistent signals); career development systems (ambiguous career paths, inadequate performance feedback); and an atmosphere in which blame, fear, and lack of trust overshadowed team commitments to solving problems. Here are some sample quotes from our interviews:

☐ "I'm frustrated. I simply can't do the quality of work that I want to do and know how to do. I feel my hands are tied. I have no time. I need help on how to delegate and operate in this new culture."

☐ "The goal of downsizing and delayering is correct. The execution stinks. The concept is to drop a lot of 'less important' work. This just didn't happen. We still have to know all the details, still have to follow all the old policies and systems."

☐ "I'm overwhelmed. I can and want to do better work. The solution is not simply adding new people; I don't even want to. We need to team up on projects and work. Our leaders must stop piling on more and help us set priorities."

Second, just before the first Work-Out session, Jack Welch traveled to GEMS headquarters for a half-day roundtable with the Work-Out participants. Here are some sample quotes from middle managers:

☐ To senior management: "Listen! Think carefully about what the middle managers say. Make them feel like they are the experts and that their opinions are respected. There appear to be too many preconceived beliefs on the part of Welch and Trani."

☐ To senior management: "Listen to people, don't just pontificate. Trust people's judgment and don't continually second-guess. Treat other people like adults and not children."

☐ About themselves: "I will recommend work to be discontinued. I will try to find 'blind spots' where I withhold power. Any person I send to speak for me will 'push' peers who resist change."

☐ About themselves: "I will be more bold in making decisions. I will no longer accept the status quo. I will ask my boss for authority to make decisions. In fact, I will make more decisions on my own."

The five-day Work-Out session was an intense effort to unravel, evaluate, and reconsider the complex web of personal relationships, cross-functional interactions, and formal work procedures through which the business of GEMS gets done. Cross-functional teams cooperated to address actual business problems. Each functional group developed a vision of where its operations are headed.

John Trani participated in a roundtable where he listened and responded to the concerns and criticisms of middle managers. Senior members of the GEMS staff worked to build trust and more effective communication with the functional managers. All the participants focused on ways to reorganize work and maximize return on organization time, on team time, and on individual time.

The five-day session ended with individuals and functional teams signing close to 100 written contracts to implement the new procedures. There were contracts between functional teams, contracts between individuals, contracts between function heads and their staffs, and businesswide contracts with John Trani and his staff.

Work-Out has picked up steam since Lake Lawn. Managers from different product lines have participated in workshops to review and implement the attitudes, values, and new work procedures discussed at Lake Lawn. A Work-Out steering committee has held cross-functional information meetings for field employees around the world. Managers throughout GEMS are reviewing and modifying their reward and measurement systems. And Welch continues to receive regular briefings on Work-Out's progress.

No two GE businesses approach Work-Out in the same way; a process this intensive can't be "cloned" successfully among vastly different businesses. But Work-Out at GEMS offers a glimpse of the change process taking place throughout General Electric.

–Noel Tichy and Ram Charan

puzzling to them. "I own the business, what are you doing here?" they say. Well, I'm not there to tell them how to price products, what type of equipment they need, whom to hire; I have no comments on that.

But Work-Out is the next generation of what we're trying to do. We had to put in a process to focus on and change how work gets done in this company. We have to apply the same relentless passion to Work-Out that we did in selling the vision of number one and number two globally. That's why we're pushing it so hard, getting so involved.

What is the essence of Work-Out, the basic goal?

Work-Out has a practical and an intellectual goal. The practical objective is to get rid of thousands of bad habits accumulated since the creation of General Electric. How would you like to move from a house after 112 years? Think of what would be in the closets and the attic—those shoes that you'll wear to paint next spring, even though you know you'll never paint again. We've got 112 years of closets and attics in this company. We want to flush them out, to start with a brand new house with empty closets, to begin the whole game again.

The second thing we want to achieve, the intellectual part, begins by putting the leaders of each business in front of 100 or so of their people, eight to ten times a year, to let them hear what their people think about the company, what they like and don't like about their work, about how they're evaluated, about how they spend their time. Work-Out will expose the leaders to the vibrations of their business—opinions, feelings, emotions, resentments, not abstract theories of organization and management.

Ultimately, we're talking about redefining the relationship between boss and subordinate. I want to get

> "People should challenge their bosses: 'Why do you require me to do these wasteful things?'"

to a point where people challenge their bosses every day: "Why do you require me to do these wasteful things? Why don't you let me do the things you shouldn't be doing so you can move on and create? That's the job of a leader—to create, not to control. Trust me to do my job, and don't make me waste all my time trying to deal with you on the control issue."

Now, how do you do get people communicating with each other with that much candor? You put them together in a room and make them thrash it out.

These Work-Out sessions, and I've already done several of them, create all kinds of personal dynamics. Some people go and hide. Some don't like the dinner in the evening because they can't get along with the other people. Some emerge as forceful advocates. As people meet over and over, though, more of them will develop the courage to speak out. The norm will become the person who says, "Dammit, we're not doing it. Let's get on with doing it." Today the norm in most companies, not just GE, is not to bring up critical issues with a boss, certainly not in a public setting, and certainly not in an atmosphere where self-confidence has not been developed. This process will create more fulfilling and rewarding jobs. The quality of work life will improve dramatically.

It's one thing to insist that the people who report directly to you, or who work one or two layers below you, become forceful advocates and criticize the status quo. They've got your support. But what about people lower in the organization, people who have to worry how their bosses will react?

You're right on the hottest issue—when a boss reacts to criticism by saying, "I'll get that guy." Now, hopefully, that guy is so good he quits that same week and shows the boss where that attitude gets him. That's not the best result for GE, of course, but that's what it may take to shake people up.

It's not going to be easy to get the spirit and intent of Work-Out clear throughout the company. I had a technician at my house to install some appliances recently. He said "I saw your videotape on Work-Out. The guys at my level understand what you're talking about: we'll be free to enjoy our work more, not just do more work, and to do more work on our own. But do you know how our supervisors interpreted it? They pointed to the screen and said, 'You see what he's saying, you guys better start busting your butts.' " We have a long way to go!

The potential for meanness in an organization, for a variety of reasons, is often in inverse proportion to level. People at the top have more time and resources to be fair. I wasn't trained to be a judge, but I spend a lot of time worrying about fairness. The data I get generally favor the manager over the employee. But we have two people at headquarters, fairness arbitrators so to speak, who sift the situation. So when I get a problem, I can smell it and feel it and try to figure out what's really happening. Managers down in the organization don't have the time or help for that. They too often say, "This is how we do it here, go do it." Work-Out is going to break down those attitudes. Managers will be in front of their people, challenged in a thousand different ways, held to account.

To change behavior, you must also change how people are compensated and rewarded. Are those systems being changed at GE?

We let every business come up with its own pay plan. It can create bonus plans in any way that makes sense. We're also doing all kinds of exciting things to reward people for their contributions, things we've never done before. For example, we now give out $20 to $30 million in management awards every year—cash payments to individuals for outstanding performance. We're trying desperately to push rewards down to levels where they never used to be. Stock options now go to 3,000 people, up from 400 ten years ago, and that's probably still not enough.

Another way to influence behavior is to promote people based on the characteristics you want to encourage. How can you evaluate executives on qualities as subjective as candor and speed?

Not only can we do it, we *are* doing it. Again, we're starting at the top of the company and, as the new systems prove themselves, we'll drive them down. We took three years to develop a statement on corporate values, what we as a company believe in. It was a brutal process. We talked to 5,000 people at our management development center in Crotonville. We sweated over every word. This will be the first year that our Session C meetings, the intensive process we use to evaluate the officers of the company, revolve around that value statement. We've told the business leaders that they must rank each of their officers on a scale of one to five against the business and individual characteristics in that statement [see the GE Value Statement]. Then I, Larry Bossidy, and Ed Hood, our other vice chairman, will rate the officers and see where we agree or disagree with the business leaders.

We had a long discussion about this in the CEC. People said just what you said: "How can you put a

GE Value Statement

BUSINESS CHARACTERISTICS

Lean
What – Reduce tasks and the people required to do them.
Why – Critical to developing world cost leadership.

Agile
What – Delayering.
Why – Create fast decision making in rapidly changing world through improved communication and increased individual response.

Creative
What – Development of new ideas – innovation.
Why – Increase customer satisfaction and operating margins through higher value products and services.

Ownership
What – Self-confidence to trust others. Self-confidence to delegate to others the freedom to act while, at the same time, self-confidence to involve higher levels in issues critical to the business and the corporation.
Why – Supports concept of more individual responsibility, capability to act quickly and independently. Should increase job satisfaction and improve understanding of risks and rewards. While delegation is critical, there is a small percentage of high-impact issues that need or require involvement of higher levels within the business and within the corporation.

Reward
What – Recognition and compensation commensurate with risk and performance – highly differentiated by individual, with recognition of total team achievement.
Why – Necessary to attract and motivate the type of individuals required to accomplish GE's objectives. A #1 business should provide #1 people with #1 opportunity.

INDIVIDUAL CHARACTERISTICS

Reality
What – Describe the environment as it is – not as we hope it to be.
Why – Critical to developing a vision and a winning strategy, and to gaining universal acceptance for their implementation.

Leadership
What – Sustained passion for and commitment to a proactive, shared vision and its implementation.
Why – To rally teams toward achieving a common objective.

Candor/Openness
What – Complete and frequent sharing of information with individuals (appraisals, etc.) and organization (everything).
Why – Critical to employees knowing where they, their efforts, and their business stand.

Simplicity
What – Strive for brevity, clarity, the "elegant, simple solution"– less is better.
Why – Less complexity improves everything, from reduced bureaucracy to better product designs to lower costs.

Integrity
What – Never bend or wink at the truth, and live within both the spirit and letter of the laws of every global business arena.
Why – Critical to gaining the global arenas' acceptance of our right to grow and prosper. Every constituency: shareowners who invest; customers who purchase; community that supports; and employees who depend, expect, and deserve our unequivocal commitment to integrity in every facet of our behavior.

Individual Dignity
What – Respect and leverage the talent and contribution of every individual in both good and bad times.
Why – Teamwork depends on trust, mutual understanding, and the shared belief that the individual will be treated fairly in any environment.

number on how open people are, on how directly they face reality?" Well, they're going to have to – the best numbers they can come up with, and then we'll argue about them. We have to know if our people are open and self-confident, if they believe in honest communication and quick action, if the people we hired years ago have changed. The only way to test our progress is through regular evaluations at the top and by listening to every audience we appear before in the company.

All corporations, but especially giant corporations like GE, have implicit social and psychological contracts with their employees – mutual responsibilities and loyalties by which each side abides. What is GE's psychological contract with its people?

Like many other large companies in the United States, Europe, and Japan, GE has had an implicit psychological contract based on perceived lifetime employment. People were rarely dismissed except for cause or severe business downturns, like in Aerospace after Vietnam. This produced a paternal, feudal, fuzzy kind of loyalty. You put in your time, worked hard, and the company took care of you for life.

That kind of loyalty tends to focus people inward. But given today's environment, people's emotional energy must be focused outward on a competitive world where no business is a safe haven for employment unless it is winning in the marketplace. The psychological contract has to change. People at all levels have to feel the risk-reward tension.

My concept of loyalty is not "giving time" to some corporate entity and, in turn, being shielded and protected from the outside world. Loyalty is an affinity among people who want to grapple with the outside world and win. Their personal values, dreams, and ambitions cause them to gravitate toward each other and toward a company like GE that gives them the resources and opportunities to flourish.

The new psychological contract, if there is such a thing, is that jobs at GE are the best in the world for people who are willing to compete. We have the best training and development resources and an environment committed to providing opportunities for personal and professional growth.

How deeply have these changes penetrated? How different does it feel to be a GE manager today versus five years ago?

It depends how far down you go. In some old-line factories, they probably feel it a lot less than we would like. They hear the words every now and then, but they don't feel a lot of difference. That's because the people above them haven't changed enough yet. Don't forget, we built much of this company in the 1950s around the blue books and POIM: plan, organize, integrate, measure. We brought people in buses over to Crotonville and drilled it into them. Now we're saying, "liberate, trust," and people look up and say, "What?" We're trying to make a massive cultural break. This is at least a five-year process, probably closer to ten.

What troubles you about what's happened to date?

First, there's a real danger of the expectation level getting ahead of reality. I was at Crotonville recently, talking about Work-Out, and someone said, "I don't feel it yet." Well, we're only a few months into it, it's much too early.

No matter how many exciting programs you implement, there seems to be a need for people to spend emotional energy criticizing the administration of the programs rather than focusing on the substance. I can sit in the Crotonville pit and ask, "How many of you are part of a new pay plan?" More than half the hands go up. "How many of you have received a management award in the last year?" More than 90% of the hands go up. "How many of you are aware of stock options?" All the hands go up. And yet many of these people don't see what we're trying to do with the programs, why we've put them in place. The emotional energy doesn't focus often enough on the objectives of the bonus plan or the excitement of the management award; it focuses on the details. The same is true of Work-Out. We'll have too much discussion on the Work-Out "process" and not enough on the "objective" to instill speed, simplicity, and self-confidence in every person in the organization.

When will we know whether these changes have worked? What's your report card?

A business magazine recently printed an article about GE that listed our businesses and the fact that we were number one or number two in virtually all of them. That magazine didn't get one complaint from our competitors. Those are the facts. That's what we said we wanted to do, and we've done it.

Ten years from now, we want magazines to write about GE as a place where people have the freedom to be creative, a place that brings out the best in everybody. An open, fair place where people have a sense that what they do matters, and where that sense of accomplishment is rewarded in both the pocketbook and the soul. That will be our report card.

Reprint 89513

Muscle-build the organization

Andrall E. Pearson

Most top managers know they should be doing a better job of building the superior organization they want. They may not, however, know what more successful managers are doing – or how to do it themselves. And while most would agree that their business's success hinges on the quality of its people, very few executives are willing to adopt the tough, aggressive approach to managing people that's required to produce a dynamic organization.

The only way to make a business live up to its potential is to get tough.

The hard truth is, only an aggressive approach can make a big difference, quickly. But it has its costs: at least initially, managers have to be willing to sacrifice continuity for a thorough shake-up. Nevertheless, most top-notch companies have been through the experience; it's what transformed the company into an outstanding organization. And once the transformation has taken place, things can settle down without a loss of momentum.

In my 15 years with PepsiCo and 20 years of consulting for other corporations, I have seen that "winners" – IBM, Hewlett-Packard, Marriott, Avery International, among others – emphasize "people development" as the way to "muscle-build" their organizations. By stressing the identifying and grooming of talent at every level, these companies eventually create a huge gulf between themselves and their competitors. They also hold on to most of their best managers even though other companies may recruit them aggressively.

If you think you do a good job of managing people, try stepping back and asking yourself the following questions. They're a solid indication of whether people development is your company's number one daily priority.

Do you maintain consistent, demanding standards for everyone in your company – or are you willing to tolerate a mediocre division manager, an uneven sales force, a weak functional department head?

What are your hiring standards? Are you bringing in people who can upgrade the quality of your company significantly, or are you just filling holes? Are you willing to leave a vacancy open until you find an outstanding candidate – for months, if necessary?

Are you hiring *enough* people? Does your organization have sufficient depth – a bank of talent to draw on – or do you sometimes promote people you know will never really produce outstanding results?

How effective is each area of your company at identifying high-potential managers and developing them quickly? Are promising people rotated carefully to expose them to different problems and functions?

Now a professor of general management at the Harvard Business School, Andrall E. Pearson was president of PepsiCo for 15 years. Before that, he was a managing director of McKinsey & Company.

Do you know specifically where your organization's biggest performance problems are? Are you taking steps to solve them, or are you looking the other way?

Do you make measurable progress each year in the quality of your senior management group and in the people heading each functional area? Are you generating clearly better quality executives and backups – not just people whose bosses assert are better managers?

As the above questions suggest, traditional approaches to people development – like promotion from within based chiefly on job tenure – are no longer good enough. A company that uses experience as its primary criterion for advancement is encouraging organizational hardening of the arteries – especially if that experience came in an undemanding environment. Businesses today need better, brighter managers with a broader repertoire of skills – a repertoire people cannot master by working their way up the steps of a one-dimensional career ladder. Mergers and acquisitions, new technology, price pressures, and the information explosion all require a stronger and more savvy management team, people who can innovate and win in an uncertain future.

Ironically, as the need for more capable managers has heightened, the talent pool has shrunk. More and more of the most promising future business leaders are choosing the service industries – Wall Street, consulting, and smaller entrepreneurial companies – rather than moving into the big manufacturing enterprises.

These trends all call for upgrading the organization: strengthening your company's entire management group from top to bottom and attracting and preparing future leaders through new approaches – in effect, muscle building. For most companies, I believe that this aggressive approach is the only way to make a business live up to its potential.

Muscle building an organization requires five separate but interrelated steps:

1 Set higher performance standards for everyone – *and keep raising the standards.* Recognize that performance can always be improved, and cultivate a spirit of constructive dissatisfaction with current performance among all executives and managers.

2 Develop managers through fresh assignments and job rotation; keep everyone learning. Don't let high-potential people stay in the same position or the same functional area too long.

3 Adjust every facet of the work environment – corporate culture, organizational structure, policies – to facilitate and reward managers' development, rather than thwart the upgrading effort (as many formal systems do).

4 Infuse each level of the company with new talent. Bring in seasoned managers to solve organizational problems, to serve as backups for management succession, and to lead by example.

5 Use the personnel department as an active agent for change. Make personnel executives partners in the upgrading process. Expect as much from them as from other top managers.

Let's look at each step in more detail.

Keep raising standards

The heart of any management upgrading process is the establishment of higher performance standards across the board. This responsibility rests with the top manager – the CEO or division general manager, depending on the company. If you're a senior manager and you delegate this task, you will convey the message that managerial development is not really that important, and every manager will set different standards.

Raising performance goals entails analyzing the company's current situation (where you are today versus where you want to be), establishing higher expectations (ways of bridging the gap), selling the entire management team on the upgrading process, and developing an action plan.

Step one is the situation analysis – looking at every important position in the company and asking, "What do we expect of this job? How should this position be moving our business forward? How close does the incumbent come to meeting the ideal?" In other words, you will be judging people against the company's mission and priorities. This questioning will indicate where the organization's weak links are and will give you a good sense of which executives already have high standards and which are most skillful at developing other people.

The way to get started is to sit down with your top executives – division managers and key staff leaders – and ask these reviewers to assess everyone who reports to them. You should also ask them how they could enhance their *own* performance.

Here are some of the questions you should explore:

Who are our best performers, and how are we going to make them even better? How can we stretch them and accelerate their professional growth?

Which senior managers and department heads tolerate marginal performance? Which do not emphasize enough their people's development?

Where are our biggest performance problems, and what are we going to do about them? (You cannot build muscle in your organization unless you are willing to replace marginal performers.)

Which groups of managers (e.g., marketing managers, operations managers) have the necessary mix of talents and skills to achieve more ambitious goals? Who in each group is promotable, and who is not?

For example, I'd be interested to find out specifically what each manager did this year to change the *results* of his or her unit. I'd look for measurable things like formulating or implementing a new competitive strategy, successfully launching a new product, or quickly cutting costs in a downturn. I'd be less interested in plans a manager has for the future, or a laundry list of routine programs he or she implemented, or personal characteristics like how smart someone is – all of which are difficult to relate to better performance.

I'd also be interested in how each manager compares with people the reviewer regards as future stars. Usually, people are better at comparing and ranking subordinates than at measuring someone's performance in a vacuum. By comparing people with star performers, you start to set higher standards and expectations. And if a unit has no stars (or only a few), you can also start to enrich the mix of talent there.

Nobody admits to promoting people on longevity. Most companies do and get organizational hardening of the arteries.

With a fix on each manager's current performance and development needs, you can then take a look at each executive's potential. A single question asking how far each person can advance (measured by the number of job layers) will usually start a lively and productive discussion, especially when a manager is ranked as high-potential yet has remained in the same job for four or five years.

You should repeat your questioning with all important department heads. Ideally, you should gather in-depth information on at least two or three levels of people under you. Your personal involvement is the best way to galvanize top managers into action – into recognizing your commitment to big changes in the way the organization operates. In implementing a management upgrading process at PepsiCo, I developed firsthand knowledge of the strengths and weaknesses of well over 100 executives. Going through this process, unit by unit and manager by manager, is obviously hard work, but there is no easy way to establish and enforce tougher performance standards and focus everyone's attention on management development.

I should add that the work is not only time-consuming but also emotionally charged. It leads to heated discussions, especially early on, when standards are likely to differ widely. Using elaborate performance-appraisal forms and systems, as most companies do, is easier, but these systems are usually a triumph of form over substance – an annual exercise to be gotten over with quickly. A simple, informal, face-to-face approach is what's needed to boost performance. You must be willing to engage in frank, tough-minded discussions of each manager's weaknesses – and you must convince each person to use equal candor with subordinates.

You are likely to find that many executives are initially either unwilling or unable to give you useful staff evaluations. For example, a division manager might say that everyone in the division is doing a pretty good job. If this happens, you will have to bear down and force the manager to draw distinctions – say, to identify who the single best performer is. It is also helpful to ask the executive to categorize the managers into four groups, from poor to superior, and then ask for a specific plan for the people in each group. Always focus first on the bottom group. The manager should specify who should be replaced, who should be reassigned, and when these decisions will be implemented.

Rooting out the poorest performers will foster a climate of continual improvement. If everyone in the bottom quartile is replaced, the third quartile becomes the new bottom group and the focus of subsequent improvement efforts.

The human tendency to avoid confrontation allows companies to fall into the trap of complacency and subpar performance. Upgrading the organization, by contrast, requires managers to make tough decisions: to fire some people, demote or bypass others, and tell poor performers where they stand. No one enjoys delivering bad news, but good managers will understand how critical it is to the company's long-term success – particularly if the CEO personally sets the example.

Some managers might object that this relentless scrutiny – and the inevitable firings – will demoralize employees. My experience suggests precisely the opposite. Top performers relish the challenge of meeting ever higher goals. What does demoralize them is a climate that tolerates mediocrity; under such circumstances, they may slow down their work to the tempo of the organization – or they may leave the company.

After you have completed your preliminary situation analysis, you are ready to formulate the specific actions you will take over the next 9 to 12 months to muscle-build your organization. What are your goals for each key manager and each department? What are the implications of those plans for recruiting and job assignments? This action plan sets the stage for a more demanding and results-oriented environment, one in which measurable progress will occur.

In my experience, focusing on a limited number of high-impact results, conducting comparative evaluations, and separating current performance from potential will produce far better effects than focusing on personal traits, making exhaustive MBO lists, or using rigorous forms.

The analysis, of course, does not stop here but should become an ongoing process, a day-to-day questioning. What's working well? Where can we improve? Over time, you may wish to supplement your face-to-face interviews with surveys to gather this kind of information.

Worship success & potential

The situation analysis is the cornerstone of your upgrading effort. Having identified how well your managers and divisions are performing, you are now in a position to determine how best to deploy your people. If you want to grow fast and improve fast, you have to develop people fast. And the secret to that is to produce challenging, fresh, *taxing* assignments.

It goes without saying that you want to put the best qualified person into each important job (and to move marginal performers aside so they don't block new talent). What may be less obvious is that you want to keep every high-potential manager constantly challenged and learning. Make sure that talented people don't stay in one job too long. Most people need about a year to master a new assignment; after four years, they're usually just repeating what they've already done, and they may go to sleep on the job. In most companies, people work in a single area for years, moving slowly and ponderously up the career ladder. By the time they reach senior positions, many have run out of steam – they've become "deadwood."

Just reassigning a top performer isn't enough. You don't want a talented person simply to repeat the same experience in a different region or at a somewhat higher level. You need to round out executives' experience through challenging new assignments that will give them a broader business viewpoint. Entirely different positions can accomplish this – for example, moving someone from domestic operations to international, putting a manager in a new functional area, or letting a high achiever engineer a turnaround.

Keep raising standards. Keep rooting out the lesser performers.

At PepsiCo, we thought nothing of making the CFO of Frito-Lay a general manager of Pepsi-Cola in Canada, or promoting the North American Van Lines CEO to head up corporate planning, or putting a good, hands-on Pepsi marketing vice president into restaurant operations. We tried to make sure that every division president served in at least two operating divisions and in at least one staff assignment (not just in line jobs). We also moved promising managers into our best run divisions to minimize business disruptions and expose them to better work environments.

Large companies should rotate their managers through different divisions both to keep them challenged and to help the organization prepare future leaders who understand its many facets. Companies that have a number of smaller divisions or a significant international business can easily move people around like this. Managers in these enterprises have many opportunities to be tested and to learn in free-standing situations at lower risk.

Decisions about reassignments are best made once a year as part of the annual performance review, not on a piecemeal basis throughout the year. Making a series of moves at one time allows you to consider the needs of the whole organization and to deploy your entire pool of talent most productively. Also, when assignments are shuffled all at once, the company has time to settle down and assimilate the changes. In the real world, or course, you will also be faced with a few piecemeal decisions, but that doesn't negate the approach.

The aim of rearranging things is to make the best corporate use of all your managers, instead of asking each business unit to do the best it can with existing resources. To be sure, you take some chances when you bypass traditional channels of promotion. Moving someone to an entirely new division is not without risks: the new unit may resent your interference, or – worse – a person may fail in the new job.

To prevent resentment and resistance, don't just foist your selections on your operating people. Take particular care when implementing this portion of the upgrading process, and choose candidates whose odds of succeeding in a new division are high. Operating managers must realize that these people are top performers and not someone another area wanted to get rid of. You should also give your operating managers veto power over candidates, or give them a slate to choose from. Eventually, they will accept and support "corporate musical chairs" as they realize they're getting better qualified people for their openings.

If you promote on the basis of potential and not just on experience, you're bound to make some mistakes. The safest route is to promote someone already in the department rather than an outsider with less experience in the function. But you'll never shake up the organization enough if you stick to safe choices. If you see one of your assignments not working out, face it quickly, and try to find another slot for the person. Over time you'll learn which jobs require pertinent experience (there are some) and which ones don't (there are many of these).

There is one other risk in rotating people throughout a company. You are running a business, after all, not a finishing school for executives. Continuity and experience are important in building relationships and relevant skills. The priorities shouldn't be one-sided in either direction. The company needs a balance. Avoid moving people so much that you destroy continuity and nobody really gets developed, but also be as careful as you can to keep people from getting stale.

Unclog the organization

The way a corporation is organized and runs can either facilitate or thwart the upgrading process. Unfortunately, organizations often become so complicated over time that some of the things I've recommended here simply won't work. If companies have tightly drawn "empires," for example, they'll have difficulty transferring executives across divisions. For that reason, a new emphasis on people development often calls for a complete transformation of the work environment.

Consider the ways in which a multilayered organizational structure can impede performance. With broken-up jobs, no one has clear-cut responsibility or a feeling of ownership and as a result, people may sit back and wait for the group to solve problems. It's difficult to assess individual performance. Decision-making mechanisms can be so complicated that people dissipate all their energy simply trying to get a question answered.

For reasons like these, a slow-moving, bureaucratic environment usually flushes talented people out the door faster than it brings them in. Innovators can't thrive in a highly centralized organization. If you want more original thinking, you have to decentralize responsibility throughout the company and get rid of red tape. Give people the freedom to stick their necks out and to take independent action.

Here are four suggestions for creating a climate conducive to executive development:

1 Keep your organizational structure as simple as possible. With fewer layers, there can be more individual responsibility, less second-guessing, clearer decision making, and greater accountability for results.

2 Break down organizational barriers. Emphasize that managers are corporate assets rather than the property of a single division or function.

3 By the same token, formally encourage cross-fertilization. Expose your best managerial prospects to top functional leaders. Some companies conduct reviews where all the senior marketing vice presidents, for example, evaluate prospects for marketing posts. In other corporations, the executives attend personnel reviews in other divisions.

4 Finally, make sure that every unit is rewarding its best achievers appropriately. This may sound obvious, but most businesses do a poor job of relating pay to performance. Sometimes better performers receive larger raises than less promising people (personnel policies or other factors don't always encourage this), but the differences may be so slight that they're demotivating. Nothing frustrates high-potential people more than hearing a lot of praise at their reviews and then learning that their efforts won't be rewarded accordingly. In the more demanding work environment you're creating by muscle building, it's especially important to peg pay to performance.

Create a nucleus of leaders

If you want to make sweeping improvements in your organization, you'll have to bring in fresh talent. The upgrading steps I've described are all crucial, but they take time to implement and bear fruit. An essential ingredient in the process is to bring in several high performers *quickly*—to fill important posts and to develop a talent pool you can draw on for promotions later.

Simply deciding to look outside the company for the next two or three openings isn't the answer. That's like trying to empty the ocean with a thimble; you'll never get anywhere. You may also be tempted to bring in new talent only at the entry level, especially if your employees tend to make their careers in your company. But are your present managers capable of supervising top performers? I recommend that you introduce new people at the highest levels of your organization and let the upgrading trickle down.

In a large, decentralized enterprise, the best way to start this talent infusion is to hire a group of proven managers without having any particular jobs in mind for them. (In football, this is called drafting for talent, not for position.) Ultimately, these people will be fed into the system as openings occur, but initially they can work directly for you or another senior person on special projects – assuming the role of in-house consultants. They can be assigned to divisions or functions that are in particular need of help, or to new endeavors. The important point is that proficient managers will be in place (setting an example for others) and learning about your company (preparing for more specific assignments).

This approach worked well at PepsiCo, where we brought in seven "floaters" over a three-year period. Within nine months, they were all working in key jobs, and five of them eventually ended up running big divisions. As another example, we felt we had too few promotable individuals in our food-service division, so we wanted to build a broader bank of talent. We considered 200 food-service executives, interviewed 50 of them, and brought in the best two we could find. Within two years, one was running a division and the other held an important operating position. Ernie Breech had similar success at Ford when he brought in the "whiz kids" (including Robert McNamara and Tex Thornton).

Nothing frustrates high achievers more than just getting praise.

As these examples show, you can bring in people with assorted backgrounds or you can concentrate on a single area, like corporate finance. Your goal may be to get the best financial people you can find and give them a group of divisions to follow. They will not only make important contributions as in-house consultants but usually an operating unit will snap them up quickly, and they'll end up serving as a division CFO or even running a unit or company themselves.

Hiring people to serve as general resources may sound like an expensive proposition. But the cost is almost certainly less than you would pay for a consultant to handle the same special projects, and this method promises a significant impact on the upgrading process. Also, a cost-conscious CEO can usually eliminate enough low-impact current jobs or managers to pay for the floaters.

Eventually, you'll be able to focus your recruiting at the lower levels of management. Here as elsewhere, you must make the commitment to work consistently and effectively to develop the best staff possible. This goal usually means emphasizing campus recruiting – year after year, at the best schools – rather than just hiring people from other companies. It means that recruiting must be a top-management priority.

Make personnel a partner

You can't improve an entire organization by yourself. As you would expect, you certainly need the support of all your executives and managers. As you might not expect, your other partner in the process is the personnel department. I'll talk about each of these in turn.

Muscle building an organization is impossible without the active involvement of your line managers. But how do you convince a busy general manager to shoulder a new set of responsibilities? You need to do more than express your own commitment to the upgrading process: you have to be unrelenting in your emphasis on people development.

Make it clear that you are asking executives to do more than just preside over annual reviews. (And if you feel someone isn't emphasizing even this part of the process enough, try attending a couple of review sessions with subordinates.) Every time you see or call a manager, you should stress your interest in the key people and their individual performance. Ask specific questions. What has been done about the marginal production manager? What progress has there been in the Cleveland office? What projects is the new recruit working on? After a few run-throughs, the answers will be ready before you ask the questions.

You can deepen your executives' involvement in other ways, for instance, by asking them to showcase their "comers" at periodic business reviews or to nominate people to serve on special task forces. You should also make time for observing the best people in action during your field visits.

Commitment from line managers often doesn't come easily; you have to create it, nurture it, even push it. You're asking them to rethink their job priorities and make more difficult decisions. The personnel department can be a valuable ally in this effort and serve as a burr under the saddle of resistant managers.

Personnel people are often seen as peripheral to the real action in a company–a group of paper shufflers who develop benefits packages, collect evaluation forms, and process paychecks. But these activities are not their most important reason for being. Outstanding personnel people can be a force for positive change in the organization. They can help ensure that line managers handle their people responsibilities properly, and they can help the whole company make the best possible use of its assets.

Unfortunately, business leaders rarely recognize the potential of the personnel function, so they often fail to staff the department with high-caliber people. Their low expectations then become a self-fulfilling prophecy.

Personnel executives can facilitate organizational muscle building in several ways:

☐ They can push executives to make consistent, demanding evaluations of their subordinates. This might include, for example, pointing out differences between a criticism-shy manager's performance appraisals and other managers' evaluations of their people, and giving advice on how to deliver bad news in an appropriate way.

☐ They can force managers to take action on marginal performers (reassignment, coaching, allowing time for improvement) and insist that poor performers be replaced.

☐ They can help search out the best people in the company and the best slot for each person. They can encourage executives to take risks on high-potential prospects. (Superior personnel executives, plugged into every part of the company, are especially valuable here.) One of the most offbeat successful deployment decisions we made at PepsiCo, for example, was to shift our trucking company president to head up the corporate staff. Another success involved appointing an international division area vice president as chief of restaurant operations and marketing. Our corporate personnel vice president spearheaded both moves; if he hadn't prodded neither would have happened.

☐ They can encourage executives to focus on results and *heap* rewards on the best performers. (Some personnel systems set rigid limits on compensation, so pay increases average out, and no one is motivated.)

If you want valuable assistance from your personnel department, you will probably need brighter, more highly skilled personnel executives than you may have now. The good news is that if you give personnel more responsibility and integrate it with other executive functions, you should attract better people.

The full-court press

The five-step upgrading process I advocate is undeniably a huge undertaking. It requires time, energy, money, and possibly the restructuring of the entire company–in short, a full-court press.

You can't achieve the results I'm talking about by implementing just one part of the process or by working to improve your organization gradually. Nor can you hire a few MBAs or a new marketing vice president and expect the organization to change to its roots. A piecemeal or incremental approach won't foster the broad-based involvement, ownership, and conviction that make real progress; you'll move one step forward, one step back, and you'll never get off dead center. Your goal is to advance.

Some CEOs may feel that management muscle building is not worth the effort it takes. As is true with other improvement programs, the companies most in need of upgrading will probably be the ones least likely to attempt it. Many company chiefs who have implemented a systematic people-development program, however, have told me that it became the most rewarding part of their jobs. Muscle building makes a difference on the bottom line, in the company's strategic success, and in the way people feel when they come to work in the morning–including the CEOs.

Reprint 87408

Red Auerbach on management

An interview by
Alan M. Webber

Former Boston Celtics star Bob Cousy calls him "Arnold." But most die-hard basketball fans know him as "Red." Hanging from the rafters of the Boston Garden are 16 green-and-white championship banners, testimony to his managerial genius.

He is Arnold "Red" Auerbach – inspiration and leader of the most successful sports franchise in America. For 36 years, as coach, general manager, and now president of the Boston Celtics, Mr. Auerbach has practiced his style of management in an enterprise in which the difference between winning and losing is very clear and very public. His management philosophy, based on the values of loyalty, pride, teamwork, and discipline, is applicable to managers in any field. And the results he has attained – measured in athletic and economic terms, or even just in the number of victory cigars he has savored – demonstrate his ability to make this philosophy work.

Mr. Auerbach is the author of *On and Off the Court* (Macmillan, 1985), written with Joe Fitzgerald. This interview was conducted in his Boston office by Alan M. Webber, managing editor at HBR.

HBR:

When you started here in 1950, there was no such thing as "Celtics pride."

Auerbach:

Right.

"I don't believe in statistics. You can't measure a ballplayer's heart."

Thirty-six years later, everybody talks about it. It's at the heart of the Celtics' mystique. What is it?

It's the whole idea of caring. I'm in contact with the Frank Ramseys and Ed McCauleys and Bones McKinneys who played for me 35 years ago. I know where they are, what they do. If they want something, they call me and if I want something, I call them.

There's a family feeling. Two people in particular evidenced it for me. One was Wayne Embry, who played at Cincinnati for nine years and came here to finish his career. He never talks about Cincinnati. He talks about Celtics pride and the Celtics organization.

The other was Paul Silas. One of the best compliments I ever got was from Paul Silas. One day he came over to me and said, "I heard a lot about this Celtics pride and I thought it was a bunch of crap"—because he was an old veteran when he came here. "But," he said, "I was wrong. I feel a part of it and this has been the happiest part of my career." It was super. When you hear it from the players, it really makes you feel nine feet tall.

What are some of the things that explain this special feeling?

Well, it started way back, when Walter Brown owned the team. I had this theory, which we still use. And that is, a player's salary is determined by what the coaches see and what I see. What determines a player's salary is his contribution to winning—not his statistical accomplishments.

I don't believe in statistics. There are too many factors that can't be measured. You can't measure a ballplayer's heart, his ability to perform in the clutch, his willingness to sacrifice his offense or to play strong defense.

See, if you play strong defense and concentrate and work hard, it's got to affect your offense. But a lot of players on a lot of teams, all they point at is offense. Like in baseball they say, "I hit .300 so I should get so much money."

I've always eliminated the statistic of how many points a guy scores. Where did he score them? Did he score them during garbage time? Did he score them when the game was on the line? Did he score them against good opponents? There are so many factors.

So part of the Celtics' system is the way you set up the salaries?

Well, it's not just the money reward, it's more than that. It's like Larry Bird always says before a big game: "I'll be ready and the other guys will be ready and we're going to win this thing." Not "I'm going to win it." He says, "*We're* going to win it." Larry Bird gets as big a thrill out of making the pass as he does making the shot.

What are the other factors?

One important thing is trust within our organization. I really believe that loyalty is a two-way street. Unfortunately, in most businesses managers expect loyalty from employees but are very reluctant to give loyalty.

We've built up an organization where we care about our people. That doesn't mean that you can't make trades. You must have a certain amount of flexibility so if you feel you can improve your club, you go ahead and make a trade. But over the years we've made very few trades. Anybody who's been with us for more than five or six years will usually finish his career here. And when a player is on the tail end of his career, we don't just say, "We paid you, you played. See you later."

Most of our players have self-retired. They tell me when they don't think they can play anymore. The Jones boys, Cousy, Russell, Havlicek, Sanders, Nelson, Heinsohn–they all announced their retirements with no pressure from me whatsoever. People who come here realize that if they produce and do the job as they should and are happy here, we'll do our best for them. And we're interested in what they do when they leave here, when their careers are over.

What else goes into the relationship with the players?

I think the players know that if I make a decision, we're all going to stand with it. The players won't con me because I don't con them. They don't give me what we call false hustle, when a guy just goes through the motions but he's not really putting out much effort.

"I've turned down a lot of trades where I might have gotten a better player but I wasn't sure of the chemistry."

How do you discipline your athletes?

We like our players to play for fun and to be happy rather than afraid. It's like that in any business. If you have employees who work through fear, you're not going to get any ingenuity out of them. You're not going to get any employees who will take a gamble or come up with ideas. All you'll have are robots that are going to do their jobs, have a low-key approach, stay out of trouble. They'll put in their hours and go home. But I'd rather have it the other way.

So we talk to people. We don't fine them indiscriminately. A lot of teams have rules that say if you're late or miss a plane, you get fined. We have rules, but we temper them with mercy. We talk to people. And we never threaten employees specifically.

What I used to do when I coached was this: I wouldn't say that if they did something I'd fine them a thousand dollars or I'd suspend them; I'd just say that if they did something I'd bust their hump. So then they'd wonder, what is he going to do?

How do you motivate the players?

Pride, that's all. Pride of excellence. Pride of winning. I tell our guys, "Isn't it nice to go around all summer and say that you're a member of the greatest basketball team in the world."

Of course, we used to do funny things. I mean, how many times can you go in there and say, "Hey, let's win one for the Gipper?" So one day I said to one of the players, Frank Ramsey, "Ramsey, give them a motivating talk." So he walked up to the board and he put down on it, "If you win, $8,000. If you lose, $4,000." And they all broke up.

But the biggest motivating force you can have is the championship ring.

And the Celtics players have always responded to this kind of approach?

You see, in sports you have so many things that aren't expected. There's so much uncertainty. So when players find themselves in a situation where management has a great deal of integrity and they can depend on my word or anybody else's word in the organization, they feel secure. And if the players feel secure, they don't want to leave here. And if they don't want to leave here, they're going to do everything they can on the court to stay here.

I've turned down a lot of trades where I might have gotten a better player, but I wasn't totally sure of the chemistry of that new player coming in. Even though he might possess golden ability, his personality and the way he gets along with teammates might be things you just don't want to cope with.

When you are thinking of making a trade or acquiring a new player, do you consult the players?

Sometimes, sure. Our players are quite intelligent and they want the Celtics to be as good as possible. So I'd talk to a Cousy, a Havlicek, or Russell, or Bird and say, "Hey, we've got a chance to get so and so. What do you think?" Why not ask them? I've never had the ego to think that I know it all.

The coaching staff is also involved in every decision. I would never take it upon myself to force any player down the coach's throat. Because if I give a player to the coach and the coach doesn't want him, he'll resent it and the production of the whole team will suffer.

Now that you're president of the Celtics, what is your relationship with the coaching staff?

It's simple. I don't interfere with the coaches of the team. If they have a problem or something is on their minds, they come to me and we discuss it. But it's only when they ask. Because the worst thing a guy in my position can do is interfere. You see it on so many other teams, where the general managers feel they know more than the coaches and the scouts and they really interfere. I think the players sense that, and it breeds discord. It affects the team's chemistry.

You have a reputation as a tough negotiator.

Not really.

No?

Yeah, I have a reputation for being a tough negotiator, but it's not like that. I just don't like it when a guy comes in with a player who's worth $100,000 and he wants a million, figuring we'll negotiate and he'll walk away with $500,000.

What I'd say is, "Now look, this is what the guy is worth, based on his abilities and his contribution to the ball club. We might give or take a few thousand, but I'm not interested in a million dollars. That's it. And there's nothing you can do to change my mind. So don't come in at one million. Come in at two million. Come in at three million. It won't do you any good." I'd say, "We're fair. Now if the player pays his dues and performs, we'll pay him more. But he's got to earn it first."

And you don't deal in perks with your players?

Not at all. I tell them, "Look, I'm not in the car business. I'm not in the real estate business or the banking business. How much does it cost for you to play basketball? Let's set a figure and do that. You want a car, buy a car."

I could tell you stories of guys who make a million dollars and want a $10,000 bonus for making the All-Rookie team. I tell them, "I'm paying you the highest money a rookie ever got and if you don't make the All-Rookie team I have to be dumb."

You place such a great emphasis on teamwork and Celtics pride. Does it bother you that there's a players' union?

It did at first, sure. I think they've done some good things for the players, no question about that. But they don't concern themselves with ownership. They want this, they want that, and you realize that if you give them all of it, you'll lose money. But they don't care. They don't want to know about your problems. They're interested in feathering their own nests. They figure, what's the difference? So the owner sells out. There's always someone with the ego out there who'll buy another franchise, mainly because of this ego factor and the idea of national recognition.

Well, eventually that could stop too. A lot of these super-wealthy people who indulge themselves in sports say they've got so much money they don't care if they lose five million dollars a year. Then as soon as they lose five million dollars they want to get out. They all want to get out, they run like thieves. It's not really the money. It's the fact that they spent the money, they lost the money, and they still didn't win.

But there's got to be a happy medium. There's got to be a meeting point where the players realize that if they get everything they want, the owner can't stay in business.

Speaking of owners, you've worked for two, both named Brown – Walter and John Y. Brown.

They're like day and night. Walter Brown was one of the finest human beings I've ever been associated with. I learned a lot from him. Hell, I worked for him for 16 years and never had a contract.

You never had a contract? How did you do business?

At the end of every year I'd say, "What's the deal for next year, Walter?" He'd say, "What do you want?" Sometimes I'd tell him I didn't want any-

"The biggest motivator you can have is the championship ring."

thing. We didn't make any money and the club was just pretty good. Sometimes I'd come in and say that I wanted more money. He'd say, "Fine, what else do you want?" I'd say, "Nothing." We'd have a discussion of no more than a minute.

We'd end up making the deal in the washroom every time. His office door was always open and there was always somebody in there. I used to get mad. I'd say, "For crying out loud, can't we sit and talk?" And he'd say, "All right, let's go to the bathroom and get the thing done."

What about the other Mr. Brown, John Y.?

The other Brown, he had a tremendous ego, like he knew it all. He used to call up different general managers around the league to pick their brains, and they'd lie to him. They'd feed him all this information and then they'd call me up and ask, "Hey, what does that guy really want?"

And he'd make deals. Well, he made one great big deal that could have destroyed the team, without even consulting me.

You worked for 30 years to build the team and the franchise. Could one owner really destroy it?

He did ruin it. We just happened to put it back together again, luckily. One wrong guy can ruin it so fast your head will swim.

How does one person ruin the whole franchise?

For instance, you make a wrong move that costs you a few million dollars. If you make a trade for a player who's getting a million dollars a year and he doesn't produce, all of a sudden you're stuck paying three or four million dollars for an unproductive situation. That happens all the time in the league, and most of these guys shrug it off. To me, a player like that is a distraction.

What was your approach to putting the team back together again?

I had to start from scratch. I picked out the best team in the league and said, "We've got to put a team together that's competitive with that team." Well, there was no way we could do it right away. You set a goal, you try for two or three years, and you say the hell with it, if we've got to suffer another year, let's do that. So we took Larry Bird, even though he wasn't eligible to play for another year. Then we made the deal for Kevin McHale and Robert Parish. And the owner, Harry Mangurian, knew what had to be done and was behind me. He had a private plane in those days, and we flew out to Minnesota just to take a look at Kevin McHale, so Harry was with it.

With all the money involved, the owners, the big contracts, do you look at professional basketball as a business or a sport?

At the back of your mind, you can't help but think that it's a business. But basically I've always felt that it's a labor of love. I've always put the chemistry and the performance of the ball club first. My prime concern has always been to have a competitive basketball team.

If you have a team that people like to see because the players are charismatic and they hustle, they play hard, they play as if they enjoy it – when you've got that, you draw people and you make money. Then the business practices fall into place.

You've gone from being coach of the Celtics to general manager and now to president. Have you changed your thoughts on how to run the organization?

Not at all. I still try to answer all the letters I get because that's the way I always did it. I would always tell the people in the front office that I didn't want to see any special treatment of the rich people buying box seats, any more than the guy buying a $3 seat upstairs. I don't want to see any meanness toward the lesser customers. They're the backbone of our business. One thing we have here is manners. That person buying the tickets is our bread and butter, and we don't forget it.

Too often, when people become executives they think that gives them a key to the toilet nobody else has. All of a sudden their heads get bigger than their shirt size. I've never operated that way. My door is open. Guys come in to shoot the bull and we talk.

That doesn't mean you can let them get so close that they lose respect. You have to have some sort of distance without being a snob. Too many executives become snobs, their egos are so big. They lose touch, they forget what got them there. After a while they don't even care about names. All they do is get the reports every morning and look at the bottom line.

"That person buying the tickets is our bread and butter and we don't forget it."

Do you think managing the Celtics is like managing any other business?

I do. People say that I could run any other business. They used to put in the paper that I should take over the Red Sox or manage the Patriots. But that doesn't make sense. My knowledge of the product isn't there.

That's one of the big problems in sports today. The old adage is true, a little knowledge is a dangerous thing. Lots of owners who have been successful in one thing think they can pick up something new in a few months. Then they can't understand why they're not successful in the new business. They don't realize that they don't have a complete knowledge of the product.

How did you get a knowledge of the product?

Well, I paid my dues. I started as a coach, and while I was coaching I was also the general manager, the road secretary, and the scout. I was working 16, 17 hours a day. We'd play in New York on Thursday and in Boston on Saturday. I'd tell somebody to handle practice and I'd go scout, because I had no scouts. We had no movies, no video. Today we have six guys doing what I used to do.

You've been part of the Celtics for more than 36 years. Is there Celtics pride after Red Auerbach? Are you the center of the whole thing?

No, it's a team. Everybody right now is a cog in the machine. If you take out one part, you just do the best you can until you can replace it. There was a

Celtics team before Larry Bird, there will be a Celtics team after Larry Bird. There was a Celtics team before me, and there will be a Celtics team after me. How good, I don't know. But it'll be there.

So what is Red Auerbach's secret recipe for creating America's most successful sports franchise?

I think it all stems from the fact that the players' livelihoods depend on their contribution toward the Celtics, not toward themselves. And after a while they believe in this.

Take Bill Walton. He contacted me when he was a free agent and asked if I could possibly get him. So I asked him why he wanted to play with the Celtics. He said it was not only because we had a team that was a contender and he could get along tremendously with the guys we had. On top of that, the Celtics' chemistry and reputation made it a team he'd always dreamed of playing for – which I felt was very kind. In fact, when he was with San Diego, he came up here to my office to see me. He wanted some Celtics T-shirts for his kids because to him this was what a sports franchise should be.

"It's a business. But basically it's a labor of love."

So it worked out that we got him. And one day he told me that he was down in the dumps. I asked him what was wrong, and he said he didn't feel like he was contributing to the team. I told him, "Of course you're contributing." "But I'm not scoring," he said. "That's the trouble with you," I said. "You're worried about statistics."

I told him that we didn't care about what he scored. All we were interested in was what he contributed. Did he roll down? Did he play defense? Did he run the court? Did he pass?

He asked, "You mean you really don't care about scoring?" I told him, "Not at all. It won't affect you one iota."

You could see his face light up. And from that point on, he was a different guy. He was always great to begin with, but this made him even better. He became loose. And he never looked to see what he scored. All he looked at was, did we win. And it was "we," not "I."

Reprint 87201

Photographs on pages 84, 85, 88, 90, courtesy of *The Boston Globe*; page 86, Wide World Photos, Inc.; page 91, UPI/Bettmann.

RISKO

"Consensus is getting people to believe that you've got the right facts and the right reasons to make the right decision."

Consensus, Continuity, and Common Sense:

An Interview with Compaq's Rod Canion

by Alan M. Webber

In February 1982, Rod Canion, Bill Murto, and Jim Harris, three Texas Instruments alumni, founded Compaq Computer Corporation, launching what has become the fastest growing company in U.S. business history. In 1983, its first full year of operation, Compaq recorded revenues of more than $111 million–a record for the most successful first year of sales. In 1984, Compaq achieved sales of $329 million–a record for the most successful second year of sales. In 1985, Compaq's sales of more than $503 million made it the first company in U.S. business history to reach the Fortune *"500" in less than four years. In 1987, Compaq passed the $1 billion mark in annual sales, hitting this mark faster than any other company. In 1988, sales passed the $2 billion level. And in 1989, Compaq's worldwide sales approached the $3 billion barrier.*

Behind this remarkable financial performance is Compaq's unique management process. The company's corporate culture is based on teamwork and consensus management and a continuous effort to maintain the benefits of a small company, even as Compaq experiences phenomenal growth. But what is most intriguing about Compaq is a series of counterintuitive notions that combine to create the company's management process. For example, the CEO of the country's fastest growing company insists that he is not an entrepreneur. While the company's product-introduction strategy depends on speed to market, Compaq believes absolutely in a slow, methodical, decision-making process. In an industry that is driven by innovation, Compaq defines innovation as staying within the boundaries of accepted industry standards. Because the company's labor costs are so low, says the CEO, the company must hire its people very carefully. In a company that has achieved such remarkable financial results, cost ranks relatively low on the list of manufacturing priorities.

In this interview, conducted by HBR editorial director Alan M. Webber, Rod Canion, Compaq's founder, CEO, and president, explores these surprising notions and the management approach that guides his company's rapid growth.

DRAWINGS BY ROBERT C. RISKO

HBR: *Compaq has spent a lot of time defining and developing its culture. How would you describe your corporate culture?*

Rod Canion: Compaq stresses discipline, balance, continuity, and consensus. That's the way to survive in an industry that changes as fast as ours does. There are lots of values behind these characteristics, but perhaps the most important is teamwork. That means treating other people with respect and expecting to be treated with respect.

No management system can force people to do things they don't want to do. So when we started Compaq, our basic philosophy was to create an environment where people can stay enthused about the company and not be frustrated by red tape and unnecessary burdens. When you come to work day after day after day for a year, superficial things wear through quickly. You find out that either you enjoy work and get lifted by it or you get dragged down by it.

It's not how hard you work. People work as hard at Compaq as at any other company, maybe harder. But work here isn't drudgery. It doesn't use up their energy on negative things. It doesn't mean fighting off people who attack you in the company or filling out forms or doing unproductive work. People don't enjoy that, and they'll leave eventually. But if you spend 80% or 90% or, if you're really lucky, 98% or 99% of your time on productive things, you leave work feeling that you've accomplished something.

Why is the corporate culture so important to you?

Our culture is designed to keep the characteristics of a small company alive while the company grows. In 1983, we were growing by leaps and bounds. We saw bureaucracy creeping in and development cycles stretching out. At that point, I realized that the company was getting too big for me to be everywhere or for the management team to mandate and enforce short development cycles through strict planning and reporting. Trying to force short development cycles on people would have failed miserably.

I concluded that what we really needed to do was tell people what was good about what they had been doing. I wanted to make them aware of the fact that they'd worked together as a team, that they'd done things in parallel. I wanted to get them to look at what we'd been doing that had worked and consciously try to keep the small-company advantage. We started doing that in 1984, and we've kept doing it. That's what our quarterly company meetings are all about. We get everybody together at a companywide meeting to talk about Compaq. Typically, we hold four meetings over two days at a nearby church that holds about 2,000 people. We go over the past quarter's performance, show a couple of videos, address issues as varied as speeding on campus or smoking in the offices, and then answer questions. Everybody takes it as a personal job to keep the culture–to keep the good qualities of a small company as we get big.

What's the secret to continuity?

You can't have continuity unless you retain people. We're able to learn as a team and then build on stable layers of new people, year after year. Low turnover is fundamental and distinguishes Compaq from lots of our competitors, particularly those in Silicon Valley. Most companies would point to compensation plans, stock options, and bonuses as the way to keep people. But really, they're just there to prevent people from being stolen. It's not pay or stock or anything else that keeps people. It's whether they're drained or charged emotionally. People stay when they enjoy what they do. People stay when they fit the culture, when they are working in a supportive, helpful environment, and when they get fulfillment from working as part of a winning team. It's dissatisfaction, more than money, that leads people to leave.

I learned that lesson early in my career. Halfway through my tenure at Texas Instruments, I left to go to a small company here in Houston. I did it basically for money. I wasn't looking for a job. They came to me and showed me all this money, and I thought, "That's great." Six months later, I realized that there's a lot more to life than money. Money is important, but even more important is enjoying what you do and being really excited about it. So I went back to TI. Compaq wouldn't be here today if TI had continued to be a challenging place to work. I enjoyed most of my career there, and it was only in the last year that I really got frustrated. That was the critical factor in my deciding to leave.

"Money is important, but even more important is enjoying what you do and being really excited about it."

But can't you live with a little bureaucracy as long as the company keeps growing? Growth has a way of curing all ills.

I would say that growth *hides* all ills–until the growth stops or slows down. At Compaq, we know that growth is a two-edged sword. It does a lot of good things for a company, and it's an environment that you want to maintain. But depending on growth as the antibiotic for whatever ails you will eventually get you into serious trouble. In fact, growth can be a disease, rather than a cure. We're trying to manage growth, and whether or not it's fatal, by managing the culture.

> "Depending on growth as the antibiotic for whatever ails you will eventually get you into serious trouble."

That doesn't sound like the ideas of a typical entrepreneur.

I never viewed myself as an entrepreneur, either when I quit TI or when I started Compaq. I always thought of an entrepreneur as someone who can't work for anybody else and has a burning desire to make his or her own idea known. That just didn't fit me or any of our team. And our not being classic entrepreneurs has been a real benefit for Compaq. The typical entrepreneur has the problem of dealing with all the things success brings, things he or she didn't really want in the first place. But because we were really more typical businessmen starting our own company from scratch, when we did grow successful, we had the skills and orientation necessary to manage that growth.

We've talked about continuity; what about discipline and balance?

Our entire orientation toward customers and technology–and the process that brings the two together–depends on discipline and balance. Our management process is designed to meet customers' needs, use the latest technology, and–most important–get to market quickly. The last part of that–getting to market quickly–allowed us to come from behind in the early days, to pass the competitors, and to continue to be out in front of our bigger competitors who don't have short development cycles. To accomplish that in a way that doesn't burn out our people requires discipline and balance.

Where does the sense of discipline come from?

I think it comes from our roots in engineering. Both Jim Harris, the vice president of engineering, and I were engineers, and Bill Murto, our former vice president of sales, had worked closely with us. That background created a sense of tough-minded pursuit of facts, of pushing until you get to what you think is really the right answer. That attitude was there initially. It was the way people operated with each other–and it grew. It wasn't viewed as threatening because it went hand in hand with the consensus process. But consensus doesn't work unless you have the discipline to keep digging for the facts that you need to make a good decision. Consensus isn't getting everybody to agree to vote for the same thing. Consensus is getting people to believe that you've got the right facts and the right reasons to make the right decision.

How important is the consensus process to Compaq's mode of operation?

It is fundamental. Our management process is based on the concept of consensus management. The real benefit of the process is not that you get the answer but all the things you go through to get the answer. You get a lot of facts, you get a lot of people thinking, and the result is that everybody owns the decision when you get through.

Originally, we used consensus management at the top to address the really tough, critical, long-term decisions. But as people participated in the process, they could see how to use it at all levels. Today it permeates the company all the way down to the manufacturing floor. When something isn't working right, the teams get together and try to figure it out.

Isn't that quite a lot to invest in a decision-making process?

It's what makes Compaq so successful. I remember when I was moving into the ranks of management at TI. I was worried about making the wrong decision. So I talked to one of my mentors, and he said, "As long as you're right 51% of the time, you're OK." I accepted that answer at the time.

Today I'd say that you need to be right 100% of the time. You may not achieve it, but that should be your goal–to be right all of the time. You need to keep striving for that goal, which means paying attention to every detail and putting everything in its proper order. Being right all of the time also means that you don't just do the best you can as an individual. You use all the resources that are available to you. You use the whole team. And the team keeps pushing and digging until everyone can agree on the decision.

If you do the best possible job, then the best the competition can do is tie you. Our basic philosophy is to push harder and more thoroughly, to push until we get more facts and the best answer. It also means recognizing that there are times when the right decision is no decision. I used to hear the saying, "Any decision is better than no decision." But that didn't seem right to me because when you make a decision, it ripples, it propagates. If that decision has to be changed, then other things have to be changed too.

What role does the boss play in this process?

That's one of the key differences in the consensus process. The normal way a company works is that a team comes to the boss at the end of the process and presents its results. So if the boss has something to contribute, he says, "No, we really want to do it this way." Since he's the boss, he usually gets his way. But a lot of bad things happen right there. The people feel that he's changing the decision just because he wants to or because he can. Also, the boss doesn't have all the information they do, so his critique may not even be correct.

At Compaq, the consensus process does not assume that because I'm the boss, I have the final answer. It's built around a team, and any time there's a team of people, you expect everybody to contribute in one way or another. If I'm going to contribute an idea, experience, or knowledge, the best time for me to do it is early in the process rather than at the very end. That way people don't think of it as getting my stamp of approval; they think of it as getting my contribution.

What's an example of the decision-making process making a difference at Compaq?

Take our approach to the laptop market. The first time we looked at that market was back in 1984. Following our usual methodical approach, we did some market research to find out what was out on the market and what the technology allowed people to do. We were researching companies that took the latest, smallest technology and did the best they could with it. Then we tried to figure out the number of potential customers there were for that type of product so we could make a go or no-go decision. In parallel, we were doing a number of other things, including preliminary design work and even prototyping for our own laptop.

Now in the laptop case, the go or no-go decision came down to one meeting. And what made it particularly interesting was that I was the driver behind the project. I liked having a laptop with me, and I wanted us to produce one that was better than anything else on the market. At this meeting, a fairly young researcher presented her facts and recommendations.

Her conclusion was that there was a market for a Compaq laptop, but it wasn't very big. We looked at how she had come up with her numbers, and we came up with a set of facts we could all agree on. In the end, we concluded that while we could sell some laptops, those sales didn't justify the effort we were going to put into it. There were better opportunities, like the desktop line. So in spite of a strong desire on my part to go into the laptop market, the process worked and we decided not to do it.

Yet here you are in the laptop market now.

Sure, because that meeting was not the end of the story. We decided to focus on other opportunities–on getting into the desktop market, which turned out to be the right decision. But we continued to look at laptops, which is also part of the process. We did several more prototypes and more market research, and the next time the issue came to a head was in early 1986. At that time, the laptop market was beginning to grow with Toshiba. We considered getting into it then.

> "Every time we spot an industry preconception, we see it as an opportunity and test it."

But once again, the laptop was up against another opportunity, the 386 desktop product, which provided a tremendous differentiation opportunity, a chance to establish real leadership. So again, we decided to focus our resources on that product. And again, I'd say that our process produced the right decision.

What led to the decision to launch the laptop?

The way we finally developed our laptop reflects another important thing that distinguishes Compaq—our attitude not to accept the general preconceptions of the industry. Every time we spot an industry preconception, we see it as an opportunity and test it. Most of them may be right, but often enough they're wrong. We feel that if we follow our processes—and we're confident they're right—we can go against the industry's conventional wisdom.

In the case of the laptop, all of the products that came out in the last part of 1989 demonstrated a set mentality. Every one of our competitors came out with a small, notebook-size computer with a floppy disk and no hard disk. The reason was obvious: you couldn't get a hard disk into a computer that size. The conventional wisdom was that if it can't be done, nobody will do it. And if nobody else does it, you're safe if you don't do it.

We came at it another way. We said, we're not going to offer a computer that doesn't have a hard disk in it. So much of the market today demands it, we've got to deliver it. Let's figure out what it takes. Sure enough, we found out we could do it. So when we finally made the decision to go with our own laptop, we were able to use technology to meet our customers' needs and be the first to market. And again, we were fortunate to make the right decision.

The laptop was one success that went against conventional wisdom. How important is that approach to Compaq's success?

A lot of the things that helped Compaq move out in front went against generally accepted opinion. I think that gets back to discipline, thoroughness, and our decision-making system. A part of the consensus process is not just coming up with the best decision that the group can make today. It's being willing to recognize when you really don't have enough information to make the right decision. So you say, "Time out, let's go get more information." And you keep doing that until you have enough information to make what the group believes is the right decision.

Another part is keeping an open mind so that people feel that it's OK to ask questions and test assumptions. In many company cultures, if you question people, they think that you're trying to shoot them down. The result is that people won't speak up. They may speak up if it's important but not if it's just a little deal. But then a lot of those little deals add up, and they can end up getting you off the right track.

Is there something in particular that distinguishes the way you approach a problem?

We work hard to ask questions. If I had to characterize our way of thinking, it is "Why not do that?" It's practically an inside joke. If somebody says that we can't or shouldn't do something, the automatic response is, "Why can't we do that." If there's a good reason, then that's the end of it. But if the "reason" is just a blanket statement or a remark in the trade press that "this is what everyone is thinking," we know that's not a good reason.

We can see today that what separated Compaq from the pack were decisions that other companies didn't make. We're testing ideas, getting people to think in a different way, and asking questions. We're looking for the assumptions that aren't justified. As I listen to people, I listen for what fits together, for where the holes are, or for the one assumption they've made that may not be right on. It comes to the point where the more traditional a thing is, the more you question it. If it's traditional, maybe you're just accepting it without really testing it.

"Conventional wisdom says you can't hire away a guy with 20 years experience at IBM."

How did that attitude get started?

We've always been caught up in the idea of testing boundaries. You never know unless you try. At the beginning of 1983, we were just starting to ship our first product, and we needed to find a new vice president of sales. We sat down and asked ourselves, if we could have anybody in the world to do this job, who would we get? It seemed obvious that he or she should be somebody who had been through it, who knew all the dealers, and who had a lot of experience.

Only one person fit that description: the IBM PC sales manager. Of course, conventional wisdom says you can't hire away a guy with 20 years experience at IBM. It's a safe company, a good job, a key role. You can't get him to leave that and come to a startup. But as luck would have it, when I ran into him at a PC conference, I approached him, and he didn't turn me down. A month later, we had gone through the process, negotiated with him, gotten him comfortable with a small company, and hired him.

How has this attitude affected the way you do business?

It's one of the things that has distinguished Compaq. For example, to some people, a slow, methodical process conflicts with speeding a product to the market. That may seem to be true because of history or other people's expectations. In fact, we've heard a lot of criticism from other companies that like to run and shoot. They announce a product early, but then something goes wrong, and they end up with six-month delays. There is a very strong, fundamental belief at Compaq that following a methodical approach as quickly as you can almost always leads to the best and fastest solution. When you seem to be moving slowly, if you're taking careful steps that turn out to be right, you get where you want to go faster than by speeding along and making mistakes that slow you down or permanently derail you.

Is it true in technology as well?

That's exactly what happened with our decision to go with the 386 processor. What was working in our favor was our mind-set and attitude. The industry tends to follow certain preconceptions about how things ought to work. One of those is that IBM is the company that always has to bless a new processor design. It's interesting how quickly that attitude evolved. After all, when IBM entered the PC market, there were already a lot of companies out there with "better" products. But IBM dominated and became the standard. Any company that jumped out in front of IBM risked being incompatible. In fact, we realized that IBM had done such a good job of setting the standard that it wasn't an IBM standard any more–the industry itself was now supporting the standard. So the key to any next product was to be compatible with existing standards and offer improvements.

In the processor area, there weren't a lot of choices. Intel was developing the next step beyond the 286, the 386. Because of our attention to compatibility all along, we understood where the risk areas and the safe areas were. We looked at the 386 and concluded that we could offer a compatible product that ran all of the software and delivered the advantages of speed and power that the 386 processor had. And we could do it first. We could use conventional wisdom about IBM's leadership to take a position ahead of IBM. And we could do it without sacrificing compatibility.

It sounds as though Compaq adopted a long-term orientation toward the business right from the beginning.

Our business changes so fast that the only way to survive is to think for the long term. When things change as rapidly as they do in our industry, the long term comes sooner rather than later. So thinking long term turns out to be just a commonsense thing to do. We have an aversion to making bad short-term trade-offs, seemingly for a short-term good.

When you think that way, and it becomes a part of your culture, it affects everything you do. For example, you don't try to squeeze the last dollar out of a supplier or try to trick a dealer to get a small advantage, because those things never last. They may last for six months, but problems will catch up with you the next time around. If you want to be around for the long term, you have to invest in developing a supplier, developing a dealer. You have to create a stable, fair, and win-win situation every time you can.

"When things change as rapidly as they do in our industry, the long term comes sooner rather than later."

There's another element to the long-term focus. A company that wants to be a leader for a very long time has to apply its limited resources, energy, and people to the most important things. Dealing with short-term issues, such as constantly changing suppliers or dealers, wastes energy and resources. It keeps you from getting on to other opportunities.

If your focus is on the long term, how do you set company plans?

We set directions rather than goals. We pay more attention to managing the direction we are going in, how we are making progress, and how we are doing things than we do to setting a specific goal and then meeting it. In other words, someone who is meeting goals but doing it in the wrong way–not building a team that could keep it going year after year–might have to be replaced. But someone who isn't meeting goals but is really doing all the right things to get us there over the long term may actually be a hero because he or she is laying the pieces in place to get the job done right.

How far do you take this idea of setting directions rather than goals?

You shouldn't get the idea that we don't have plans. In order to be able to buy land and build buildings, we do have to plan. But the plan doesn't drive the company. The plan is a tool that we use to communicate with groups that need coordination. We have certain revenue targets for a year, for example. We have a goal, but we all know that it's a goal for planning purposes and that the numbers are wrong.

We say that a lot: "These numbers are wrong. We just don't know if they're high or low." Saying it out loud reinforces the idea that those aren't magic numbers that we have to do whatever it takes to hit.

We learned that from the beginning when it became clear that we had no way to set and then meet company revenue goals. Our first year, we had revenues of $111 million. When we started, if we had set a revenue goal for everyone to hit, it certainly wouldn't have been $111 million. At the outside, it might have been $50 million.

If we had passed the $50 million goal in the third quarter, everybody probably would have coasted on to the end – at least, that would have been the temptation. On the other hand, what if we had set that goal and come in at $35 million? Now, $35 million would have been a phenomenal first year. But everybody would have said that we didn't meet our goals.

That's why today we accept that things change. What's really important is that we're doing the right things in manufacturing and marketing and throughout the company – the things that will give us maximum growth. We believe those things will work over the long term – even if they seem not to be working now. You don't just abandon them to hit the numbers. You have to have consistency and continuity; you can't switch back and forth. You can't tell people to think long term and next quarter tell them to make their numbers. You train people by all your actions over time. You communicate more strongly with your actions than your words.

> "It wasn't cost versus flexibility. It was how we were going to respond to the market."

How would you describe Compaq's approach to competitive manufacturing?

There's a whole science to our manufacturing approach, and it begins with carefully setting priorities. What do we want our manufacturing organization to gear itself to do? When we asked ourselves that question, quality turned out to be number one but keeping costs low was not number two. In fact, cost was way down the list, after flexibility in shifting the product mix and speed in bringing products to market. We geared our manufacturing to the change that is such an important part of the industry, rather than to trying to change the industry. Our approach was to stress flexibility and speed, rather than assume that the market wouldn't change.

Or take our view of our work force. Since we have relatively low labor costs, we feel we should hire our people very carefully. Some people might consider that counterintuitive, but we think it's common sense. After all, if you look at a typical computer that we build, the actual human labor that goes into it compared with the material that we buy outside is pretty small. So we feel that we can afford to increase that percentage with slightly higher labor costs if the result is reduced quality problems and more efficient teamwork. Rather than squeeze labor costs down by 10% and reduce the quality of people, we are willing to increase it by 15% and get the best people who are going to make everything work better.

How did you come up with these manufacturing priorities?

Our manufacturing priorities grew out of the consensus process, out of different teams bringing up issues for discussion. The marketing people would look at our costs and tell us that we needed to lower them. Our factory people would say that we could have lower costs, but that would mean that we'd have to give up some flexibility. We talked about it, gathered facts, and finally concluded that to get lower costs on a repeat product basis, we'd have to build in a pipeline, which automatically reduces flexibility. In the early days, IBM, the King Kong of the industry, had a manufacturing philosophy that believed in 90-day windows during which nothing changed. They tried to get dealers to give them a 90-day order that didn't change. But of course, in the computer industry, that isn't the real world.

The dealers never had the right amount of inventory; they had either too much or too little. They would cut way back on their orders, or they would double their orders. So it was clear that in the PC market, a pipeline wouldn't work; there just wasn't the stability. The environment forced us to decide that there was real value in being able to switch our production from one model to the next – say, from one desktop or portable to another – to get the sales that existed. We wanted to be able to deliver whatever the dealers ordered. The way we looked at it, it wasn't cost versus flexibility. It was how we were going to respond to the market.

If quality is the top priority, what is the Compaq idea of quality?

Quality isn't whether or not your products work. Quality is how people do their jobs. Quality is defining your job and then meeting the expectations. When you do that, you raise everyone's consciousness that everything is important. Every piece of the company is important.

How did you arrive at that definition?

I think that attitude goes back to the first two or three years of the company, when there were relatively few people. Back then, there was a lot of opportunity, certainly a lot more than we could possibly handle. Everyone in the company had to organize his or her own tasks, and we had to decide how many people we were going to hire and which areas would get the people. We realized that there shouldn't be any jobs in which it didn't matter whether you were there that day or not. We were counting on everyone, no matter the function or part of the process. It's important, or it's not there.

> "In any situation where we're looking for creativity, we begin with the customers' needs."

We try to communicate this feeling throughout the company. It's not one little piece that you could look at and say, "That's it." The feeling has to be everywhere. It's in the factory, in the way it looks. It's an open, pleasant factory with trees in it. The Cokes are free. And that's not by accident, that's by design. We have company picnics. We have company meetings. Those events mean different things to different people. It's a half day that you get to do something that's different and maybe a little fun.

How would you describe Compaq's approach to innovation?

In any situation where we're looking for creativity, we begin with the customers' needs. We always start by trying to figure out what we must not change in order not to violate the needs of customers. They define the boundaries, the framework of things that are fixed. Then, in the areas where we can innovate, we try to be as creative as we can.

This has really been our approach to the whole product area: innovating within a framework. We knew from the very beginning that we had to produce not only a good hardware product but also one with good software. And that meant the product would have to be compatible with the IBM PC. So we told our engineers–we drilled it into their heads–that they couldn't violate anything that would prevent the software from running. Be creative, but don't violate these fundamental rules.

That approach has made the difference. Early on, a lot of companies had products that the industry magazines reviewed as being more innovative than Compaq's products. It amazed industry experts that these products didn't sell. It took a long time before people understood why our products sold and other people's didn't.

Do you apply this notion of innovation in other parts of the company as well?

We had the same attitude when we opened our Scotland factory. Our approach reflected a clear and thorough understanding of our target. We wanted to create a model of success for any foreign factories we would build in the future. The thing we worried about the most was that something wouldn't work. Here, in Houston, we live in an ideal world, a controlled, self-contained factory environment. Since we were going across the ocean to a different culture, we wanted to be conservative about everything. We decided to take what worked and transplant it carefully to the new factory. The Scottish teams were eager to improve on the process. But we told them, don't improve it now, let's get it up and running with no problems. We can improve it later.

What is your approach to new-product development?

The whole new-product cycle from the concept definition, research phase, design, testing, and into manufacturing has been the heart of the company's success. It's the foundation of everything else. It has meant having the right product at the right time–consistently, over and over again. The reason for it, I believe, is our use of a process that doesn't rely on luck or the vision of just one or two people.

> "Leadership to me is about not being held back by your competition, and also having credibility and clout with the customers so they'll go with you."

Our process involves a team that deals with new-product ideas. There's a core–people who are involved all the time–and others who are part of the team, depending on their area or the type of product. But it's not just a matter of focusing on a specific product. The team also deals with long-range strategic issues, for instance, how RISC-processor technology is going to affect the market. Some people see that issue as black and white. We see it as a force that will affect things in many different ways. The team also looks at what our competitors are doing. We identify things we don't know or aren't sure about and ask a team to research carefully a specific question, gather more information, and then revisit the question a few weeks later. It's a building process. It's not one 15-hour meeting. It's five 3-hour meetings over a period of months, where we build our knowledge and understanding until finally everything we need is there to make a decision.

What is it that makes a company a leader in a certain industry?

To be a leader, you have to do more than just get out in front. A lot of small companies go for the headlines by announcing a product first. That works to get headlines, but it doesn't work well to get sales because you have to combine being first to the market with having credibility with customers so that they'll follow you. Leadership to me is about not being held back by your competition and also having credibility and clout with the customers so they'll go with you.

Reprint 90404

HBR ARTICLES • CUSTOM HBR ARTICLES • SPECIAL COLLECTIONS • BOOKS • VIDEOS • CASES • HBR ARTICLES

• SPECIAL COLLECTIONS • BOOKS • HBR ARTICLES • CUSTOM HBR ARTICLES • VIDEOS • CASES •

CUSTOM HBR ARTICLES • SPECIAL COLLECTIONS • BOOKS • VIDEOS • CASES • HBR ARTICLES • CUSTOM HBR ARTICLES